BRITISH SOCIAL LIFE IN INDIA

1608–1937

BRITISH SOCIAL LIFE IN INDIA

1608–1937

BY

DENNIS KINCAID

GYAN

Published by

GYAN

Gyan Publishing House
5, Ansari Road
Daryaganj, New Delhi-110002
Phone: 011-47034999, 9811692060
E-mail: books@gyanbooks.com

Distribution Network
gyanbooks.com
India, USA, Canada, UK, Australia

ISBN: 978-93-6208-303-6 (HB)
First Published, 1938

2nd Impression 2024

Printed at: Gyan Press, Delhi.

BRITISH SOCIAL LIFE IN INDIA 1608–1937
Author: DENNIS KINCAID

BRITISH SOCIAL LIFE IN INDIA

1608–1937

VESTIBULE OF DUPLEIX' PALACE AT PONDICHÉRY

From a Plan at the Ministère des Colonies, Paris

BRITISH SOCIAL LIFE IN INDIA

1608—1937

BY

DENNIS KINCAID

LONDON
GEORGE ROUTLEDGE & SONS, LTD.
BROADWAY HOUSE: 68–74 CARTER LANE, E.C.

PREFACE

MY son Dennis left this book not quite finished. His friend Mr. David Farrer very kindly undertook the task of completion. Dennis was very anxious to place on record that Chapter IX was based on notes supplied by his mother. Acknowledgment is due to Mrs. Kipling and Messrs. Methuen & Co., Ltd., for permission to quote from Rudyard Kipling's *Departmental Ditties* on pages 228 and 229.

CHARLES A. KINCAID.

ILLUSTRATIONS

PROLOGUE

ON April 4, 1579, Father Stevens of the Society of Jesus sailed from Lisbon for the East Indies. He was the first Englishman known to have reached India. His name is still remembered with gratitude and affection by many Indians; for he was one of the earliest writers in Marathi, one of the pioneers of that language which he considered the most graceful and elegant he had ever come across; and he was the only European who has ever written a considerable poem in any Eastern language. The son of a rich London merchant, he was an ardent Catholic, and after studying the classics at New College he went to Douai to be trained for the priesthood. He came under the influence of Campion and entered the Society of Jesus. He felt drawn to the mission-fields of the East, enthralled by stories of St. Francis Xavier's triumphs and all the romance of Jesuit endeavour in the China Seas, which excited his imagination in the same way that tales of Elizabethan seamen in the New World stirred the young Protestant apprentices he had known at his home in London.

The voyage was long and wearisome, and it must have been with great relief that he saw at last the long green coast-line of the Konkan, islands of moist sweet grass, the red soil and heavy trees, and far inland the jagged line of the Ghats. The ship rode into the calm waters of Goa Creek and on a hill rising from the dark jungle Father Stevens saw the great golden city, saw the walls and gateway, the white mass of the cathedral, the twin blue towers of St. Francis' convent, the vast façade of St. Augustine completed only seven years before. The landing stage was in a palm-shaded inlet just below the cathedral, and new arrivals entered the city by a gateway known as the Gate of the Viceroys, a square triumphal arch with heroes in Grecian armour posturing in their niches. A wide road led past the cathedral into the centre of the town.[1] One would have imagined that for some time the Jesuit enthusiast would be too much moved by all that Catholic splendour to have thought of mundane concerns ; yet if we can judge by the letter written to his father soon after his arrival [2] almost the first thought that occurred to him was that here in India was a fine market for English trade. It is strange and typical of the divided allegiance of so many of the best Englishmen of that age, that Stevens, who spent the rest of his life in the territories of a king intermittently at war with England, and many of whose friends and contemporaries at Douai were most cruelly executed by the English Government, nevertheless remained sturdily devoted to English interests. He never seemed to tire of helping Englishmen in trouble, though most of those he met in Goa must have caused him some anxiety. He had, however, only himself to blame for their presence, for his letter to his father excited so much comment and interest that some merchant adventurers set out for Aleppo in the *Tyger* [3] meaning to make the journey to India overland across Syria. In 1583 four of these Englishmen arrived in Goa : Leeds, Newbery, Fitch and Story. They were under arrest and were " examined whether they were good Christians ", by which, of course, was meant good Catholics. They were

[1] *La Vieille Goa.* Germano Correia. Imprimeire Rayal.

[2] Quoted in Hakluyt's *Voyages.*

[3] An echo of the popular interest in this expedition is in Shakespeare's

" Her husband's to Aleppo gone
Master of the *Tyger* . . ."

ready to profess any creed and Stevens lent his support to their claim to be Catholics, though he must have known very well they were not. They must have remembered enough Catholic jargon to enable them to pass muster, and it is most improbable that the examining ecclesiastics knew enough about the Elizabethan settlement to distinguish Anglican characteristics. Once certified to be "Good Christians" by the authorities, the English visitors must have found little curiosity about their real religion among the laity, for the commercial and military circles in Goa were as casual in religious practice and as vague in theology as their heretic guests. Indeed one of the earliest parties of Portuguese soldiery in India sat through a service in a Hindu temple of Kali, the Dark Goddess, under the impression it was the shrine of a local black Madonna.[1] Leeds not only professed Catholicism, but offered to become a Jesuit on condition of his being given a contract to paint the frescoes in one of the new churches then under construction. The contract finished, he announced he had no vocation for the religious life and, having married an Indian girl, opened a shop in Goa. The other English visitors wandered about the streets, commenting on the umbrellas and palanquins of the local officials, and on the contrast between their own bright clothes and the eternal black of Portuguese male attire.[2] They shook their heads with Protestant self-righteousness at the *Strapado* for the correction of heretics, an engine of torture displayed in the chief square,[3] and passing on with muttered comments on "those most zealous bigots and notorious hypocrites" they visited the churches, "which were richly endowed to maintain the Luxury of a great Number of idle Drones", and admired

[1] K. M. Pannika, *Portuguese in Western India.*
[2] Correia, op. cit. [3] Fryer, *New Account of the East Indies.*

the famous bells, "all christened and dedicated to some Saint, having a specific power to drive away all manner of evil Spirits, except Poverty in the Laity and Pride in the Clergy, but to those that are not used to Nocturnal Noises, they are very troublesome in the Nights". They were surprised that there were no stained-glass windows (which argues in them a certain Catholic instinct) and were very careful not to come into conflict with priests as did Mr. Hamilton's friend who refused to make a present to some passing friar of a fine fish he had just bought; whereon "the Priest gave him a Reprimand in scurrilous Language, and the Gentleman using some tart Language to the Priest he let fly the sharp Dart of Excommunication, that pierced him so deep that it cost him above 7 pounds Sterl".[1]

When tired of Goa they wandered inland. Mr. Story entered the service of the Mogul Emperor as a jeweller. Mr. Newbery journeyed slowly to Persia and there disappeared. Mr. Fitch strolled serenely through Burma and the Shan States and arrived in England in time to be present at the foundation of the East India Company on September 24, 1599.

This first party of merchant-adventurers was followed by numerous others. These forerunners of the Nabobs were strangely diverse in character. There was Mildenhall who tried to supplant the newly-formed East India Company by a company consisting of himself and his friends. He lived three years at the Mogul court at Agra and then visited Persia where he "learned the art of poysoning by which he made away three other Englishmen . . . but himself tasted of the same Cup and was exceedingly Swelled, but continued his life many months with Antidotes".[2]

[1] Hamilton, *New Account of the East Indies.*
[2] Quoted in Foster, *Early English Travellers.*

And there were the two musicians Lancelot Canning, a virginals-player, and Robert Trully, a cornet-player, who hoped to make their fortune by introducing the Mogul court to Western music.[1] They were allowed to perform before the assembled court. Canning played first, but the faint watery music of the virginals had no attraction for Jehangir's flamboyant court and the audience became restive, at which Canning nearly " dyed with conceipt ". It was left for Trully to uphold the reputation of European music. The first notes of his cornet caused a sensation. The Emperor asked if he might try this gorgeous instrument, and, finding it hard to manipulate, ordered all his musicians to learn the cornet. The Imperial Chief Bandmaster was annoyed at the favour shown to a foreign musician and insisted on trying the cornet after the Emperor. He blew so hard that he injured himself internally and died. In spite of this dramatic scene, Jehangir's interest in cornets soon waned and Trully only received fifty rupees for his entertainment. So Trully wandered south, hoping to repeat his success at the court of Golconda. Finding that his offers of a cornet-recital awoke no enthusiasm there, he decided to become a Musulman " which was kyndlye accepted by the Kinge. So Tryllye was circumcised and had a newe name given him and greate allowance from the Kinge ".

But openings for English trade were won, not by the salesmanship of these wandering bagmen but by the rash and nonchalant bravery of a series of fighting seamen. In their choleric defiance of opposition there is a familiar ring. When the Musulman allies of the Portuguese sent Middleton a warning letter he replied, " You sent me a foolish paper, what it is I know not, nor care not. In God is my trust, and therefore respect not what the devil or you can do with

[1] Purchas, *His Pilgrimes*.

your charms." When the Moguls revoked their first permission to settle in Surat, English ships blockaded the coast of Gujarat, attacking the pilgrim-ships bound for Mecca till the Mogul Governor capitulated. And when the Portuguese opposed English penetration, the English, in face of extraordinary odds (" the *Dragon* alone made their Admiral and Vice-Admiral turn back and fly before her, we having had but one man slaine " [1]) swept Portuguese shipping from the Indian seas, and in spite of the Viceroy's exclamations against " these thieves, disturbers of States, a people not to be permitted in any commonwealth ",[2] actually blockaded Goa. However, English and Portuguese interests were too closely allied for long hostility and the two nations presently concluded a treaty which was " carried out with the greatest punctuality by the English ", wrote the Viceroy of Goa, " very different," added the Viceroy, " from the Dutch." [3]

[1] Letter from Thos. Aldworthe.
[2] Thomas Kerridge.
[3] Danver's *Report on Archivo da Torre do Tombo.*

CHAPTER I

IN 1608 English merchants had received permission to settle for trade; they built a factory and in 1618 established the hierarchy and precedence of their community, the chief of the company taking the title of President in imitation of the Dutch.

Surat lies twelve miles up the River Tapti in the warm and fertile plain of Gujarat. Few boats came up the river to Surat, and these few were always flat-bottomed coasting vessels. The ocean-going European merchantmen anchored at the port of Swally. There you might count the masts of several hundred ships, only a minority of them European; Arab dhows with red sails and Chinese junks and Mogul vessels carrying pilgrims to Jiddah, the port of Mecca.

European travellers found the customs examination a tedious ordeal. Every trunk, box and parcel had to be opened and sometimes shoes and hats were removed and peered into.[1] The customs officials wandered about with a retinue of black slaves carrying whips to dissuade intending smugglers. They were little kings in their own domain and levied duty on articles at their own valuation. They insisted on levying duty on the buttons worn by Europeans in their coats, not only on their first arrival at the port but each time they left their ships. This was particularly annoying for the pursers of English ships who often had to make several visits ashore to arrange for reprovisioning the ship and, as one of them complained, " in a short time the very intrinsick value of the buttons would be spent in

[1] Thevenot, *Voyage*.

customs ". If the customs officials found anything specially attractive in the foreigner's luggage they would put it on one side, pretending that they were not sure of the rate at which customs-dues should be levied on this article ; and the owner never saw it again.

Emerging from the customs shed the new arrival hired a conveyance to take him to Surat. There was a wide choice in carriages. You could travel in " a chariot drawn by two Buffaloes attended by olive-coloured Indian foot-boys who can very prettily prattle English " as did Mr. Herbert, who would one day abandon commerce for a career in the parliamentary forces and become one of Fairfax's commissioners ; or you could engage a great coach, such as most of the English merchants used, drawn by two white oxen " with circling Horses as black as a Coal, each Point tipped with Brass, from whence came Brass Chains across to the Headstall which is all of Scarlet, their flapping Ears snipped with Art ".[1] Jangling and jolting the carriage carried the traveller through the alleys of the port. Beggars stared at the foreigner and clamoured for bakshish. But, as Dr. Fryer noticed with relief, you were not troubled " with Boys so rude as in England ". Their chief fault was their Eastern curiosity. They followed every foreigner with inquisitive comments and would " presently upon their punctilio's with God Almighty and interrogate " the traveller. Otherwise " they are very Respectful ", continued Dr. Fryer, " unless they get Drunk when are they Monarchs and it is Madness to oppose them."

It was relief to come out into open country and enjoy the prospect of wide green fields, richly cultivated and, in their evidences of efficient husbandry, almost reminiscent of the farm-lands of England were it not for the hundreds

[1] Fryer, *New Account of the East Indies*.

of peacocks that clustered about the stagnant pools and an occasional camel moving jerkily in the shadow of dusty palm-groves. The roads were shady with over-arching banyan-trees and the traveller would remark the green parrots chortling and screaming as they flew from tree to tree, and on the branches " an infinite number of great Bats, hanging by the Clawes, making a shrill Noise ". He would be lucky if he were not offered, by officious guides, the startling information that " this Fowle ingendreth in the Ear ".[1] Then in the distance you saw Surat Castle " well-walled, ditched, reasonable great and faire with a number of faire pieces of ordnance, whereof some of exceeding greatnesse. Before this lyeth a pleasant greene in the midst of which is a Maypole to hang a light on "[1] and all round " very many noble lofty Houses, flat at Topp and Terraced with Plaster ". The road led through the gardens of the city, which lay outside the city walls. In these the Indian merchants wandered on warm evenings " to take the Air and feast in pleasant Summer houses ". There were many fountains and rivulets of fresh water and " Grottoes descending underground by huge Arches and Stone Steps shaded by Trees on each hand ".

And so, passing through the clamour of the streets thronged with as cosmopolitan a crowd as you could find anywhere in Asia, the traveller reached at last the English factory and must have felt a sober satisfaction to note that it was

> built of Stone and excellent Timber with good carvings without Representations, very strong for that each Floor is Half a yard thick at least, of the best cement, very weighty . . . with upper and lower Galleries, or Terras walks. The President had spacious Lodgings with noble Rooms for Counsel and Entertainment.

---

[1] Finch's narrative of Purchas.

From the roof rose a number of flag-poles with English flags moving in the wind. This dignified exterior was, however, somewhat spoiled by the confusion and uproar in the court-yard where " the Packers and Warehouse-keepers, together with Merchants bringing and receiving Musters, made a meer *Billinsgate*, for if you make not a Noise they hardly think you intent on what you are doing ".[1]

The head of the factory was the President and he lived in almost as great state as the Mogul Governor. Outside the door of his bedchamber stood servants with silver staves and when he appeared they followed him from room to room. If he went downstairs a picket of liveried guardsmen sprang to attention in the hall, and if he left the factory " Bandarines and Moors under two Standards marched before him ". He was provided with " well-filled stables for pleasure or services " and he had his own chaplain, physician, surgeon, linguist and mint-master. At his entry into the dining-room trumpets blew and while he sat at table violins played softly. All the English merchants dined together in the hall of the factory, the President at the head of the table and the others seated in order of seniority. On certain Church festivals, however, they dined in the gardens outside the city. They went in solemn procession, the President and his lady in a palanquin with banners ahead, the Council in ox-drawn coaches of special splendour, each having " a Four Square Seat, inlaid with Ivory ", and the other factors on Arab horses whose saddles were of embroidered velvet and whose headstalls, reins and cruppers were of solid silver. All the dishes and drinking-vessels were of massive silver. Each diner was attended by a page with a silver basin and ewer, so that he might wash both before and after the meal. A peculiarly English grace

[1] Fryer.

prescribed by the elders of the Council was intoned by the chaplain. " We, Thy unworthy creatures do most humbly implore Thy goodness for a plentiful effusion of Thy grace upon our employers, that we may live virtuously in due obedience to our superiors. . . ." Generally there were many and various courses. " Cabob " was a favourite dish, not unlike a goulash ; " dumpoked fowl ", that is, chicken boiled in butter and stuffed with raisins and almonds ; " mango achar and sony sauce ". On Sundays for dinner there would be " Deer and antelopes, Peacocks, hares and partridges and all kinds of Persian Fruits, Pistachoes, Plums, Apricots, Cherries ". But meat was sometimes scarce and though the senior merchants never went without, the common sailors had to fast twice a week and content themselves with saffron rice. Beef was unprocurable. Captain Downton had attempted to start an abattoir but Hindu humanitarians had bribed the Mogul Governor to prohibit this ; pork was, of course, unheard of in Musulman territory ; and so the English had to satisfy their seventeenth-century appetites with mutton and chicken. At first some of the young factors tried to supplement this meagre diet by shooting doves and pigeons but the tender-hearted Hindus would implore them not to do this, and would as a last resort offer them money to spare the poor birds. This method of persuasion was so successful that it became a regular practice for impecunious young sportsmen (and the contrast between their splendid style of living and their small salaries was responsible for general indebtedness among all the junior factors) to take out a gun near some rich Hindu's house and talk loudly and ferociously about the number of pigeons they would massacre that afternoon till the Hindu ran out with tears in his eyes and money in his hands. Only on Sundays were European wines served at table ;

on weekdays they drank Persian wines from Shiraz and, more commonly, arak. Arak was evidently an acquired taste and the French traveller Bernier was surprised at the English liking for it. He described it as " a drink very hot and penetrating like the brandy made of corn in Polan. It so falls upon the nerves that it often causeth shaking hands in those that drink a little too much of it." On the other hand Captain Symson attributed to arak various medicinal properties. It was " good for the gripes . . . in the morning laxative and in the evening astringent ". But he added that immoderate indulgence in arak made drinkers " so restless that no place is cool enough ; and therefore they lie down on the ground all night which occasions their being snatched away in a very short time ". Occasionally the factors dined with Muhammadan friends and found the pulavs and birianis delicious. These meals were, however, of enormous length and coffee was served between courses. And once they could persuade their hosts to ignore the Prophet's ban, they found Musulman heads stronger than their own. They were " not content with such little glasses as we drink out of, nor Claret nor Rhenish (which they call Vinegar) but Sack and Brandy out of the Bottle they will Tiffle till they are well warmed ".[1] But Western science could still score a minor success, and Indians who first witnessed the opening of a bottle of beer expressed a George II-like surprise at the bubbles and froth. " It is not ", they cried, " the sight of the drink flying out of the bottle, but how such liquor could ever be put in ".[2] On occasion, however, the effect of beer and brandy on the temper of a Muhammadan unused to alcohol was unfortunate. A party at the Mogul Governor's was interrupted by the host falling

[1] Fryer.
[2] Price's *Memorials*, quoted in Douglas's *Bombay and Western India.*

into a sudden rage with some dancing-girls and ordering their instant decapitation, there in the dining-room, before the eyes of the startled English guests. Whatever their opinions, however, the guests cannot have ventured on too open an expression of disapproval, even when they left the palace, for there were spies everywhere. The chief of these in Surat was called the "Harcarrah" and he sent his reports direct to Delhi. He

> harkens to all kind of news, whether true or false, listens to everything that happens, whether of moment or no account and reports to the Great Mogul whatever is done or spoken of; but with so soft a pen that nothing may offend, considering the profound veneration due to such a powerful prince whose frowns are mortal.

Fortunately, perhaps, the Harcarrah was even more interested in comets and earthquakes and other portents than in seditious gossip. He related, with some concern, that in a village near Surat "a monster without a head and with his eyes placed in his breast every night cryed out with a horrid noise, 'Destroy and kill'. At hearing this read the King (Aurangzeb) said calmly, ''twas the twelfth century, when the Prophet foretold strange things in nature should happen'."[1]

On holidays the factors amused themselves with archery and musket-shooting; or they would stroll round the bazaar, the temples and the old palaces. They were interested in Indian religions, though, like most foreigners, it was the seamy side of Indian religious life that intrigued them. Mr. Hamilton was excited by the stories he was told of a sect called the "Molacks who observe *heathenish* customs. They have a yearly Feast, but the time of its celebration is only known to themselves, wherein, after much Mirth and

[1] *Surat Factory Records*, 1698.

Jollity, each Sex withdraws to a Room. The women take each a Handkerchief and go in the dark promiscuously among the Men." They admired the earnest attachment of Hindus to their faith, their quiet and reverent worship (or " decent cringings " as Mr. Hamilton put it). But the extravagances of the Yogis excited their laughter and exasperation. " I have seen a fanciful Rascal ", exclaimed Mr. Hamilton, " seven Foot high with a large Turband of his own Hair wreathed about his Head, and his Body bedaubed with Ashes and Water, sitting quite naked under the Shade of a Tree, with *pudenda* like an Ass." And if they chanced upon a conjurer in a corner of the bazaar they could not resist joining his audience. Then as now the mango-trick was a popular feature of the performance. Dr. Fryer relates how he saw some conjurers

> present a Mock-creature of a Mango-tree, arising from the Stone in a short space (which they did in Hugger Mugger, being very careful to avoid being discovered) with Fruit Green and Ripe ; so that a man must stretch his fancy, to imagine it Witchcraft ; though the common Sort think no less.

Was it real fruit ? To test this a friend of Mr. Ovington's " pluckt one of these Mangoes and fell sick upon it, and was never well as long as he kept it till he consulted a *Brahmin* for his health, who prescrib'd his only Remedy would be the restoring of the Mango, by which he was restord to his Health again ".

Many of these young factors must have been pretty rough diamonds, for one of the earliest resolutions of the Company was " not to employ any gentleman in any place of charge ". And when the King began to negotiate for a place for a penurious but deserving knight, the Company fell into a panic at the prospect of this aristocratic recruit and petitioned the King to " be allowed to sort theire business with men of their own qualitye ". They were particularly afraid of the martial propensities of seventeenth-century gentlemen ; like their cousins in the London counting-houses they regarded soldiers as unrighteous and lewd men who would trouble the godly tenor of their lives. And soldiers provoked fighting, and fighting led to unnecessary expense. Look at the Portuguese, they said, " notwithstanding their many rich residences they are beggared by keeping of soldiers ". This did not mean that every clerk and factor was not prepared to buckle on a sword and shoulder a musket as readily as the London apprentices who defied Rupert's squadrons ; when they spoke of soldiers they had in mind the ferocious mercenaries who thronged the London taverns, bragging of skirmishes in the Low Countries and always ready to pick a quarrel, a very general pest in seventeenth-century Europe. Another reason for prejudice against aristocratic employees was the fear that they would not be amenable to the discipline imposed on all servants of the Company, whose way of life resembled that of students in a well-conducted college. All had to sleep in the factory whose gates were only open from dawn till dusk. With the coming of night the Company's servants retired into a virtuous seclusion, congratulating themselves on their self-imposed remoteness from the tumult beyond their gates, where like some great City of the Plain, Surat awoke to new liveliness in the cool of twilight ; and in addition to the strains of music and song there came faintly through barred windows, to the ears of the factors the noise of police activity ; for their Superintendent's " Business is to scower the Streets and Brothels of Idle Companions ; so that all Night long he is heard by his Drums and Trumpets, shouting and hallooing of his Crew in their Perambulation ". Any youth returning to the factory after sundown was fined five weeks' salary, which was distributed among the poor. Absence from prayers, which were held twice daily, was visited with a fine of half a crown on weekdays and five shillings on Sundays.[1] Oaths were penalised at a shilling a time, and there was a variety of punishments for being drunk " and thereby prostituting the worthiness of our Nation and Religion to the calumnious Censure of the Heathen ". Even the maximum amount to be drunk was regulated and though the allowance would appear to be liberal—" not more than half a pint of brandy together with one quart of wine at any meal "—yet no doubt there were found many to grumble at the restriction. But wine was not the only refreshment, for as Mr. Mandelslo noted, " at our ordinary meetings we took only Thé which is commonly used all over the Indies as a drug that cleanses the Stomach and digests the superfluous humours ". It was not drunk with milk, though sometimes candy sugar was dissolved in it, but the factors with more delicate palates brewed it with a variety of spices and " the more curious with conserved lemons ". A few packets were sent home to friends in England where there was an outcry against this " hay water " ; but the doctors, as usual scenting profit in a new drug, were loud in their advocacy of its qualities. For long, however, it was considered an oddity and in an order despatched in 1664 it was included in a cargo of oil of cinnamon, " rarities of birds, beasts or other curiosities ", and some years later Leadenhall Street remarked as though with indulgent surprise that " very good *tea* might be put up in tutinneague Pots ".

Sundays must have been tedious ; for in addition to the services there were two sermons read out by the President. But there were compensations on " the great Feasts of

[1] In money of that time.

Christmas, Easter and Whitsuntide " for then, as a contemporary wrote, " we have the Solemn Service, publike Feasts and noe great busynes permitted to be done in the factory house and all the country people know why we are soe solemn and feast and are Merry. Soe allsoe for Gunpowder Treason Day," though one cannot help feeling that Indians must have wondered at this persistent observance of an abortive plot when in their own country similar plots were of such frequent occurrence that they were forgotten in a very short while. Besides these celebrations, " we have very strikt Fasts kept upon Ash Wednesday, Good Friday and the Thirtieth of January ". Even if other members of the Factory omitted to observe the religious calendar it was incumbent on the President to fast every Friday ; not that, as it was hurriedly explained, " our Fasts are as the Romanists " ; nevertheless they involved, " a meane dyett, nay generally none untill night, but Prayers and Retirement ". And the frivolous were not encouraged. A Mr. Sturdivant found himself in hot water as a result of a report that " he hath a straggling humour, and delighteth in Tobacco and Wine ". Interest in the arts was regarded with some suspicion, and when Mr. Lenton ventured on an ode he was told " the Court did not well relish his conceits and desired him neither to print them nor proceed any further in making verses ". Nor was the local council the only tribunal of taste ; for Leadenhall Street kept a close eye on the morals and behaviour of its employees and had occasion even to comment on the factors' pets. " The Tygar ", for instance, " you keep at the expense of a Goat a day, we looke upon as a superfluous vain Charge."

So to judge by the rules of conduct prescribed for the English merchants in seventeenth-century Surat it would be difficult to find another community of such sobriety and discipline. Unfortunately the rules represented an ideal of conduct and often had little relation to reality. Even at the beginning of the seventeenth century Sir Thomas Roe found most of the English liable to frequent bouts of drunkenness and to " other exorbitances proceeding from it ". Sir Thomas, of course, felt deeply on the subject of Surat liquor since his own servant's drunkenness had caused him some embarrassment. The man, probably sick to death of shipboard rum, had no sooner arrived in Surat than he discovered a taste for the Armenian wine which was served him in the first *buvette* he entered. After slaking his thirst he staggered out into the sunlit streets at the same moment as the Mogul Governor's brother went by with a great train. Swaying into the middle of the road he addressed the Mogul nobleman with a " How now, thou heathen dog ? " Fortunately the Governor was in a good humour and when Sir Thomas hurried to apologise he dismissed the incident with a smile and a suave gesture. This was not poor Sir Thomas's only trouble with a servant, however ; his valet at Delhi tried to escape punishment for disobedience by interesting a Mogul Prince in his case ; and the whole court was involved in the affair which Sir Thomas refers to disgustedly in his diary as " Jones His Lewdnesse ". After Sir Thomas, the Italian traveller Della Vallee reported that not only the junior factors drank to excess but that the President himself, as soon as he awoke in the morning, shouted for " burnt wine " which he " drank frequently to comfort the stomach, sipping it little by little for fear of scalding ". Nor was drunkenness the only accusation levied against the foreign merchants, for from Terry we learn that the " natives who are very square and exact to make good all their engagements used the word Christian as a synonym for cheat. . . ."

The prejudice against employing gentlemen rapidly declined after the fall of Charles I. The Company had to appease the voracious appetites of the Parliamentarian oligarchs by enrolling as many of them as possible among their shareholders and finding jobs for their stupid nephews. With the return of Charles II courtiers succeeded to the privileged position of the revolutionaries; and a new, almost aristocratic, tone becomes evident in the communications of the Company's servants. " We thought it necessary ", they wrote when recounting Streynsham Master's resistance to the Marathas, " to maintaine your honour and that of the Nation (which wee had hitherto reputably preserved) from any scandall that might be cast upon us of deserting the Towne in Time of danger."

The changes in manners that marked the Restoration in England had their effect on the life of the Surat factors. The almost conventual life of the first half of the century was disturbed by a new spirit of atheism and indifference, and in spite of President Oxinden's order from England for " a large Table in a frame gilded and handsomely adorned with Moses and Aaron and in ye midst and at ye Topp God's name writt ", the prevailing sentiment of many of the sceptical or lazy juniors was expressed by Shem Bridges of Bengal who exclaimed " that we have divine service once on the Sunday is as much as can be expected in these hot countries ". Instead of attending the President's sermon the young factors preferred to spend their time with their fighting cocks, especially imported from Siam, or with their other pets with which the factory was crowded—we hear of innumerable fantail pigeons, Basra turtle-doves, tame cockatoos and a performing cassowary. They were less interested in pomp and ceremony than in comfort and while the officials stationed at Swally, the port of Surat, had been formerly satisfied with tents they now demanded bungalows. Private rooms began to be furnished with an elegance that disturbed the directors, and what was to be said of Mr. Young who sat up till two or three " in drinking of healths . . . thus perverting or converting to an ill private use those refreshments intended for the Factory in general " ? The court of Directors became increasingly anxious at the " riot, prodigality, carelessness and folly and expensive and vicious habits " and soundly denounced its employees as " incorrigible Lumber " most of whom ought to be dismissed " in a summary way, without formality of tedious, impertinent examinations or other trumpery ".

But as threats were more often uttered than put into effect the factors attended office when they chose and in the evenings strutted about the gardens of Surat in their vast hats of velvet and taffeta with bunches of feathers, followed by troops of servants in elaborate liveries. The uniform of one's servants was an important matter and even visitors had to decide how they would dress their retainers. Sir Thomas Roe, after some thought, chose for his servants an elaborate outfit, including " red taffeta cloaks guarded with green taffeta " as the proper dress for an English ambassador to the Great Mogul. The extravagance of European costume, the ruffs " of twelve, yea sixteen lengths, set three or four times double ", the slashed silks and heavy folds of lace, always impressed Indians with awe. A Mogul noble inquired politely if Dr. Fryer slept in those grand clothes of his ; and when an English mission visited the Maratha court, their enormous Caroline wigs caused a sensation. At sight of them the King stopped his palanquin and begged the foreigners to come nearer so that he could feel with his own fingers those prodigious ringlets. Considering that this interview took place in the middle of the hot weather it is difficult not to admire the stoic endurance of those English envoys, sacrificing all comfort in their determination to do their country credit by their fashionable appearance. A certain prejudice against any concession to the severest climate as being unworthy of English hardihood lasted until the first half of the nineteenth century, and General John Jacob, whose long residence on the upper Sind frontier certainly qualified him to speak as an expert on tropic heat, was loud in his disapproval of modern concern with the dangers of heat-stroke. Certainly the gentlemen in the seventeenth-century Surat would have earned his approbation, for their clothes seem to have differed in no respect, not even in lighter materials, from those worn in London. It was in vain that the Company issued sumptuary decrees directing with a shrewd combination of Puritan sobriety and protectionist zeal

> that for the encouraging good husbandry, by preventing the vaine and immoderate excess of apparell . . . no apparell or outward garments, to wit, Tunicks, vest, Doublet, Breeches be used or worn, of what quality, nation and condition soever but such as are made of English manufactures, of silke, wooll or cotton.

The Company's employees were less interested in the country of origin or material of their clothes than in their approximation to the latest fashions at home. They begged their friends in London for advice on dress. No present was more gratefully received than some example of the recent fads and fancies of the smart world, and Mr. Christopher Oxinden was delighted at his sister-in-law's gift of " a small box in which is a crevat and cups and riben of the newest mode with a border of lace for your nightcap ". In return they would send Indian curios and these would often take a strange form in that superstitious age when people expected material benefits from Eastern magic and not the mere spiritual advancement of modern parlour-occultists. Sir Streynsham Master sent in all seriousness to his daughter, Lady Coventry, along with the most elaborate directions for use, " in an *Indian* silk Bag and Paper, an Eagle Stone good to prevent miscarriages of women with child, to be worne about the Necke ". But other presents were less outlandish and fantastic and the " Japan dressing-box " which Mrs. Nicks sent home to " her dear garlls " sounds like a sinister forerunner of those countless Oriental knick-knacks with which in subsequent centuries so many English drawing-rooms were to be encumbered.

It must often, however, have seemed a sad waste of all this male finery that there were so few women to admire the feathered hats and watered silks and lace cuffs. English women were rare and though on festive occasions the local Armenian and Portuguese ladies might sit at table with the English merchants such reunions were not encouraged, for there was no knowing when some Englishman might wish to marry a Portuguese and then the children " thro' their father's neglect, brought up in the Roman Catholic principles to the great dishonour and weakening of the Protestant religion ". The Dutch merchants of Surat had no such foresight and often married Papists. Many of those Portuguese women had started for India as the intended wives of officials in Goa ; for the Portuguese Government, in its concern for the morals of its employees in the East, used to send out annual batches of women who had failed to find husbands at home and, that the obedient officials might not cavil at such trifles as lack of physical attraction, sent with them substantial dowries. These women, however, as often as not were provided by fate with other husbands in other parts of India, their ships being captured by Musulman pirates and themselves despatched to the slave-market at Surat. A famous beauty of seventeenth-century Surat was a Donna Lucia who, having arrived at Surat in this manner, attracted the attention of a rich Dutchman. They were married by the rites of the Dutch Reformed Church ; and all the foreign merchants in Surat attended the wedding dinner. It was a most successful marriage and the English merchants related, as a proof of the Dutchman's unreasoning devotion, that he allowed his wife to practise her religion, though in private. Some of these Portuguese captives brought to Surat reached even more exalted stations ; in the previous century one had become an Empress and another the wife of a Mogul Chamberlain, the renegade Bourbon, founder of the house of the Bhopal Bourbons. Some, however, were bundled into the harems of local officials and never heard of again. Senior members of the English Company discussed the dangers of these Papist women and warned susceptible juniors against their seductive charms. But no one seems to have thought of the emotions of these mild convent-bred girls looking forward to a quiet and dutiful existence as wives of minor civil servants, caught away suddenly from their curtain-shaded cabins and their stout duennas and paraded through the cosmopolitan bazaars of Surat with less ceremony than a herd of cattle. Probably piracy in general was so common a peril that men had little thought to spare for such everyday occurrences. The worst pirates, indeed, in the Indian Ocean then were English ; and many of the Company's servants had clandestine relations with these savages. And when the Governor of New York, Lord Bellamont, at last persuaded the Home Government to realise the disgrace of the increasing power of the pirates, it was unfortunate that the man they selected for the expedition was Captain Kidd.

This officer left New York in 1696 with 155 seamen and the blessings of the Government and within a few hours of sighting the shores of India had developed into the most ferocious of all the pirates. A number of other English vessels joined him so that he was soon in command of a formidable fleet; and even the Company's vessels were often in danger of capture. A year after Kidd's arrival in Eastern waters the *Dorill* fell in with one of his ships. Solomon Lloyd relates, "wee could discerne a fellow on ye quarter deck wearing a sword. As he drew near this hellish imp cryed, 'Strike you doggs,' which we perceived was not by a general Consent for he was called away. Our Boatswain in a Fury ran upon ye Poop unknown to ye Captain, and answered that wee would strike to no doggs as hee." Then on the pirate ship "one stept foreward on ye forecastle beckoning with his Hand, and said 'Gentlemen, wee want not your ship nor Men, but Money.' A parcel of Blood Hound rogues then clashed their cutlasses and said they would have it or our Heart's blood." [1] Nevertheless the pirate vessel was driven off after a violent cannonade lasting three and a half hours, and the Company's ship proceeded safely on her way.

Of other Europeans in Surat the English took little notice. The French of course talked too much; with the Portuguese there was the religious difficulty; but the Dutch in spite of their faults had some qualities in common with the English. They were good hosts for instance, regaling Dr. Fryer with "good soops of brandy and Delf's beer till it was late enough"; and among their number were some whose drinking abilities excited awe even among the English as they did respectful admiration among their own countrymen, who celebrated their anniversaries in suitable manner. In the cemetery for instance

[1] Hedge's *Diary*.

" OUR STATION "

A Mid-Nineteenth Century Impression

there was the tomb of a great Dutch drinker. At the top was a great cup of stone and another at each corner. Dutch drinking parties used to frequent this tomb, brewing their punch in the large stone basins ; remembering their departed companion they sometimes forgot themselves.[1]

The English might extend to their Dutch rivals a faint cordiality that they denied to other Europeans but they seldom troubled to learn their language ; and when Albert de Mandelslo from Holstein visited the English factory expecting that his knowledge of Dutch would be of service to him there he found that only the President knew anything but English. Nevertheless, the English did their best to entertain their guest ; the President asked him to supper, offering him, however, only fruits and preserves, since he was unaccustomed to a heavy meal at night " out of a fear of overcharging his stomach, digestion being slowly performed, by reason of the great heats " ; and he attended the " divertisement " in the great hall of the factory on Friday when healths were drunk to wives in England. " Some made their advantage of this meeting ", he noted, " to get more than they could well carry away, though every man was at liberty to drink what he pleas'd, and to mix the Sack as he thought fit, or to drink *Palepuntz*, which is a kind of drink consisting of *aqua vitæ*, rosewater, juice of citrons and sugar." On the Sunday he accompanied the English to a garden outside the city where they amused themselves by " shooting at Butts " and challenging his hosts to a competition, he won £5 in wagers. After this gesture of hospitality the English must have been glad enough when their guest left them and they could return to the insular routine of their life with a sigh of relief.

It was to this curiously self-centred community that the sudden news of the cession of Bombay came with a shock of

[1] Ovington's *Surat*.

surprise. They were not so well informed on world politics as Lord Clarendon who at that moment was congratulating himself on the acquisition of a valuable island " with the towns and castles therein which are within a very little distance of Brazil ".

CHAPTER II

IF the English were surprised at the cession of Bombay the Portuguese colonists were appalled ; and it is amusing to find the Viceroy of Goa employing the arguments of retentive imperialism to which recent debates on colonies have accustomed us. It was not because of Portuguese material interests that he opposed the cession ; it was because " I see in the island of Bombay so many Christian souls which some day will be forced to change their religion by the English." [1] The natives, however, with that common but irritating blindness of conquered races to the superior qualities of their present masters, welcomed the change. They sent a deputation to the English, advocating an early occupation and criticising the theocratic centralisation of Portuguese rule, under which " none could with liberty exercise their Religion but the Roman Catholique, which is wonderful confining with rigorous precepts ".

After prolonged debate, the new possession was formally handed over by the Portuguese to Mr. Humphrey Cooke, " whom ", as the Viceroy remarked indignantly, " I know in Lisbon as a grocer." [2] This would not seem so serious a charge in English eyes, but for the fact that he appears to have been a very bad grocer ; and Oxinden dismissed this episode in the new Governor's life with the scornful comment " he was a pretender to be a merchant ". Worse than these antecedents, however, were his manners. The Portuguese found his attitude, during the difficult period of exchange of administrations, more than tiresome ; he was " full of

[1] Danver's *Report*.

[2] Danver.

boasting and bravado ". Worse still, his secretary was " an Awful Heretic " against whom the Portuguese had a special grievance, for he was really a Greek who had been a Catholic, served under the Portuguese Government, written a treatise in Arabic which he dedicated to the Viceroy of Goa, and now he turned up in Bombay pretending to be an Anglican and bearing the English name of Gary. It was unfortunate that when Gary (after Cooke had been ignominiously arrested for debt, escaped from jail and fled to the hospitality of the Jesuits in Goa) became Governor of Bombay he showed his zeal for his new religion by forbidding ministers of the Inquisition to make arrests in Bombay. " This is most insolent ", complained the Viceroy, " and as those who go there are those with open consciences our places and towns are being deserted "—a revealing commentary on the sincerity of the spectacular mass-conversions in Portuguese territory. But Gary's devotion to liberty did not extend beyond hampering the activity of the Inquisition, and in the exercise of his judicial functions he showed himself, as Dr. Fryer said, " a Person of Mercuriall Brain ". Being generally drunk his decisions were often odd ; one Tuesday he condemned a man to be hanged, the sentence being instantly carried out, and on the following Friday he called out the same man's name in court and finding no response, fell into a rage and directed the man's arrest for contempt. He quarrelled with the Home authorities who complained of his " Vaine glorious Boastings, seeking to magnify himself by debasing us (soe much as in him lay) " [1] and finally appointed another in his place. He settled down as a planter on the island.

None of the royal governors was very successful and the King was glad to hand Bombay over to the Company in

[1] Forest, *Home Series*, 1, 222.

1668, the governors thereafter being appointed by the Company.

The first of these governors was Goodyer, a modest man who had not looked for so high an office; as his friends remarked, "the unexpected charge much troubled him". He took up his residence in the old palace of the Portuguese governors which was

> a pretty well Seated but ill Fortified House, 4 Brass Guns being the whole Defence of the Island. About the House was a delicate Garden, voiced to be the pleasantest in *India*, intended rather for wanton Dalliance, Love's Artillery, than to make resistance against an invading Foe, for the Portugals generally forgetting their pristine vertue, Lust, Riot and Rapine are the only remarkable Reliques of their Ancient Worth.[1]

As if to avoid similar censure the English began, with a great display of vigour, introducing conscription among the startled natives, and forming them into train bands under English officers. They had to march to the beat of drums and learn musketry drill. To most Indians of the merchant class these manœuvres, modelled on the training of the regiments of London apprentices, were quite inexplicable. But Indians have always regarded the actions of their rulers as mysterious and for some time they seemed not to have realised that these parade-ground evolutions had any relation to war, for we find the Company repeatedly insisting, "They must be made used to firing lest in Time of Action they should start at the Noise or at the recoil of their armes." When the stricter Brahmins and banias found out the purpose of these wearisome exercises there was a great outcry and finally they were allowed to contribute money instead of serving. With their money the Company hired a regiment of obedient Germans. For the Governor's bodyguard were

[1] Fryer.

recruited 300 Bhandaris, or fishermen, armed with clubs. They were the only fairly stable military forces in Bombay, for though English soldiers were being constantly sent out as reinforcements they either died of scurvy on the voyage or of drink soon after arrival. But there always seemed to be just enough Englishmen to provide the sentries outside the Governor's residence. Their hours of duty were regulated by sand-filled hour-glasses and each time the hour-glasses ran out gongs were tolled. Probably the regularity of their duties kept them fitter than most of the English soldiers, for whom the hours of parade were very variable and for whom, outside their barracks, there was no possible amusement within their means except drinking. When drunk they often engaged in a little amateur highway robbery ; which was at least less dangerous to the public than the sudden desire of a corporal to tie a " fired bandoleer " to a dog's tail—but in the struggle the bandoleer was thrown into the air and came down among a pile of thirty-five barrels of gunpowder, resulting in a heavy loss of life. Even if the soldiers left the punch-shops with the most innocent intentions there was no knowing when they might not stumble into trouble. On an April evening, for instance, a young trooper cantering light-heartedly down the road nearly rode over a Mr. Braddyll, who told the fellow to be more careful. The trooper replied, " God damn you. If I had a pistol I would shoot you through the head for a farthing." Mr. Braddyll's rejoinder " Would you so ? " was not very spirited and the trooper naturally replied " Yes I would." Alas, Mr. Braddyll was a member of the tribunal before whom the trooper was arraigned for his insolence and it must have been with sober satisfaction that Mr. Braddyll signed the order directing that the trooper should receive thirty-nine lashes. Nor were the officers much of an example to the men in the matter of sobriety, though of course their peccadilloes were viewed more indulgently. It was no doubt regrettable that Captain Wyatt, returning to barracks at dawn, should have, in a sudden access of drunken rage, thrashed a soldier for no imaginable offence, and then drawing his sword run him through the body and finally, when he was dead, trampled on his face; but the Company felt that loss of his commission was perhaps sufficient punishment, for a gentleman would naturally feel this disgrace keenly.

It is probable that many of the deaths which pious travellers ascribed with gloomy relish to "that accursed Bombay punch", were really due to the ordinary diseases of the East aided by the antics of contemporary surgeons. The favourite method of treating cholera was to apply a hot iron to the ball of the patient's foot; if he winced that was a proof he would recover, if he gave no sign of pain then all hope should be abandoned; and the doctor, having delivered this diagnosis, pocketed his fee and drove round to the next patient's house. With the advance of science new methods came into favour and for a time the following treatment was recommended by the medical profession as invaluable in all fevers.

> Take an iron ring about an inch and a half in diameter and thick in proportion. Then heating it red hot in the fire, extend the patient on his back, and apply the ring to his navel, in such a manner that the navel may be as a centre to the ring. As soon as the patient feels the heat take away the ring as quick as possible when a sudden revolution will be wrought in his intestines.

Cholera was considered to be due to eating fish and meat together and its treatment consisted in applying a red-hot iron to the heel "so close that it touches the quick". How many cures resulted from these methods of treatment are not recorded; and the Company was, as always, less interested in the physical, than in the spiritual, health of their employees. It was a pity that there remained in the island as evidence of Portuguese occupation, so many Catholic churches " thwack'd full of young blacks singing vespers ", and it was decided to build a Protestant church of " form proportionable to the small churches in England " so that the heathen should " observe the purity and gravity of our doctrines ". Five thousand pounds were collected for this purpose, mostly from the Company's servants " freely and conscientiously ", and it was disappointing that the whole amount should have been embezzled by the Governor, Child.[1]

But, even though no Protestant church was built for some decades, houses were being constructed all over Bombay. The Portuguese colonists who had remained in the island however much they might rail at the heretic administration, profited by the new comparative security from pirate raids to build palaces and " banqueting houses " and in the comments of English officials a certain jealousy of these " rich Dons " is discernible. Parsis were building country-houses on Malabar Hill and there was already a zoo " to keep the Company's antelopes and other beasts of delight ". The English were proud of their houses which so exactly resembled gentlemen's residences in London. Life was easy, for if the pay of Company's servants was comparatively small all lived beyond their means, depending on supplies from local money-lenders. Indeed while each ship from Europe was surrounded as soon as it entered the harbour by a small fleet of rowing-boats piled high with fresh fruit and vegetables, curios and silks, the first people to climb on board and welcome the new-comer to India were the money-lenders ; and though the lordly young European, pleasantly

[1] Hamilton.

THE COLONEL

self-conscious of his new breeches and well-fitting coat, might affect to despise as effeminate the rustling muslins and gold ear-rings of the banias he was glad enough to accept the offer of an immediate loan and to scribble his signature at the bottom of a document which the money-lenders with many compliments, salaams, and deep bows laid before him.[1] With almost limitless credit life was easy even for the most junior clerk. No work was done after one o'clock [2] when everyone went home for dinner which was eaten in wigs and flowered coats, to the accompaniment of violins and the gentlemen toasted each other with Madeira or Shiraz wine, served in cups of rhinoceros horn which was an antidote against poison. After dinner there was a long siesta and in the evening the hairdressers came to attend to gentlemen's wigs before they left their rooms for an evening ride or formal visit. Servants were mostly (except the butlers who were Parsis) slaves from Malabar. These were so cheap that they were presently exported in great numbers, though never with the reckless indifference to morality that characterised some other slave-dealing companies ; the directions being always careful to insist that " you should send near as many female slaves as male, because the male will not live so contented, except they have wives ". And sometimes orders for especial slaves were received from highly placed persons in England —once even from King Charles himself who

> desired to send to India to provide for him there one male and two female blacks, but they must be dwarfs of the least size that you can procure, the males to be seventeen years of age and the females fourteen, giving the commander great charge to take all care of their accomodation and in particular of the females, that they be in no way abused in the voyage by the seamen.[3]

---

[1] Hodge's *Travels*. [2] Forbes's *Oriental Memoirs*.
[3] Letter to Surat, quoted in Anderson's *English in Western India*.

As in Surat, the younger merchants paid great attention to their clothes and often astonished newcomers, who had provided themselves with serviceable suits of "hodden gray" appropriate for distant travel, with the elegance of their bottle-green coats, black velvet taffetas with gold embroidery, buff waistcoats and breeches and at their throats necklaces of amulets to guard against the many ills of the East, especially the stones they called "snake-stones" which were held to be an infallible protection against the cobra. Their talk was generally of dogs—bulldogs, "sleuth hounds and gray dogs". They held coursing matches on Malabar Hill and Dr. Hove had the satisfaction at one of these matches of starting a hare "as large as an European one". But sometimes in their excitement they stayed out all day in the heat and, their hats in spite of feathers and lace affording little protection against the tropic sun, developed heat-stroke or, as Ovington more elaborately expressed it, "the ambient air mixing with the natural, when it is fermented and charged, commonly proved too much for their constitutions". The richer or senior factors went farther afield for their sport; and for their amusement, the Company in 1692 started a pack of twenty hounds at Karwar, each hound to receive two pounds of rice a day (but no meat apparently), and the factors who visited Karwar were agreeably surprised at the hospitable manners of the local natives who welcomed them "with pretty black female dancers, who are very active in their dancing and free in their conversation". If one could not afford visits to Karwar or coursing-matches on Malabar Hill there were always the public whippings, floggings, brandings and bastinadoes which the new English courts awarded so plentifully and which provided a free entertainment for the idle. It was especially interesting when the victims were women, for the judges of those days suffered no pangs of sentimentality or chivalry. A Hindu woman found guilty of theft was ordered thirty-nine lashes to start off with, to be followed by further instalments of thirty-nine lashes every day thereafter until she revealed where she had hidden the stolen property. In the middle of the eighteenth century a woman who abetted her lover in the murder of her husband was sentenced to be burnt alive. There was on occasion no prejudice against the use of torture if a conviction was required and the requisite evidence deficient. In 1720 the most respected Hindu in Bombay, Rama Kamati, was arrested on a charge of corresponding with Angria, the pirate chief. There was no evidence against him except a roundabout story by one witness who said he had been told by a dancing-girl he visited that Angria himself had told her that Rama had written to him. This fantastic piece of hearsay evidence was not enough for the court to convict on, so by order of the Governor himself, Rama's servant was put to the torture. After his thumbs had been wrenched off "the smart thereof" caused him to make a statement implicating his master. Rama was sentenced to perpetual imprisonment and all his property was confiscated.[1] At the time this case was the talk of Bombay, and as with most Frenchmen at the time of the Dreyfus trial, the general feeling among the English was that there could not be so much smoke without a fire and that there must be something in that story of the man who knew the dancing-girl who knew Angria. But when Rama died in prison eight years later he was forgotten, and though it was sub-

[1] For a full account of the trial see Malabari, *Bombay in the Making.* Though torture was not again resorted to to procure evidence, death by torture remained common all this century. In Calcutta in 1789 some robbers were tied down, their right hand and left foot hacked off, the stumps dipped in hot butter and the men left to die.

sequently discovered that the case against him was entirely false, having been got up by his enemies, that was little consolation to his impoverished family who never received any restitution.

The pirate Angria was a bugbear to the English in the early eighteenth century and even Europeans were on occasion accused of sympathy with him in the same way that accusations of Bolshevism were bandied about in post-war England. A seaman called John Stanmore had been attacked by his captain with a cane and had muttered that "it was a little way to Angria", which exclamation was held to amount to high treason. Poor Stanmore threw himself on the mercy of the court, pleading that he had had nothing to eat or drink all day and had been kept long hours at work; but the court with exclamations of horror at the "vile and dangerous principles" which must have prompted any cordial reference to Angria, sentenced Stanmore to receive, for three days in succession, thirty-nine lashes at each of the gates of the city in turn.

Stanmore's punishment would have been heavier had his pleading not suited so exactly the humour of the court. Indians often pushed the court to real severity by their, to English eyes, frivolous pleadings. A man charged with "knocking down a woman and taking from her ear a gold joy" was so rash or ignorant of English morality as to try and justify his assault on the ground "that his designe was only to lye with her". The court, deeply shocked at such a defence, which they dismissed as "Impudence", to show their disapproval of such pleadings condemned the man to three days' steady flogging, to branding with hot irons on the face and to perpetual imprisonment.

The trials that caused most public excitement were those for sorcery. The laws against magic were ferocious and since most Indian (but not English) physicians were classed as sorcerers and large rewards were offered to informers, there was a constant stream of charges and counter-charges. Even an old Hindu woman who had admittedly cured a number of children with her herbal remedies was given eleven lashes to discourage her traffic with Satan. Trials for sorcery continued till the seventeen-seventies when they suddenly declined, possibly because the then Governor, Thomas Hodges, was himself interested, so rumour ran, in black arts and kept a private wizard whom he consulted several times a day.

After watching a buxom woman stripped and flogged for exchanging bets on the result of a case in the corridors of the law courts, it was pleasant to resort to one of the punch-houses which were springing up all over the city. One would be careful to examine the bowl in which the punch was brought, for, by a new Government decree, "if the Clerk of the Market's seal is not on any Bowle, it may be broken and payment of the punch lawfully refused", which was comforting to apply when one had drunk the punch. And after several bowls of punch the talk would perhaps turn on the charms of the last shipload of women from England—for the Company had now copied the Portuguese custom of drafting out a supply of women to their possessions in the East. They were classed as "gentlewomen" and "other women". They were not given dowries but were guaranteed their "diet" during a year in India. Trouble arose if they were still at the end of the year without husbands or sufficient money to pay their fare home. It was obviously impossible to leave them to starve, but the reluctance shown by the Company to provide them with a proper allowance and the continual haggling and bargaining had its inevitable result in a rapid deterioration of the visitors' morals. Then, with what magniloquence the President and Council dealt with the situation! "Whereas some of these women are grown scandalous to our nation, religion and Government interest, we require you to give them faire warning that they do apply themselves to a more sober and Christian conversation." And when even these Olympian thunders were ignored, "the sentence is that they shall be confined totally of their liberty to go abroad and fed with bread and water."[1] In an age without shorthand the length and circumlocutions of letters exchanged between Bombay, Surat and London argue a pleasantly aristocratic leisureliness (even when real anger breaks through the suave periods as when attention turns to Mr. Watson, "that scandalous Chaplain—let him have no solace from us, he is no more our servant, banish him the Island . . .")

Of course if women arrived in the marriage-market with dowries of their own, there was no longer any question of prevailing on the Government to support them if they failed to find husbands; the difficulty was to prevent senior Government servants interesting themselves in the dowries. A Miss Ward had actually £3,000 of her own and the Governor, Sir John Gayer, decided that a lady with that capital was just the wife for his son. Unfortunately before he made known this decision she had fallen in love with, and married, a junior clerk. The Governor declared this marriage void and succeeded in marrying her to his son. But presently she had an affair with a schoolmaster "who", in Mr. Hamilton's words, "was ordered to teach her to write good *English*, but, neglecting those Orders, he taught her something else, and was discovered Practising, by a

[1] Letters from President and Council to Deputy Governor December 18, 1675, and January 17, 1676.

watchful Mother-in-law; and the poor Husband's Head aked as long as he lived", in spite of his father's causing the schoolmaster to be arrested and sent home in chains.

Occasionally all Bombay was fluttered by some exotic romance. In 1685 a Company's servant, "a young beautiful English gentleman", while on a commercial mission, attracted the fancy of the Queen of Attinga, a very wealthy ruler, who offered to seat him on her throne. "But he modestly refused so great an honour. However, to please Her Majesty he treated her with the same Civility as *Solomon* did the Queen of Ethiopia or Alexander the Great did the Amazonian Queen, and satisfied her so well that she made him some presents."[1] She lived in the pepper country of the southern coast; and her territories were already becoming famous for the big-game shooting that visitors from England found there. Two young noblemen intending a short visit stayed there three years, delighting in the variety of game, in the mystery and beauty of the great forests and in the simple hospitality of the jungle folk. But generally as the eighteenth century progressed it was the English settlements on the east coast that attracted travellers. Surat declined rapidly with the collapse of the Mogul empire, and cultured English visitors inevitably reflected on the fate of Tyre when they rode through the almost deserted bazaars. Bombay itself was continually menaced by Maratha power and by Malabar pirates. They were "scrambling and unquiet times" and the senior officers were seldom men of ability or, if the number of alleged embezzlements are any guide, of ordinary honesty. The Members of Council continued to dine in great state but they could no longer afford to offer the hospitality of the Company to junior employees, who now had to seek

[1] Hamilton's *New Account.*

refuge in taverns and punch-houses. So weak were the armed forces that an envoy from the King of Persia had to be sent away without setting foot on the island lest he should relate to his master the nakedness of the land. In May 1707 there were only six servants of the Company in Bombay, and of those Henry Coster was "wholly disabled by his unaccountable sottishness to hold a pen". And the main occupation of the English merchants seems for the next few decades to have been the prosecution of various internecine feuds. The appropriate note was struck by Gayer when in 1703 he described Sir Nicholas Waite of Surat as "That Grand Apostate of the infernal regions" whose only concern was "to cut our throats at one stroke to promote his unbounded Luciferian ambition. Had we not assurance", he added a little unconvincingly, "of the hellish contrivances of the forenamed Monster we should not write in such a Stile." Quarrels arose quite unexpectedly and over the most trivial matters. When a Muhammadan prince asked for the loan of an English doctor the Governor, Sir John Gayer, concluding that the native assistant surgeon of the Government Hospital could be spared, directed that "that black fellow" should be sent to the prince. This decision was arrived at without consulting the head of the hospital, Dr. Skinner, who vented his rage by sending a long letter of personal abuse to the Governor. Sir John sighed and remarked, "This most scurrilous answer shows the Pride and Factiousness of that vain man." Another doctor, by name Maxwell, having been dismissed on account of his "lewd debauched life" settled down contentedly in Cochin as a receiver of stolen goods.

Quarrels raged in the Council chamber. Mr. Mewse, the Third Member of Council, who was considered "unfit for virtuous conversation", broke another member's head

THE JUDGE'S WIFE

with a bottle of wine. The Right Honourable the President Stephen Cott went further than this ; he not only broke a bottle on the head of Mr. Peachey who had accused him of laxness in Sabbath observance, but directing a shrewd kick at Mr. Peachey's person " regularly doubled him up ". Taking advantage of Mr. Peachey's temporary disablement he soundly " cuffed " him, and as Mr. Peachey limped from the room he threw a slipper after him. He followed up the triumph by publicly taunting Mr. Peachey whenever he met him ; he instigated one Robinson to give Mr. Peachey a beating and while this was in progress he leaned over a balcony and laughed provokingly ; he pursued Mr. Peachey and gave him, as Mr. Peachey complained, " on my right side a blow which was a stoppage to my breath " ; finally he had Mr. Peachey arrested and put in prison just " to plague him." It is perhaps not surprising to learn that during this period the Provost Marshall was so unfortunate as to fall into delirium and have to be confined and denied access to alcohols ; while the Council sighed over " having too many such as he is in one fort " and opined that it would be " much better to be rid of such a scabby sheep ".[1]

The eclipse of Bombay during the eighteenth century by the more prosperous settlements of the east coast is forcibly expressed by a minute of the Council in 1825. " For a century and a half Bombay has been of little importance to the Company. . . . A settlement on the coast of Africa could scarcely have been a subject of less consideration." But before considering those more prosperous settlements of Madras and Calcutta the story of Mrs. Draper, whose association with Sterne has made her more familiar to most English readers than all the generals and presidents who were her contemporaries in Bombay, may be briefly considered.

[1] These details from P. Anderson's *English in Western India.*

Eliza was born in 1744 at Anjengo, in Malabar, where her father was employed in the English store. A district of jungles and mudflats and endless creeks; a village of thatched cottages hidden among tall palms that hissed and swayed in the warm damp wind. There was no school here for Eliza and one can only suppose that it was from her parents that she learnt her varied accomplishments. She was ugly, and yet even as a child there is evidence of her extraordinary charm. The tree under which she used to rest after her evening stroll along the beach was known for a century as "Eliza's Tree". The Abbé Raynal who met her long afterwards in Bombay wrote ecstatically of her fascination. "Anjengo," he exclaimed, "you are nothing but you have given birth to Eliza!"[1] and the Abbé knew all the most accomplished women in Paris in that great age of conversation, wit and charm. And James Forbes, who so seldom praised without qualification, admitted with a sigh that a description of her attraction was beyond his powers. "Her refined tastes and elegant accomplishments need no encomium from my pen." But in Anjengo there were few to admire her and she must have been grateful to Mr. Daniel Draper who, on a visit from Bombay, proposed to her. Gloomy, pompous and twenty years older than Eliza, he must nevertheless have seemed a most desirable husband both to Eliza and her parents, for he was a great man in Bombay, Secretary to Government and already spoken of as destined to the highest posts. She was happy with him at first and when, some years later, he suggested a visit to England she was enraptured. On the ship were two Bombay friends, Commodore and Mrs. James. The Commodore was something of a hero, for he had attacked and broken the power of Angria; while his

[1] *Histoire Philosophique des-Deux Indes.*

wife was a woman of culture with many friends in literary London. Among them was Lawrence Sterne, and she enjoyed " the almost unique distinction of being the only woman outside his own family circle whom Sterne never approached in the language of artificial gallantry, but always in that of simple friendship and respect ". Soon after they arrived in London, Mrs. James gave a dinner-party and among the guests were the Drapers and Sterne. Sterne fell instantly and desperately in love with the ugly but fascinating girl from India, and she was swept off her feet by his tempestuous and tragic style of wooing (so different from Daniel's formal expressions of affection). He affected to believe her still unmarried and would write—

> Pray, Eliza, do not think of giving yourself to some wealthy nabob, because I design to marry you myself. My wife cannot live long—she has sold all the provinces of France already. And I know not the woman I should like so well for her substitute as yourself. Tis true I am ninety-five in constitution and you but twenty-five—rather too great a disparity this ?—but what I want in youth I will make up in wit and good humour. Not Swift so loved his Stella, Scarron his Maintenon, or Waller his Sacharina as I will love thee and sing thee, my wife elect."

Eliza who knew nothing of Sterne's life believed all this rigmarole. " I believed Sterne," she cried, " implicitly I believed him ; I had no motive to do otherwise than believe him just, generous and unhappy." In the letters they exchanged she called him " mild, generous and good youth " and he called her his " Bramine ". But when Mr. Draper's leave came to an end Eliza had to follow her husband back to Bombay. Sterne's letters became increasingly hysterical. " Eliza, from the highest Heaven, my first and last country, receive my oath ; I swear not to write one line in which my friend may not be recognised." They were not destined to meet again, for soon after Eliza's return Sterne "was taken ill at the silk-bag shop in Old Bond Street"; he was carried home to his lodgings and there "put up his hand as if to stop a blow and died in a minute". Mrs. Sterne and her daughter, finding some copies of Sterne's letters to Eliza, tried to blackmail her with the threat of publication. Eliza wrote in alarm from Bombay to Mrs. James. "To add to my regret for his loss, his widow has my letters in her power (I never entertained a good opinion of her) and means to subject me to disgrace and inconvenience by the publication of them." Although this threat never materialised, the rumour of Eliza's correspondence with an eminent man of letters had, as Eliza complained, "somehow become extremely public at this settlement" and in her constant alarm lest the rumour should reach Daniel's ears she must have been very grateful for his sudden transfer from Bombay to Tellichery where he had been appointed chief of the factory. She was happy in this new station and tried to forget the past. She began to interest herself in her husband's work and even worked as his amanuensis. She enjoyed her new importance as wife of the head of the factory, she was flattered by the deference of the Indian employees and merchants, and in her letters she extolled their superior culture, describing the place as the "Montpellier of India". She wrote that

> the Country is pleasant and healthy . . . our house a Magnificent one, furnished too at our Master's expense and the allowance for supporting it Creditably what you would term Genteely, tho' it does not defray the charge of our Liquors which alone amount to six hundred a year. . . . Our Society at other times is very confined as it only consists of a few Factors and two or three Families; and such we cannot expect great intercourse with, on account of the heavy rains and terrible thunder and lightening to which this coast is peculiarly subject six months in the year. 'Tis call'd that of Malabar

> . . . Mahé is not more than seven Miles Distant from us (Yet very few civilities pass between us and the Monsieurs) and Cochin (a Sweet Spot) about two Days' Sail.

Unfortunately for Eliza's virtuous resolutions Daniel received a new promotion and was recalled to Bombay and appointed Member of Council. Once more Eliza attracted admiration and when she appeared at balls at Government House in hoop and farthingale factors and cadets besieged her for dances. There was not, of course, much competition; there were only thirty-nine ladies in the station, thirty-three of them married, five widows and one " Winnifred Daires, Unmarried Woman " as she was somewhat ungallantly described on an invitation list. The Governor was then Hornby, and his interest in magic and the fact that he was " ignorant not only of the first principles of Government, but of the ordinary knowledge requisite for a gentleman " [1] did not prevent him from giving a series of successful balls at which Eliza was always the chief attraction.[2] The Drapers now lived in a house at Mazagon, called Belvidere, a long yellow building, formerly a Portuguese convent, on a mound overlooking the sea and pleasantly shaded by palms. Cadets and factors would walk along the sands in the mornings to call on the Drapers (morning calls were then fashionable), and would sit and talk in the airy drawing-room. They were probably very cheerful, for the first morning visit of almost every cadet was to some other cadet's quarters where he would be welcomed with draughts of punch and of " arrack and water, which, however cool and pleasant at the moment

[1] Donald Campbell, quoted in Douglas's *Bombay and Western India*.

[2] The Indians were interested in the powder, paint and towering head-dresses of ladies bound for these balls. But the patches caused them acute anxiety, and one Indian sent a message to Mr. King expressing sympathy for his wife's black boils.

was succeeded by the most deleterious effects."[1] Then, sufficiently refreshed, they would set out on their calls, not without some jeers at the few virtuous youths " who devoted their morning hours to music, drawing, literary improvement and other rational pursuits ". Probably the visits and compliments of the young factors and cadets would have kept Eliza amused without involving her in any serious entanglement, but for the sudden interest that the severe and frigid Daniel began to take in the housekeeper, Mrs. Leeds. Eliza noticed that when he went to his bedroom for his afternoon siesta, he used to call for Mrs. Leeds to help him put on the " Conjee cap " that he wore in place of his wig when resting. It always appeared to take Mrs. Leeds a long time to help him with his cap and Eliza had to protest against " your avowed preference for Leeds to myself ", but Daniel paid no attention. It is difficult to blame Eliza for finding compensation in the ardent suit of a naval officer called Clark ; and when Daniel's middle-aged infatuation for Mrs. Leeds made life at Belvidere intolerable for Eliza, she let herself down by a rope from her bedroom window and took refuge on Clark's ship, leaving behind a pathetic note for her husband, " I go. I know not whither, but I will never be a tax on you, Draper. I am not a hardened or depraved creature. The enclosed are the only bills that I know of, except six rupees to Doojee, the shoemaker." She was received with enthusiasm in literary circles in London and now, no longer troubled by scruples over their effect on Mr. Draper, authorised the publication of Sterne's letters to her. She died in 1778 and was buried at Bristol. The epitaph on her tomb " In her Genius and Benevolence were united " is a curious contrast to that on the gravestone of Sterne, " Ah ! Molliter ossa

[1] Forbes.

quiescant." Daniel, having become President of the Bombay Council, retired in great affluence and lived very virtuously in St. James's Street where no one had heard of Mrs. Leeds.

CHAPTER III

IN 1639 Mr. Day obtained leave from a Hindu prince, the Naik, " out of our spetiale Love and favour to the English to build a fort and Castle in or about Madraspatam " which long South Indian name the English soon shortened to Madras. The official reasons for the choice of this site, as conveyed to the Surat Council, were that it provided " excellent long Cloath and better cheape by 20 per cent than anywhere else " which inspired the Surat Council to " hope of a new nimble and most cheape Plantation ". But the gossip-loving Hamilton believed that " the Gentleman who received his Orders to build a Fort on that Coast, chose that Place . . . because he had a Mistress at *St. Thome* he was so enamoured of that made him build there, that their Interviews might be the more frequent and uninterrupted ". Apart from Mr. Day's convenience, the proximity of St. Thome was generally considered a nuisance by the senior factors—

> not in respect of any hurt the Potugalls can doe the ffort but because of the many idlers, both men and women, who frequent the ffort so much that divers of the English Souldiers are married ; which must necessarily be tolerated, or the Hotshots will take liberty otherwise to Coole themselves.

And even if Hamilton's story of Mr. Day's mistress in St. Thome be an exaggeration there was little of the Puritan about Mr. Day.

> " 'Tis no strange thing," said Captain Trumball, " for Mr. Day to be drunke. Drinkeinge with Moores and Persians at Ballisara hee soe disguised himself in theire presence that they

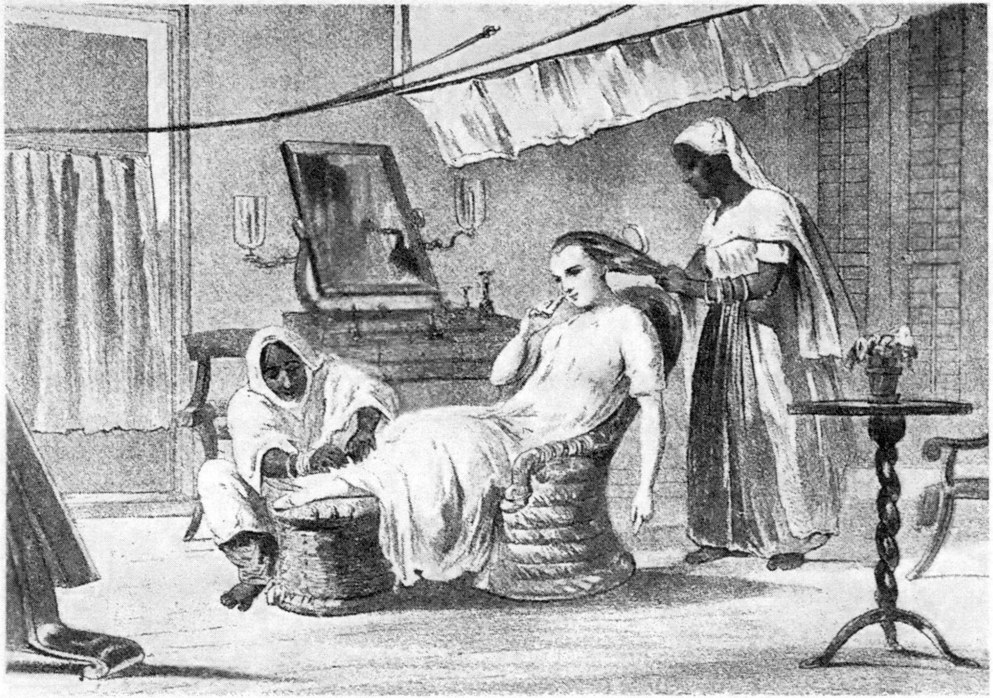

THE MAGISTRATE'S WIFE

> sent him away in a Pallankeene out of which he fell by the way. . . . And another tyme hee made himselfe soe drunke he Rann into the Sea."

Day had two assistants. The first, Cogan, after building the fort, returned to England to fight for the Royalist cause, leaving behind two sons, one of whom entered the service of the King of Golconda and became his " Chief Gunner " and the other " is Runn away to St. Thome and there is turned Papist rouge and goeth every day to Mass with his wife ". The second assistant was Harry Greenhill, to whom Mr. Day was grateful for taking his mistress off his hands and establishing her in a " very faire house with orchard and garden " and " at the christening of his seconde childe there was shott off 300 brasse bases with three volleys of small shott of all the Souldiers in the castle and 13 gunners from the fort ; but the powder was paid for by him." [1]

Greenhill succeeded Day as Agent, or head of the factory, and one of his first concerns was to strengthen the garrison which up to then had only numbered fifty. A Mr. James Martin applied for the post of commander of the garrison, and a commission sat to consider his qualifications. He was called in and " severall questions were demanded of him, where hee had been bred a souldyer and in what quality ". Mr. Martin " declared that hee did commannd some Tennants of Mr's the Archbishop's in Yorkshire ; but that hee never was a commissioned Officer ". It is not surprising that " an objection was made against him by a Gentleman present ". But this objection was overruled and the commission rashly decided " to entertaine the said Mr. Martin to command their Souldyers at the Coast at the yearly salary of 40 l." Rashly I say, because within six months of his appointment a formidable indictment had

[1] *Indian Records Series*, Madras, Vol. I.

been drawn up against him by his colleagues entitled "Captain Martin's Abuses and Blasphemies". This portentous document began thus :—"Imprimis, the said James Martin hath bitterly inveighed aginst Independents, Presbiterians, Protestants and Papists ; and . . . hath inveighed against Governor Cromwell" (the year is 1652) "in this manner, how that before those Warres begunne he was a pore cowardly fellow and would take a Cuff on the eare from any man." But the real gravamen of the charge was that "James Martin hath frequented Punch houses in Companie of the private Souldiers and hath played with them at Cards". Instead of being abashed by this last revelation of a taste for low life Martin replied, "I am forbidden to keepe company with the souldiers, though some of them be as good as those whome the Agent hath made his greatest Companions and" he added, warming to this topic, "what is the Agent but the sonn of a greased Butcher?" In spite of these spirited exchanges this truculent officer kept his command till his death more than two years later.[1]

As in Bombay there were both sepoy regiments and "City Train bands"; but the latter were only called up on the rare occasions when a Maratha attack seemed imminent, and then hasty instructions were issued that they should be at once "instructed in Millatary Exercise so as to acquaint them with the Points and Bullwarks". The chief difficulty in maintaining a proper garrison was that no one ever knew when to expect reinforcements from England; when they had been demanded they never arrived, and when least expected or needed several troopships would suddenly appear and unload some hundreds

[1] Full details of Martin's period of command in *Indian Records Series*, Madras, Vol. I.

of half-naked and scurvy-rotten recruits, causing the Agent to wonder how on earth to feed them " seeing all provisions being still very scarce and deare and none of the publicke houses will be persuaded to entertain or dyet them ". Moreover they had immediately to be provided with " a Coat each, one Capp, two pair of breeches and three shirts " and the only satisfaction the Government derived from this unexpected outlay was that they could stop the soldiers' pay until these clothes were paid for. Generally the soldiers went about the streets in rags and saved their new clothes for Sundays, when, as had been ordered by a recent decree, they had to " weare English apparell ". They had no uniform at first, until the idea suddenly recurred to the London authorities, and was explained in an almost interminable lecture, that—

> It being found here in Europe very convenient for the Soldiers to have coates of one collour, not only for the handsome representation of them in their exercise but for the greater Awe of the adversary, besides the encouragement of themselves, we have thought that our Soldiers with you should be put into the like habitt, for though it be hott in the daytime yet the night being coole (which it is so rarely in Madras, but the droning voice never pauses to consider this) it may bee a meanes to preserve their healths.

After much more in this strain the letter concludes " And cause the turning up of the coate sleeves to be frill'd with something of a different coler ". After all these expenses the Government were not going to follow the costly Bombay experiment and import women for their white subjects. Instead they decided to " induce by all means our Soldiers to marry with the Native women because it will be impossible to get ordinary young women to pay their own passages " ; that is, of course, passages out from England to Madras.

The garrison was needed not only to defend the town against external assault but also, in the absence of organised police, to preserve order in the settlement itself. In 1652 occurred the first communal riot with which British authorities had to deal. Two castes in Madras, the Belgewars and Berewars, were on bad terms. One day " a Belgewar told a Berewar that he was not worth a Cash ". The latter countered with what must be the feeblest retort in history, " that if himselfe were not worth a Cash, the other was not worth two Cash ". However poor as a debating point, this reply provoked a riot and the garrison had to intervene.

While the arrival of recruits from England was, for the recruits, a dismal experience, civilians generally landed in the highest spirits. They had been charmed with the first view of the city, the white buildings among green trees, the wide clean sweep of sand and the blue hills in the distance. The soaring imagination of a Royal Academician[1] even compared the appearance of Madras to that of some " Grecian city in the age of Alexander ". The passengers disembarked in surf-boats built of planks lashed together, paddled by the fishermen. As the boats approached the rolling line of surf the oarsmen jumped out and carried their passengers on their shoulders through the leaping spray. If the passengers were ladies, this task was chivalrously undertaken by young officers from the garrison who always hurried on board each ship from Europe to see if there were any ladies disembarking at Madras whose acquaintance they might make. After the passage through the spray the new arrivals were glad to set foot on shore ; but they found the sand " scalding hot " and hurried towards the long palm-avenues from whose cool shade they could admire the gardens and green rice-fields beyond

[1] Hodges.

the city walls, the square fort against whose walls the waves broke in a line of foam, the house of the President with its dome and fretted balconies.[1]

The President, whose palace was grander than any Government building in Surat or Bombay, lived in a style appropriate to his residence. "His Personal Guard consisted of four hundred Blacks, besides a Band of fifteen hundred men ready on Summons. He never goes abroad without Fifes, Drums, Trumpets and a Flag with two Balls on a Red field." [2] He and the Members of Council were shaded from the sun by scarlet umbrellas, but any ordinary person who used an umbrella was fined. There was never a public table as at Surat or at first in Bombay; but the President dined in solitary state or with the Members of Council, while the younger men had their meals in taverns.[3] Of the life of the factors, Myddelton wrote: "This is an expensive place and from the drunkennesse thereof good Lord deliver me; all gamesters and much addicted to venery." Not that Myddelton himself was averse to liquor for, as he complained, "Sacke is too deare, yet wee have other goode drinke to remember our friends withal." [4] The favourite sports, he found, were hawking and cock-fighting. The game-cocks were armed with penknife blades instead of gavelocks which made their encounters even more savage than usual.

Public events and festivals were celebrated with great magnificence. The news of the marriage of the Prince of Orange with Princess Mary was greeted with prolonged drinking of healths and firing of salutes. The accession of James II was celebrated by processions down the main streets of the city (the Indians being all ordered to decorate

[1] Details from Fryer's *New Account*.
[2] Fryer.
[3] Letter of Sawcer to the Hon. Company.
[4] Myddelton's Letter.

their houses, which must have made even more puzzling the order three years later to show the same pleasure at this king's fall), processions in which marched all the

> Chief Merchants and Gentul Inhabitants, Elliphants carrying our Flags, the kettle Drums and Musick playing before them. After that went twelve English Trumpets with Silk Banners and six Hoeboys all in red Coates playing by turnes all the way.

The ambassadors of Persia and Siam were received in solemn audience by the President and offered their congratulations on the royal accession ; they were invited to " a Banquet and Dancing ", which gave them " great satisfaction " ; though, accustomed to the passive rôle of guests at dance-parties in their own countries, they must have found strange the spectacle of gentlemen, from the President down, posturing, pointing a toe, bowing and retreating, and the ladies with their broad Caroline shoulders and high, scarcely-hid breasts, smirking and quizzing behind their tinselled fans. But the evening ended with fireworks and bonfires which must have been more to their taste, and more familiar as a form of celebration. There were similar entertainments on Gunpowder Day when the King's health was drunk on bended knee and twenty-five great guns were fired and rockets shot off ; and on the King's birthday wine and arrack were served free to the garrison.

Till the accession of William of Orange relations between English and French in the East had been cordial ; Dr. Fryer refers admiringly to Louis XIV as " that stirring King " ; and English, French and Portuguese all combined in hatred of the Dutch. But on the accession of William III, announced in a General Letter to the Eastern agencies as " this great change that it has pleased God by his wonderful providence to make in the Government of this nation ", the English in Madras found themselves transformed into allies of the Dutch and enemies of the French. The Dutch governor of Pullicat, whose name was, oddly enough, Lawrence Pitt, hastened to Madras and " came to an anchor, paying all accustomary civilities to the place " and on his arrival in the city " the President made an entertainment for him and the rest of the Dutch people, showing him all the respect and civilities imaginable due to his quality and employ ".[1] In return an English President visited the Dutch settlement at Geldria and was

> treated with a very Splendid Dinner, the Table being spread with about 100 Dishes of Meate, and Wine of all sorts in great plenty ; five healths were drunke about at Table, and all the Canon in the fort and some at the Redoubt, in all fifty-one, fired every time ; 2 healths after Dinner while Cannon fired.

Then they all went to the garden of one of the rich Dutch merchants where they had " a very handsome supper and other divertisements of merry making till midnight ".[2]

At Madras, too, entertainments were often given in the gardens outside the walls. In these gardens were " Gourds of all sorts for Stews and Pottage, Herbs for Sallad, and Flowers as Jassamin, for beauty and delight ; cocoes, Guiavas a kind of pear ; *Mangos* the delight of India ; a Plum, Pomegranates, and *Bonanoes* which are a sort of Plantain, though less, yet much more grateful ". With their orchards and mango-groves these gardens resembled the Continental idea of a *jardin anglais*. Travellers like Fryer were interested in the exotic plants and strange trees, but there seems to have been little skill in the design of the gardens and during the hot weather when the grass disappeared and the plants wilted garden was often a courtesy title. Mr. Hickey was invited by a friend to visit a " boasted garden ". But—

[1] Consultation of 1690 quoted in Talboy Wheeler's *History of Madras*.
[2] Streynsham Master's *Diary*.

> after going over what I conceived to be a wild and uncultivated piece of ground, with scarcely a blade of grass or the least sign of vegetation he suddenly stopped and asked me what I thought of a Madras garden, to which in perfect simplicity, I answered "I would tell him my opinion when I had seen one." This answer he replied to with, "When you see one, Sir, why you are now in the middle of one." The devil I am, thought I.

There was no attempt at imitating the splendid parks at Pondicherry where everything was sacrificed to elegant geometrical designs, great square lawns with star-shaped flower-beds and long well-swept walks protected from the sun by creeper-hung pergolas, in whose shade gentlemen in high-heeled buckled shoes exchanged compliments in as leisurely and elaborate a manner as if they were at Versailles or Marly. Moreover, while the English at Madras made little effort to grow fruit, the French took the trouble to lay down vineyards in Pondicherry and were rewarded by a surfeit of delicious grapes. This was provoking enough ; but all Madras exclaimed at the mercenary spirit of the French in refusing to sell their grapes to the English for less than a rupee a bunch. When a Mogul embassy was received by the Madras authorities in some newly decorated summer-house in their gardens, it was considered a proper compliment to the guests for the President and Members of Council to wear Mogul dress ; and it must have been interesting to see those stout red-faced merchants pulling on the white satin jodhpurs and painted tartar boots and patting down their starched and transparent muslin shirts. Obviously they felt less comfortable in their costume than some of their French rivals who delighted in Mogul display. But the French adapted themselves much more easily to Indian habits than the English ; and young men fresh from France were at first appalled to find that all the ladies of Pondicherry had copied the Indian custom of chewing betel-nut which stained their lips bright-red, and that they would even testify to their favourable reception of a compliment by offering the new arrival a pinch of their own powdered betel-nuts from silver comfit boxes, putting the youth to the uncomfortable choice of giving offence to a lady or himself tasting the repulsive-looking stuff. As they naturally chose the latter alternative, they soon adopted the habit themselves.[1] Also the French colonists, in spite of the irritating power of the Jesuits, who interfered in every appointment, were mostly agnostics with no prejudice whatever against either " heathen " customs or " heathen " behaviour ; indeed, they often arranged parties to visit Hindu temples on the occasion of great festivals and watch the elaborate rites of Hindu worship.

The English occasionally gave private parties in their gardens, but this was more rare than at Surat for the country round was much more disturbed than at Gujarat. The gentlemen only unbuckled their swords when they reached the rendezvous and even while they ate armed servants kept a look-out for stray bandits. But the possibility of sudden interruption did not weaken a determination to be as comfortable as possible. In the shade of mango-trees carpets were spread and cushions and mattresses, and mosquito nets were hung from branch to branch enclosing the party in an airy tent. There would be fish and cold meat and fruit and at a picnic at which Madame Dupleix was present the duck paste was particularly appreciated.[2] While they generally rode out to the picnic in the cool of the morning, they liked to return in palanquins, shaded from the noon heat and, after a heavy meal, pleasantly

[1] *Memoirs du Chevalier et du General de la Farelle,* edited by Laurel de Farelle, Paris, 1896.

[2] *Vie de Johanna Begum* Yvonne Gaebele, Editions Leroux.

lulled to sleep by the swaying of the palanquin and the melancholy chant of the bearers.

Generally, however, parties in the gardens were of a more formal nature and the receptions of Mogul envoys were occasions of considerable pomp. The Mogul embassy of 1692 was received in the gardens with a guard of infantry and cavalry, and with " accustomary ceremonies of musick ". The envoys and the English representatives exchanged presents, the gift of Prince Kam Baksh to the English President being a horse " covered with a Velvet State cloth and furniture, the headstall and crupper imbost with plated Gold ". Then began the ceremonial reading of the Prince's letter, on behalf of the Emperor Aurungzeb,

" In the Name of God, Great and Merciful,
To you Excellent in Countenance and Elected to Great Favour
Elihu Yale . . ."

The titles must have pleased Mr. Yale, for he was a great autocrat. His butler left his service without proper notice. Yale directed he should be hanged. " But on what charge ? " the legal advisers queried ; for though hanging was, by English law, the punishment for a large variety of offences, it had not, by some oversight, been attached to the offence of leaving employment without notice. " What charge ? " said Yale " Piracy, of course." And hanged the servant was, on a charge of piracy. Born in America, where his munificence was rewarded by the naming of the famous American University after him, Yale died in England and was buried at Wrexham, where his tomb in front of the church door bears these lines :

Born in America, in Europe bred.
In Africa travelled, in Asia wed ;
Where long he lived and thrived, in London dead,
Much good, some ill he did, so hope all's even
And that his soul thro' mercy's gone to heaven.

Another Mogul embassy headed by Nawab Daud Khan in 1701 was welcomed by Governor Pitt, grandfather of the Earl of Chatham. The reception was even more splendid than that of Kam Baksh's embassy. The Nawab was met by the Governor some way outside the city. They embraced each other and Pitt presented the Nawab with " a small ball of Ambergrease cased with gold and a gold chain to it ". After exchanging a number of compliments Pitt took the Nawab into the fort and set by him " two cases of rich cordial waters and wine " and then began the drinking of healths, accompanied by salvos of artillery. The Nawab, in spite of his religion, was no teetotaller and evidently enjoyed the freedom of a town where Aurungzeb's harsh laws against wine-drinking did not run. When it was time for dinner (at which there were " about six hundred dishes, small and great, of which the Nawab eat very heartily ") the Nawab needed some more drink and so " French brandy " was set by him, and becoming increasingly good-humoured he especially commended the " dancing wenches " who postured before the diners. In the morning the Nawab was supposed to leave Madras but " having been very drunk over night, was not in a condition to go, and deferred it till to-morrow morning ". He announced he would like to spend the morning in the gardens. So the Governor " ordered immediately to beat up for the Train Bands and the Marine Company, and drew out a detachment of a hundred men under Captain Seaton to attend him and those Gentlemen of the Council who went to the Garden to receive the Nawab ". They arrived at the garden, the soldiers were drawn up in ranks ready to salute, the gunners standing to attention waiting for the word to fire the salvos of welcome. They had come in a hurry to be sure of arriving before the Nawab so as to receive him with proper honours, but it seemed that they need not have hurried. Time passed but there was no sign of the Nawab. Mogul nobles travelled slowly, of course, but as hour by hour went by, impatience changed to alarm and messengers were sent to bring news of his whereabouts. They returned to say that, while on his way " The Nawab was got into a Portuguese chapel very drunk and fell asleep ". He did not wake up till 4 o'clock in the afternoon when he sent a man running to the Governor " and desired him to send a dozen bottles of cordials ", which were duly sent. It is sad to record that the Nawab, so far from being grateful for this rousing reception, became increasingly hostile to the English after his return to his headquarters, and, in the following year, sent an ultimatum ordering the surrender of the English mint, which demand Governor Pitt dismissed as " rhodomontade stuff " ; but when the Nawab tried to enforce his demand by attacking Madras he was bought off by a present of twenty thousand rupees, " and five thousand privately " to his secretary.

Five years later the Emperor Aurungzeb died, and south-eastern India fell into confusion which was increased by English and French intrigues and only ended by Clive's conquests. But the merchants in Madras city were less concerned with the rights of the various contending armies than with the good sales of cloth they were able to effect with the different commanders for their soldiers' equipment ; reporting to the home authorities that " the fine broad cloth as scarlet, aurora, some blue and yellow is used for the inside of tents, and for covering clothes for the elephants and hackarys " whereas " Perpetuanos are only used among the meaner sort of people for caps ". The Council, on the other hand, was deeply disturbed over some recent unsuitable marriages of Englishmen in Madras. Many of these kept slave-girls, as mistresses, but this did not cause concern; it was the marriages that were unfortunate, especially when the " Young Gentlemen were of good families in England ". For instance " one Crane, was married to a Frenchman's daughter of this place on Sunday last ", and " one Dutton, an ordinary fellow, married Ann Ridley ", who was a Catholic, so, " for the preventing the like practices for the future " it was enacted, after considerable discussion, that no Christian should be married in Madras without leave from the Government.

It was unsuitable marriages the authorities objected to; they connived at less regular unions. These were so common that no social stigma attached to them, and sometimes they brought great happiness. Henry Crittleton, a Company's officer, kept a Brahman mistress called Raje; and in his will he refers to her with obviously sincere gratitude and devotion, leaving to her all his property. General Pater was so fond of his mistress Arabella that when, on her death, the chaplain refused to bury her in consecrated ground, he had her body interred in a field and then built a church over it, the church of St. Mary's, so that in spite of the chaplain she should lie in consecrated ground. These were men of means, but many a poor sailor and soldier showed a similar affection for his mistress. The sailor James Buller left his slave-girl, Noky, her freedom and fifteen Arcot rupees a month; and William Stevenson left his Maria a third of his " estate " provided she remained virtuous. When the sailors were called away on a long voyage or the soldiers ordered inland they generally left their girls with some friend. This was often a thankless task for the friend and David Young complained of one young woman to whom he had offered shelter. " Bett is making the damndest noise that ever I heard from morning to night; we can have no peace with her; and when I gave her her monthly allowance, she kicked up such a dust that I could not still it. I shall have a fine time till your return if she goes on at this rate."

In 1720 the town was intrigued by the pretentious will of young Mr. Charles Danvers who died at the age of twenty-one.

> My corpse [ran this will] to be carried from the Town Hall at seven o'clock at night. I desire that all the free merchants of my acquaintance to attend me in their palankeens to the place of burial; and as many of the Company's servants as I have had any intimacy within my life-time; that all that attend me may have scarves and hat-bands decent. I desire that Mr. Main and the charity boys, may go before my corpse and sing a hymn; my corpse to be carried by six Englishmen or more if occasion; the minister and the rest of the gentlemen following. I desire of the Honourable Governor that I may have as many great guns fired as I am years old, which is now almost twenty-one. . . . After my corpse is buried, which I desire may be done very handsomely, the remainder of my estate I desire may be laid out in rice, and be given to the poor at the burial place as long as it lasts.

It is to be noticed that this young man's pay was only £5 a year; he had been out in Madras three years, but he died wealthy. For in spite of the anarchy outside the walls (and in spite of considerable embezzlement within) the riches of the English community increased very greatly during the first half of the eighteenth century. In the letters of the Council both to England and to the other settlements, there is seldom any but vague and indifferent reference to the wars and anarchy along the coast. The accessions and depositions of Nawabs, the raids and retreats of Maratha armies, were of far less interest than an occasional scandal in the Fort, such as that caused by Miss Elizabeth Mansell's charges against Captain Cummings which were investigated at great length in solemn session of the President and Council and formed the subject of eager gossip for over a year. Miss Mansell, the niece of a Member of Council, had come out to Madras to stay with her uncle. As soon as she landed she made a formal charge of rape against the commander of the East Indiaman in which she sailed. This was, of course, a capital charge, and Captain Cummings was arrested and confined in prison till the first hearing of the case. The captain conducted his own defence and cross-examined the prosecution witnesses with some skill. His case was an admission of intimacy with Miss Mansell; but he alleged that from her arrival on board she had not ceased to pester him with her attentions, and when Mrs. Cummings was seeing her husband off at Portsmouth she was so alarmed at Miss Mansell's manner towards her husband that she "burst out into tears, which he had much ado to overcome by promises of a prudent behaviour". Rather early in the session Miss Mansell's character began to suffer; one witness admitted that at Portsmouth she was caught "playing at Tagg with a couple of footmen". Miss Mansell's chief witness was a Mrs. Mary Coales who deposed that she had often seen Miss Mansell cry and exclaim "She could never be happy" on account of the captain's behaviour. Captain Cummings put to her this subtle question: "Did she not fall into a passion *whenever I took any notice of you*?" Simpering complacently, Mrs. Coales admitted this was so. Other witnesses, cited to prove Miss Mansell's distress and despair, made increasingly damaging admissions. Mark Romney, for instance, saw her sitting on a chair beside the captain at eleven o'clock one night, and she suddenly put her arm round his neck, called him "her dear captain" and gave him a kiss. Mark Romney thought this so entertaining that he "beckoned to a midshipman, who was a small distance off, to come and look ; who put his finger to his nose but would not come ". Other witnesses admitted that Miss Mansell had been intimate with two other young men on the boat, so that at this stage the Council broke up the trial and formally acquitted the captain. Obviously Miss Mansell ought to have been prosecuted for perjury, or the captain awarded some compensation for his imprisonment ; but then the prosecutrix was related to a Member of Council and so the Captain while being acquitted was treated to a severe lecture to the effect that his " relation to this young woman would be a perpetual Blot on him ", since he had taken away her character. And when the wretched man exclaimed that she had no character even before she came on board he was " stopped from proceeding in this sort ".

Most visitors, however, arrived in less dramatic circumstances. But they were scrutinised and criticised none the less exhaustively. The charms of the young women were eagerly canvassed. An increasing number of them came to India in search of a wealthy Nabob for husband. " By this time," wrote Dalton to Clive, " I reckon you are able to give me an account of the new-arrived angels. By God, it would be a good joke if your countenance was to smite one of them and you was to commit matrimony." There were among the new arrivals plenty of rough diamonds for the self-consciously correct to laugh at, and a newcomer's table-manners were sometimes delightfully informal. The Reverend Mr. Yate, for instance, who was invited to dine with the Governor soon after his arrival, was at first surprised to find several wine-glasses beside his plate ; but when the claret came round he filled all his glasses at once and drank them off happily ; he repeated this each time the claret returned to him and presently exclaimed, " Upon

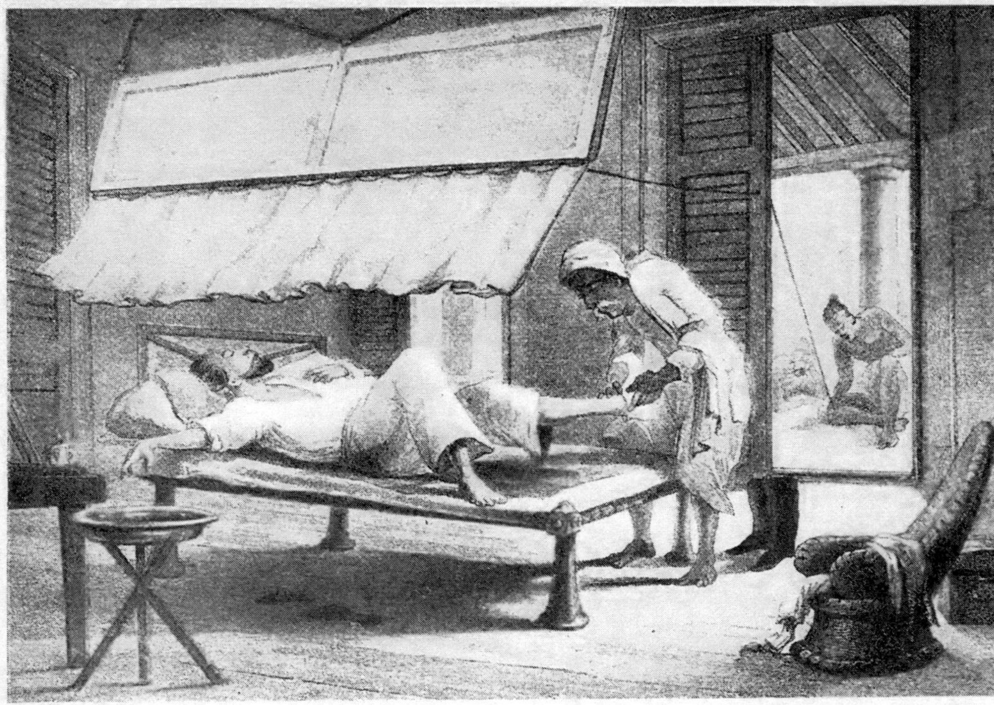

THE BEDROOM

my conscience this is the prettiest custom I ever saw in my life, and I wonder it has not been adopted in Ireland."

Then, as always, the clothes of new arrivals were a source of the greatest interest. The Company's ships when eastward bound generally put in for a few hours at Boulogne or some other French port and all the gentlemen hurried ashore to buy smart French suits. The French tailors traded on the general English ignorance and sold them a fantastic array of coats with high waists and enormous skirts or very low waist and skirts like a short kilt, and breeches of crimson satin and waistcoats hung with spangled lace, all recommended as the very latest fashion from Versailles. Then the gentlemen visited the barbers and had their hair dressed in Parisian fashion with tier upon tier of side curls and so thick a layer of pomade that at night a thick hair-net had to be worn. This was not a fashion of hair-dressing that commended itself to India, however, for the rats were attracted by the smell of the pomatum and when a gentleman was sleeping often bit through the hair-net and ate up all the hair.[1] And to go with the Parisian coiffure one had to buy a fine French hat. Mr. Hickey bought what he was told was a Chapeau Nivernois, " a little skimming dish of a hat ", which caused a sensation in Madras where very large hats were still being worn. He wore it with some complacence at a party at Government House ; but unfortunately at supper his neighbour, an elderly gentleman who had been eyeing the hat " with peculiar archness ", suddenly snatched it away and hoisted it on the point of his cane for the amusement of the assembly.

It seems to have come as a surprise and disappointment to the young officers and cadets that they could not wear

[1] Hickey.

their fashionable finery when they set foot in Madras, but had to be content with the regulation uniform. A general order had to be issued : " Except on occasions of taking some manly exercise, such as playing at cricket, fives or other game, no cadet shall appear out of his quarters otherwise than dressed in the uniform established for the cadet company." And the Commander-in-Chief had to announce that he " positively forbids officers appearing in fancy uniforms or in any but that of the corps to which they belong ".

These smart French coats and hats could only be used on gala occasions and most new-comers hurried to local tailors to order clothes more suited to the climate of Madras. As these were run up in great haste and by unskilful bazaar tailors they were seldom well cut. Mr. Hickey's friend, Mr. Rider, found his new gingham breeches far too tight, but he had no other breeches suitable for the climate and he rashly wore the new pair to fence in. There were several ladies watching the match, and it was unfortunate that during a neat lunge Mr. Rider's gingham breeches split the whole way up the back. The ladies were most tactful, however, and instead of increasing Mr. Rider's confusion by laughing at his discomfiture they contented themselves with " an interchange of arch leers ".

Towards the second half of this century there was a change in the financial interests of Madras. Trade with Manila, Java and the Far East declined and Company officials began to turn their attention to the possibilities of profit nearer home. In the prevailing anarchy of the Carnatic a prince remained in possession of his territories only if he could pay his troops. The Nawab of the Carnatic began the practice of borrowing from Madras and was followed by numerous chieftains and princelings ; they were charged 2 per cent. a month and were consequently never out of debt ; to meet arrears of interest they applied for new loans and presently there was hardly a noble of that province who was not in debt to the Company and hardly a Company official who had not benefited from the gratitude of the debtors. As these princes sank deeper into debt their politics and administration became of very urgent concern to the Company's officials ; if their debtors gained territory it was an increased security for new loans, if they lost it the security for old loans was diminished. Political control of the province, secured by Clive's victories, was the necessary conclusion to these transactions. Meanwhile the officials did well. In nineteen years Pigot received £1,200,000 in bribes from the Nawab and even the more modest Wynch pocketed £200,000. The Nawab's self-constituted banker in Madras was Paul Benfield ; through him many of the bribes were paid and he helped the Nawab to raise his loans. He became so rich that he could dictate the policy of the Madras Government. True to the tradition of Finance, he professed an ardent attachment to liberal principles of individualism. He was even prepared to fight for these principles rather than submit to Government control or even opposition. When finally the Government attempted resistance, he seized the person of the Governor and installed a body of nonentities as Council who took their orders from him and from the Nawab. Later, his wealth at last gone, the Nawab declined into a dignified figurehead. He lived in Madras and might be seen out driving most evenings. He owed everybody money and since he could not possibly pay off all his creditors he paid none. His excuses were conveyed in Persian letters of exquisite courtesy. Everyone liked him for his charming manners and his ready smile and as he grew older and more and more dignified he became one of the sights of Madras, and a positive attraction for tourists.

A French capture of the city and the looting of the suburbs by Hyder Ali, whose troopers ruined many a " Gentleman's Seat " outside the walls, were dramatic interruptions of the quiet prosperous life of Madras; but after a few angry expressions at the general barbarity of foreigners and natives, the English settled down again soon enough, rebuilt their country-houses and ordered new furniture from England. Furniture was always expensive. A bill shows that a " Europe chair " cost 27*s.*, " a dining table in two part " £6; " a Mahogany bureau " £10. There would be pictures, too, and we hear of the purchase of " 24 French pictures in crayons " and " 20 Europe pictures "; and to cover the walls " China paper ". Most East Indiamen carried consignments of furniture and glassware which the captains sold to the factors and their ladies. The captain's chief concern was to time the arrival of these consignments so that the demand always exceeded the supply; after a period of stormy weather sometimes half a dozen ships arrived together and then it was difficult to find sufficient purchasers for their consignment; they had to be sold while the ships were in port in Madras, for it would be a dead loss to take them back to England. A Mr. Douglas solved the problem by buying up a quantity of glassware and then disposing of it by raffles and lotteries. He was " a gay and dressy man ", whom you might have mistaken for a French nobleman; he always wore a sword, a number of rings, and his hair was brushed straight back from his forehead into a high crest, with three tiers of side-curls. He was a tireless dancer and never missed either minuet or country dance. His skill in dancing and his energetic flattery impressed all his partners. He would praise their common sense and business capacity and when they assented breathlessly he would whisper that as a mark of his esteem he would let them into the secret of a most exclusive lottery which was not open to the public. He always had the documents ready in his coat-pocket and seldom failed to obtain his partner's signature to an engagement to buy an expensive lottery ticket. By this method he made £100,000 in quite a short time. His dupes do not seem to have borne him any grudge. English furniture the ladies had to have, whether ordered direct from London or bought from East Indiamen captains or won in Mr. Douglas's lottery, to fill those enormous rooms in which they lay for hours on sofas drawn close to the doors hung with moistened grass screens through which the wind came cool and damp. Reading matter was scarce and there was very little light literature. In 1754 in the catalogue of the Madras library (which had been founded by the purchase of a retiring chaplain's books) there were a number of Christian Fathers, and classical authors; Blackmore's *King Arthur*; the *Lusiad*; Drayton's *Polyolbion*; *Hudibras*; a single romance called *Don Feuise*; a number of law-books and some travels. Some of the greater houses contained private libraries with Hebrew, Greek and Latin authors; Bacon and Locke, Butler and Steele and Addison; the poetry of Pomfret and Akenside. Officers on campaign often took with them an impressive number of books; *Tom Jones*, *Don Quixote*, *Gil Blas* were all popular. But few of these authors would appeal to the ladies. And their main recreation seems to have been repairing their complexions with rouge, with Venus Bloom and Mareshall Powder, freshening their hands and shoulders with Hungary water, lavender, and bergamot and changing their jewels and dresses. Even visitors fresh from the raffish extravagance of London commented on the gaudy ostentation of the ladies' diamonds and on the extraordinary colours and designs of their dresses. Not only the dresses of the ladies, for the "gay India coats" of the Madras gentlemen startled their friends in England. Even in the remotest factories inland lonely Englishmen piqued themselves on their fashionable appearance. In an age without fans or ice, when houses were built with no regard for the rigour of the climate, these flowered coats and white breeches soon required washing. As a result, gentlemen's wardrobes were remarkably large. One lawyer owned seventy-one pairs of breeches and eighty-one waistcoats. For office wear, gentlemen left aside their brocades and silks and were content with sleeved waistcoats, plain cotton shirts and breeches of dimity or nankeen. And as they settled themselves at their desks the writers would pull off their wigs and wear in their place little starched white caps.

While the gentlemen scribbled with their long quill pens or raised their voices in the law courts there was nothing much for the ladies to do till dinner-time at two or three o'clock and yet they had to wear "fashionable undress and large caps" for fear an acquaintance should call. Dinner was a welcome event. Even in the hottest weather there were eight or nine courses with a wide variety of wines such as "Mountain wine, Rhenish Syder, Galicia, Florence, Hock, Canary, Brandy, Claret and Skyrash Wine". The doctors advised heavy draughts of port in the hot weather as a specific against fever. One doctor recommended plenty of meat to strengthen the blood, but it was appropriate that he suddenly "fell dead after eating a hearty dinner of beef". In fact the doctors must have been responsible for as many deaths as in the previous century. Their charges were enormous, a gold mohur for a visit, and their one panacea was bleeding ; little children were cupped till they fainted from loss of blood. After the bleeding a ferocious purge was administered, a source of a little extra profit for the physicians who charged a rupee for an ounce of salts and three rupees for an ounce of bark. A councillor died because his doctor's assistant " negligently powdered pearl in a stone mortar wherein arsenic had been before beaten, the mixture whereof with the pearl is supposed to be the occasion of his death ". A physician sued his patient, claiming £30 for medicines supplied. These medicines consisted of six phials of " Hysterick drafts " containing " cordial waters and juleps, tincture of castor, spirit of lavender and hartshorne ". The hospitals were in a strange state and in 1794 a complaint was made that in the Presidency Hospital, " it is not an uncommon practice of the patients to form parties, often with the sergeant of the guard, to go into the Black Town, where they generally remain during the greater part of the night, committing every act of enormity ". If the huge meals and heavy drinking were not among the causes of the heavy mortality they must be held responsible for the general irritability. Though Madras never rivalled Bombay in the number or violence of its feuds, it is certain that men's tempers were short and personal assaults common. Even chaplains were not safe from attack. " What ignominy ", as an unfortunate clergyman complained, " can be greater, or reproach more severe, than to be kicked ? " But it was sometimes a clergyman who inflicted this ignominy on others. The Rev. St. J. Brown kicked a servant off a terrace twenty feet high and deprecated any attempt at rescuing him with the concise " Let him go to hell." Mr. Isaac in a petition addressed to the Company, complained that one of the Company's servants, Mr. Powell,

> came into your memorialist's house and . . . your memorialist in a polite and friendly manner invited the said Powell to sit down, but the said Powell . . . flew into an outrageous passion and . . . assaulted your memorialist by raising his closed hand over your memorialist's head, and dared your memorialist to go out of his own house and offered him a shilling so to do.

Compared with such behaviour, the conduct of Lieutenant John Holland in calling Mr. Emmanuel Samuel "an infamous coward and a detestable Poltroon" could hardly be taken too seriously and the justices let him off with a fine of fifteen pagodas.

In the evenings a drive or ride along the sea-front was the favourite recreation. The sea-wind was refreshing and there were ships in the harbour and perhaps visitors from Calcutta with the news and gossip of that greater city. Or perhaps a party would be leaving by ship. There would be a crowd of friends to see them off, the gentlemen flushed and unsteady after a round of farewell dinners. The catamarans were rowed near to shore, the ladies were carried on to them and the gentlemen climbed on as best they could. The boatmen waited till three great waves had broken and then tried to rush their frail craft over the rolling swell. Once across the belt of surf the gentlemen bowed and saluted their friends on shore and the ladies waved their handkerchiefs. It was a relief to have escaped a wetting, for one always wore one's smartest clothes on an occasion like this, with one's friends lined up on the beach and the captain of the ship waiting to welcome his guests on board with fiddles and a fanfare of trumpets.

CHAPTER IV

EVEN if the voyage was only from Madras to Calcutta it was as well to prepare for a long sojourn on board. That journey might take six weeks and contrary winds might blow one all over the Bay of Bengal. Travellers must in that century have been less easily bored than to-day, for if the Madras–Calcutta route could take so long what of the journey from England?

An East Indiaman was romantic enough seen dimly in the murk at Gravesend, with its great masts and the cargo going aboard and the merchants standing on the quay muffled in their cloaks, talking of distant lands and strange people. There were guns along the ship's bulwarks and grizzled sailors with gold rings in their ears tramped down the rain-sleek cobbles. The captain was a tremendous figure, more majestic than the commander of a warship and quite as autocratic with his passengers as with his crew; [1] but he stood there greeting his guests with the affable condescension of a rich relative welcoming his cousins at his country-house. And after the first buffetings of the Channel it was romantic to stroll on deck, to watch with one's spy-glass for the first glimpse of Madeira, while the gulls flashed overhead and the great sails swelled in the wind and the rigging sang. Dinner was generally served on the second deck and a band played while the passengers drank loyal toasts and the claret went round briskly. Presently the ladies adjourned to the round-house, where coffee or tea

[1] As late as 1818 the commander of an East Indiaman clapped in irons a lieutenant in the army for whistling in his presence.

was served. The rigging was hung with coloured lanterns, and when the fiddles struck up enthusiastic dancers hurried to the upper deck. Serious drinkers gathered in the round-house and between great draughts of Burgundy and champagne sang catches and glees till one in the morning, when supper was served. It was below deck that impressions were less favourable. Cabins were represented by canvas partitions. If there was a storm these partitions offered no obstacle to the furniture which rolled from one end of the ship to the other. Not only furniture ; for when Mirza Abutakt, a cultivated Muhammadan gentleman, was travelling—

> Mr. Grand, who was of enormous size, and whose cabin was separated from mine only by a canvas partition, fell with all his weight upon my breast and hurt me exceedingly. What rendered this circumstance more provoking was that if, by any accident, the smallest noise was made in my apartment, he would call out, with all the overbearing insolence which characterises the vulgar part of the English in their conduct to Orientals, " What are you about ? You don't let me get a wink of sleep " and other such rude expressions.

There was only one state-cabin under the round-house. But this was reserved for men, as the ship's officers had to pass through it to take soundings even at night. But while it provided the only spacious accommodation, the round-house had several disadvantages. Sailors stamped about overhead at all hours " performing the necessary manœuvres with the sails attached to the mizen-mast, specially that of working the spanker-boom ". Moreover, the poultry were kept in cages in the round-house and " the feeding with the consequent pecking twice a day " became an increasing irritation. It was lucky if there were not several goats tied in there as well. Still, one had the compensation of fresh air ; for though the Company prided itself on the regulation requiring every ship to be thoroughly washed twice a week the smells seem to have been formidable. A storm caused everyone the series of discomforts that Warren Hastings catalogued : " The Want of Rest, the violent Agitation of the ship, the Vexation of seeing and hearing all the Moveables of your cabin tumble about you, the Pain in your Back, Days of Unquiet and Apprehension, and above all the dreadful Fall of the Globe Lantern."

The pleasant sensations of novelty at sight of land waned as the ship followed the endless coast-line of Africa where savage " Caffres " lay in wait for stranded vessels. Scurvy soon appeared among the crew and there were frequent funerals. At first the passengers were pleasantly impressed by the solemnity of these occasions, filled their diaries with melancholy and philosophical reflections and commended the sober and reverent demeanour of the crew during the service ; indeed, these deaths and dramatic funerals might well be the Almighty's method of recalling to a serious and godly life those poor rough sailors who, as Mr. Forbes hoped,[1] might now examine their consciences and live more virtuously in future. The ship's officers, being hardened to such occasions, were often somewhat casual in their conduct, and a poet describes how, when

> The passengers and crew around,
> With gravest faces, look profound,
> The *service* is begun, when, lo !
> The captain's eye glanc'd down below ;
> An error in the compass spies :
> He *d——ns* the *stupid helmsman's* eyes !
> Assures him he'll be flogged, and then,
> The purser adds his own, " *Amen* ".
> The pious *pair* again go on,
> Conclude the service, and—'*tis done.*[1]

Often enough the crew was so reduced by scurvy that the

[1] *Oriental Memoirs.*

gentlemen had to work like common sailors, and then there were fewer laudatory references to the Almighty's methods.

The Cape was a welcome break in the tedium of the voyage. There was fresh food of every kind ; in particular delicious vegetables and the Cape grapes that the older passengers declared were the best in the world. It was curious that Cape wine was so execrable and so expensive. As the ship often stayed some time at anchor the passengers took lodgings in the town (the Dutch housewives welcoming the chance of letting rooms to the opulent English), and went for expeditions into the surrounding country. Word would be sent on ahead to the little Dutch inns and the travellers would find awaiting them a breakfast of eggs and bacon and cheese, washed down with Constantia wine. A favourite expedition was, as always, to the summit of Table Mountain ; the climb was tiring but its ardours were mitigated by the music of flute-players who trudged ahead, their notes often echoing strangely in narrow clefts or under overarching cliffs ; and near the summit a table would be spread in a cool cave and for refreshment there was tea and coffee, cold ham and chicken and great baskets of fruit. Every traveller admired the zoological gardens in Cape Town, reported then the best in the world ; it was pleasant to stroll down the shady arcades under tropic trees and stare at the extraordinary animals of Africa, to drink a glass of wine on a blossom-hung terrace, and then as the day grew warm retire to the cool shadow of a billiard-room and challenge and chaff the stolid Dutch farmers. The Dutch were not so stolid as never to find occasions for laughter at their guests. The London fashions especially amused them. A number of English ladies bound for Calcutta appeared at a dance at Cape Town all wearing the waistless dresses then in fashion, and the Dutch thought that these dresses made their wearers' figures laughably ugly. One humourless old farmer, however, was seriously disturbed : " Ah ! God help their poor parents," he exclaimed, " how miserable must they be upon perceiving the situation their daughters are in ! " And when a friend asked him why, he muttered, " Is it not apparent they are all with child ? "

It was a sad disappointment to the passengers if a favouring wind decided the captain to push on past the Cape. But there was always hope of an anchorage at Johanna Island ; and there the " Caffres " swarmed round the ship in their tiny craft made of single tree-trunks offering for sale fresh eggs and poultry and a wonderful variety of fruit, pineapples, oranges, guavas and bananas. They scrambled about over the piles of fruit and waved and laughed and shouted, " Englishman man very good man, drinkee de punch, fire de gun, beatee de French, very good fun." It was considered unhealthy to sleep ashore ; but if the ship had missed the Cape, there were generally affairs of honour to be settled between the gentlemen, who in the tedium of the voyage, had found many occasions to quarrel. By the time they stepped ashore, however, they had often entirely forgotten their resentment and often the cause of offence. But contemporary prejudice obliged them to make a show of a duel. Two young cadets who accompanied Hickey on his first voyage having boxed each other's ears were both terrified at the prospect of a duel. The other passengers, however, insisted ; but took the precaution of removing ball from the pistol of each combatant. There was a long discussion between the duellists and the seconds about the distance, the former suggesting thirty yards, the seconds proposing six paces. They compromised on twelve paces (despite the anguished sighs of the duellists who proclaimed such proximity " absolute butchery ") but the duellists insisted on the Fourth Mate, who had the longest legs on the ship, measuring the paces. They were about to fire when suddenly one duellist shouted that the other owed him forty dollars and that it was a little hard that he should lose his money as well as his life. When this was settled, the signal was given, both fired, and to the consternation of the seconds one of the duellists fell down. They hurried up fearful lest the pistol had, after all, been loaded with ball ; but they found the duellist alive and indeed uninjured, but full of the conviction that a ball had whizzed so close to his ear as to cause his collapse.

Once in the Indian Ocean passengers and crew alike were haunted by the fear of French privateers. At the first sign of hostile craft the canvas partitions of the cabins were removed ; all furniture, beds and luggage were swept from the decks ; women and children were hurried down to the hold, where they shuddered in unsavoury darkness while on deck the gentlemen tried out cutlasses and sketched a few defensive manœuvres and were then brushed aside by the hurrying sailors who now had more urgent duties than deference to the quality.[1] Capture by the French entailed a number of inconveniences. The French were polite enough in their way but it was regrettable that their officers dressed so shabbily ; Admiral de Suffren who looked, as Hickey contemptuously observed, " like a little fat, vulgar English butcher " received his English captives in slippers, blue cloth breeches unbuttoned at the knees and a coarse linen shirt open at the neck, with sleeves rolled above his elbows. Moreover, the French had nowhere to send their captives ; their ports were often in the hands of the English and their allies on the Indian continent were unreliable and

[1] See Mrs. Sherwood's *Autobiography* for an account of such an encounter.

disreputable. The hundreds of prisoners sent by de Suffren to safe custody with Tipu Sultan were, in spite of the latter's promises to the French, treated with great cruelty. That dark squat prince whose chief amusements were designing dresses to be compulsorily worn by his female subjects, studying and interpreting dreams, and watching a mechanical lion mangle a doll dressed in European costume, would suddenly awaken to a stern realisation of his duties as a Muslim sovereign and issue orders for the forcible circumcision of the Englishmen in his prisons. . . .

Even after arrival at the mouth of the Hooghly adventures were not all over. The passengers disembarked in a tender which sailed only by day and was tied up at night to one or other of the islands in the Gangetic delta ; but the islands had to be chosen carefully, for they abounded in tigers and, as happened on the tender which carried my grandfather to Calcutta, a tiger would occasionally be found on board in the morning and a passenger or two missing.

After the long months on board ship it must have been delightful at last to reach Calcutta, then the greatest and gayest of Anglo-Indian cities. It was the city that Clive described as

> one of the most wicked Places in the Universe. Corruption, Licentiousness and a want of Principle seem to have possessed the Minds of all the Civil Servants, by frequent bad examples they have grown callous, Rapacious and Luxurious beyond Conception, and the Incapacity and Iniquity of some and the Youth of others. . . .

It was here that Mrs. Sherwood found the material for her descriptions of

> the splendid sloth and the languid debauchery of European Society in those days—English gentlemen, overwhelmed with the consequences of extravagance, hampered by Hindoo women and by crowds of olive-coloured children, without

> either the will or the power to leave the shores of India. . . . Great men rode about in State coaches, with a dozen servants running before and behind them to bawl out their titles; and little men lounged in palanquins or drove a chariot for which they never intended to pay, drawn by horses which they had bullied or cajoled out of the stables of wealthy Baboos . . .

It was here that were made many of the vast fortunes that aroused so much jealousy and envy in England and here that the traditional Nabob flourished. The origin of many legends, General Richard Smith, was in the seventies still lording it in Calcutta society. As Sir Mathew Mite he was pilloried in Forbes's play "The Nabob" and Macaulay described this character as

> an Anglo-Indian chief, dissolute, ungenerous, and tyrannical, ashamed of the humble friends of his youth, hating the aristocracy yet childishly eager to be numbered among them, squandering his wealth on pandars and flatterers, tricking out his chairmen with the most costly hothouse flowers, and astounding the ignorant with jargon about rupees, lacs and jaghires.

For once Macaulay is guilty of no exaggeration. Smith was referred to by contemporary Calcutta in terms appropriate to a Grand Chamberlain of Byzantium. People ridiculed his manners but were terrified of his power. The most extravagant compliments were paid him by men who, when his back was turned, jeered at his "low origin". A similar deference was paid to Mrs. Smith by most of the married ladies. Dr. Hancock wrote anxiously to his wife begging her to call on Mrs. Smith the moment she returned to Calcutta to congratulate her on her safe arrival, for "the Omission might be of Consequence to me, as he is a man of great Power. You perfectly well know his Vanity and my Necessity." In spite of his extraordinary style of living, Smith always loudly professed an attachment to Stoic principles and a horror of all corruption and excessive wealth. He was one of Francis's greatest friends and people were edified by his stern denunciations of Hastings' extravagance.

It was not only General Smith's circle who were remarkable for their style of living. Fortunes were made in a few years and lost in a night at cards. There was a whist club at which stakes were very heavy, but it was crowded every night and gentlemen were disappointed if they missed a visit. A chaplain, who had looked forward to a pleasant evening at cards, was extremely irritated when he had to postpone his game "because he had a d——d soldier to bury". Francis at a single sitting there won £20,000 and on another occasion Barwell lost £40,000. "Oh," runs an entry in Mackrabie's diary for March 9, 1776, "I lost seven rubbers running. Oh sad, sad, sad." Very few were averse to considering the most blatant forms of bribery. Hastings once made up his mind to end the whole dreary squabble with his opponents in Council by buying them up for £100,000 apiece; and Clive, vexed by the incompetents for whom influential relatives in England had secured comfortable berths with the Company, had suggested buying them out as soon as they landed in Calcutta. When a certain new-comer presented himself at Government House, Clive looked him up and down and said, "Oh well, how much will you take?" Yet everyone affected to know and care nothing about money. A gentleman left his finances to his *sircar* or broker, generally a money-lender of considerable wealth but whose humble address and abject demeanour were very flattering. The *sircar* hired the servants and arranged for the daily expenses of the house, and a favourite subject for contemporary satirists was that of the lordly European lolling in a long chair, the mouth-piece of a hookah in his hand, a glass of Madeira at his elbow, while standing with bent head before him the *sircar*, ragged and servile, read out from an enormous roll of parchment the various expenses unavoidably incurred by him on behalf of his employer ; and, concluding with an account which showed he had not one penny left, he would venture to advise that the honourable gentleman should again summon that kind money-lender, who, being the *sircar's* cousin, would oblige the gentleman at a most reasonable rate.

Similarly a gentleman's house had to be stocked with an army of servants. Hickey, not a wealthy man by Calcutta standards, employed sixty-three, including eight whose only duty was to wait at table, three to cut the grass in the garden, four grooms and one coachman, two bakers, two cooks, a hairdresser and nine valets. The richer merchants employed upwards of a hundred servants and some of them were styled by most outlandish names. The wig-barber (as opposed to that superior employee, the hairdresser) was as inevitable in every fashionable house as the hookaburdar, who not only tended the gentlemen's hookahs at home, kept the silver chains and rosettes brightly polished, blew on the charcoal and renewed the rose water, but also accompanied his master abroad even to dinners at Government House, at which, after the ladies had withdrawn, the hookah-bearers entered in solemn procession, each taking up his position near his master, to whom he handed the ivory mouthpiece after unwinding the enormous coil of piping from round the neck of the hookah. It was important to arrange the hookahs properly, for it was considered an insult to step over another's hookah-snake. It was as dangerous to get between a gentleman and his hookah-bowl as it is reputed to be to-day to walk between a Mexican bull-puncher and his drink. A duel was inevitable.

Many ladies began to favour the hookah.

> The gentlemen [we read in Price's *Tracts*] introduce their hookahs and smoak in the company of ladies and . . . the mixture of sweet-scented Persian tobacco, sweet herbs, coarse sugar, spice etc., which they inhale, comes through clean water and is so very pleasant that many ladies take the tube and draw a little of the smoak into their mouths.

At receptions they sat in carefully posed attitudes with the coils of the hookah encircling their waists like Cretan snake-goddesses ; and it was a very flattering gesture for a lady to offer a gentleman the mouthpiece of her hookah for a refreshing puff.

Nor was it only the civilians in their great houses in Calcutta who required so many servants. Officers who went on active service were equally well-attended. Forced marches and rapid strategic moves were not easy when an army included so many non-combatants, but the servants were never left behind. In that perilous year 1780, when the Company's rule seemed to many to be doomed, a captain, throughout the Mysore campaign, was accompanied by his steward, his cook, his valet, a groom and groom's assistant, a barber, a washerman and " other officers " besides fifteen coolies to carry his luggage, his wine, brandy and tea, his live poultry and milch-goats.

It was often difficult to keep all these servants in order. Fortunately the law showed little favour to insubordinate employees. Records of magisterial courts are full of entries such as the following : " A slave girl of Mr. Anderson called Piggy, having run away from her master—*Order.* five strokes with a rattan and she to be sent to her master." For petty misdemeanours such as theft and drunkenness the master of the house was generally unwilling to invoke the aid of the law and would wield the rod himself. If the author of some theft was unknown a priest would be called and the servants put through the rice ordeal which continues in Indian villages to-day. The priest first delivers a homily on the enormity of theft, the torments of hell, the weary procession of rebirth in a lower life consequent on a man's dying with a sin on his conscience. He then calls for dry rice over which he mumbles mysteriously. Then each man is required to hold a small amount of this rice in his mouth for a few minutes, and the priest solemnly assures them that the rice in the mouths of the innocent will, at the end of the ordeal be found to be wet, while that in the mouth of the thief will be dry. That there is a natural and obvious explanation for the frequent success of this ordeal in revealing a malefactor does not detract from its value as a test among simple people.

But in spite of the rattans of the magistrates and the threat of the rice ordeal, many servants, especially of bachelors, looted their employers joyously. When Mr. Hickey had embarked on a ship in the Hooghly his servant Chaund, to whom he was devoted—

> —invited Gregg (the captain's English servant) to go on shore with him and get a girl, which he declined, and Chaund went by himself, but within two hours returned on board attended by *three* whores. Gregg enquiring what he could mean by such conduct which must ruin him with his master if he heard of it, as was most likely the case, he laughed at him, observing that his master would not be at all angry about the matter which, however, there was no occasion for him to know anything of. He then added that he had brought three nice girls, one of whom was for himself, one for him (Gregg), and the other for Deenoo—who was only thirteen years of age—and that he had engaged them to go down to the ship and to land them at Fulta on their way back to Calcutta. Gregg again remonstrated, but being in the prime of life and full vigour of health he could not resist the temptation thus offered, and he at last yielded to Chaund's persuasions and example, as he also did to that of participating in the good fare which the profligate Chaund produced. The evening's entertainment concluded with the whole party, male and female, getting abominably

drunk, in which state Chaund retired with two of the girls to my bed.

Not only was an army of servants considered necessary for comfort, the wages of each being little lower than that of a similar servant in India to-day, but rents were, by contemporary standards, very high. There were no hotels till 1780 when Sir Elijah Impey's late steward opened an hotel where, as the advertisement stated, " turtles are dressed, gentlemen boarded and families supplied with pastry " ; but we do not know what the charges were. Francis paid £1,200 a year for his house ; and Mrs. Fay for a small villa " in a part of the town not esteemed " was charged over £200 a year. Furniture was expensive. It cost Hickey £1,000 to make his house fit, as he considered, for human habitation. The prices of other amenities were in proportion. Admission to the pit at the theatre cost £1 and the better seats were £2 each. It cost £10 to christen a child and £40 to be married. The minimum fee for a doctor was £2. Commodities imported from Europe were sold at a fantastic rate ; ham and cheese being priced at twelve-and-six a pound. In such circumstances everyone grumbled endlessly at the difficulty of saving money. Francis angrily lamented, " If I carry home £25,000 by the severest parsimony of five years it will be the most I can accomplish." And soon he raised his ambition to a saving of " forty thousand secure ". As little of this could be honestly come by and as he was prepared to lose thousands nightly at whist there is a certain verrine magnificence in such anticipation.

The daily round of life in Calcutta resembled that in Madras. The young factor was awakened by a posse of respectful servants. A barber shaved him, cut his fingernails and cleaned his ears. For breakfast he had tea and toast and as he sat at table the hairdresser attended to his wig. When he had finished his tea his " houccaburdar softly slips the upper end of the snake or tube of the hucca into his hand ". When he drove or rode to office he was " preceded by eight to twelve chubdars, harcarrahs and peons, with the insignia of their professions and their livery distinguished by the colour of their turbans ". The hours of work were light, nine to twelve in the hot weather and ten to one-thirty in the cold. For it cannot be said that the methods of the Company's employees were very business-like. It is difficult not to sympathise with the indignation of the Directors when they learnt that some most important documents which had been lost " were picked up in a Publick Necessary House ". But every lapse was blamed on the heat. There were no fans. A drowsy servant waved a fly-whisk without appreciably stirring the air. Robes and wigs were worn in court by judges and counsel alike all through the hot weather. Nuncomar's long trial was held in June, the worst month of all, and the judges rose four times a day to retire to their chambers and change their linen.

Ladies went for an early ride or drive and then waited for callers till dinner at two. For dinner, Mrs. Fay who considered she was living cheap and was in addition obliged, as an invalid, to be content with a spare diet, sat down every day to soup ; roast fowl ; curry and rice ; mutton pie ; lamb, rice pudding ; tarts and cheese. The satirist who wrote under the pseudonym of Quiz was shocked at " the indelicate method both ladies and gentlemen eat, both at tiffen and dinner ". He was absolutely disgusted at seeing " one of the *prettiest girls* in Calcutta eat about two pounds of mutton-chops at one sitting ! " And he hurried into verse to describe his distaste for the appetites of the officers who

March to barracks where with joy,
Their *masticators* they employ,
On curry, rice, and beef and goat,
Voraciously they cram each throat.

By each plate were two glasses " one pyramidal (like hob-nob glasses in England) for loll shrub ; the other a common-sized wineglass for whatever beverage is most agreeable ". Wine was, during dinner, generally diluted with water. When dessert had been served and a few loyal healths drunk the ladies withdrew and the gentlemen sat down to the serious business of disposing of three bottles of claret each. It would have seemed oddly unsocial for a gentleman to drink less when, as Mrs. Fay wrote " every lady (even your humble servant) drinks at least a bottle ".

In spite of so much drinking, however, there were very few connoisseurs of wine in Calcutta ; as Mr. Hickey found when, to do honour to a distinguished company of guests he was able to cajole three dozen of the best claret from Baxter and Joy's " Europe Shop ". These were to be reserved until dessert had been set on the table and the servants were instructed to serve claret " of the Danish batch " during dinner. But when the good claret was introduced the only comment from the guests was " Zounds ! They have changed the wine upon us." " Well," replied Mr. Hickey, " I trust it is for the better." " No, by God ! " exclaimed some of the guests. " Quite the contrary, it is from the most delicious to execrable stuff." In spite of Hickey's remonstrances, his pleading that they should give the wine a fair trial—

> —the party unanimously decided that what they had drunk during dinner was infinitely the best, it being uncommonly high-flavoured, delicious wine, whereas the other was abominable, not fit to be drunk. Finding this opinion general, I told them I rejoiced to find they had such correct taste, especially

> as I could indulge them upon very easy terms, the wine they admired having cost me no more than eighteen rupees a dozen, while that they abused and rejected was at the enormous price of sixty-five rupees a dozen. The moment I declared the vast difference in the prices several of the party began to change their tone, some of them observing, " There certainly is a delicacy and a flavour in the English wine which the other wants." . . .

In a mess drinking would be less haphazard. There would be Madeira before dinner, and claret with the turkey which was the favourite and almost regular dish, with ham and curries and rice. When the cloths were removed each man drank with his neighbour. Then followed the toasts, each honoured by a suitable tune from the band. Thus for the Ladies the band would strike up " Kiss my lady " and for the Honourable Company " Money in both Pockets ". When the colonel left, there would be a course of savouries and drinking would recommence. And if any officer left before the rest he would be followed with shouts of " Shabby Fellow ", " Milk Sop " or " Cock Tail ".

After dinner everyone slept till the evening, when the hairdresser paid a second visit to powder and trim the gentlemen's hair and build up, for the evening *sortie*, the ladies' turban-like coiffures, heavy with bows, ribbons and bunches of flowers. The two most fashionable hairdressers were Frenchmen and their charges were fantastically high; eight rupees for a gentleman's hair-cut and four rupees for hairdressing. After the coiffure, " everybody dressed splendidly, being covered with lace, spangles and foil " and then set out for an airing. The sedate or nervous kept to their palanquins, a slow and unexhilarating method of conveyance; though the Court of Directors had, in the 'fifties, censured the practice of palanquin riding as though it were evidence of raffish luxury. " We very well know ", they

THE BURRA KHANAH—" A GRAND FEED "

wrote, " that the indulging writers with palankeens has not a little contributed to the neglect of business we complain of, by affording them opportunities of rambling." Newcomers to the country were often distressed by the odd noises the palanquin bearers made as they trudged along, supposing that these grunts, groans and hollow whispers indicated that the bearers were on the point of fainting from fatigue. A Mr. Cleveland was so much alarmed that he hopped out of his palanquin and was surprised to see that

> thereupon they set the palankeen down and immediately began to converse very cheerfully. . . . But Colonel Watson told him that it was a custom amongst bearers when carrying a palankeen to make that moaning noise, which did not at all indicate fatigue, and that the front bearer always noticed the sort of road they were passing over, pointing out any impediments as " Here's a hole ", " Here's a puddle of water ", " Here's long grass ", " Here's a parcel of bricks ".

But by the younger members of society a palanquin was voted odiously slow ; they preferred a phaeton and pair of Arabs. Francis could be seen every evening driving furiously his four handsome Arabs. Ladies often drove unattended by gentlemen, showing off their skill with the reins, an umbrella nodding over their heads, their horses " finely set out with silver nets to guard their necks from insects ".

No gentleman could hope to win a young lady's favour unless he had a smart carriage. A Mr. Calvert, having been refused by a Miss Philpott, tried to increase his value in her eyes by purchasing an English post-chaise, the four horses being driven by postillions in very rich liveries. He appeared on the racecourse one evening and drove up close to Miss Philpott's phaeton. As she never commented on his sudden splendour he said, " What do you think of my love trap ? " " Elegant, upon my word," said Miss Philpott, " quite *magnifique*."—" And what do you think of the *bait* within it?" "Do you mean to speak in French or English?" But in spite of her pert reply, which made Mr. Calvert the joke of Calcutta, Miss Philpott was deeply moved by the dashing equipage and became engaged to Mr. Calvert in a month.

Another evening recreation was boating. Pinnaces flitted down the river to return after nightfall with a coloured lantern at the prow. Families were rowed sedately in barges hung with brocades and attended by musicians. But there was no craft to compare with Mr. Hickey's, which was forty-eight feet long with a crew of fourteen, all dressed alike "in white linen jackets and trousers, with bright red-and-green turbans, cumberbands (a large roll round the bottom of their bodies) of the same".[1] Other gentlemen of means were rowed by teams of black slaves, especially imported from Bourbon or Mauritius, notable for their strength and huge physique and dressed in fantastic costumes. They were often attended by tiny negro slaves in vast turbans who blew gaily on French horns, whose resonant music mingled with the clamour of conches from Hindu temples lining the river where, as darkness gathered in the dust-laden air, the gods were saluted with gongs and offerings of heavy-petalled flowers.

If most people got drunk at dinner, supper was equally hilarious. At a party on November 3, 1775, at the Claverings all the ladies drank themselves silly on cherry-brandy and pelted each other with bread pellets. This rough game became suddenly fashionable and Barwell was hailed as Bread-pellet Champion of Calcutta, since he could snuff out a candle at a distance of four yards with a pellet. The craze came to an equally sudden end when a Captain Morrison, losing his temper at receiving a pellet unexpectedly in the

[1] Mackrabie's *Diary*.

face, threw a leg of mutton at the offender. A duel followed in which the pellet-thrower was nearly killed ; and the practice fell into disfavour.

One was often surprised by a party of guests descending on one unexpectedly. But Colonel Auchmuty had the unusual foible of inviting people to supper and then forgetting all about it. When the guests arrived, he would be blunt but hospitable. He would explain that as he was not expecting them there was little to eat, but that the cellar was fortunately full. But when they took him at his word and continually asked for fresh supplies of wine he would exclaim, " By Jesus, my choice ones, I am apt to think you have been for some time without a taste of the true stuff. The Devil burn me, but I belave you imagine yourselves in a wine merchant's cellar." But as he drank with his guests his earlier reserve would vanish. He would leap up from the table and shout to his wife, who prudently remained upstairs when guests called on the colonel, " Shela ! My Jewel, why Shela, I say, take care I say of the spoons and silver forks, count them up carefully, my honey, for by the holy Jesus we have got some tight boys to-night."

If there was a ball or reception, people generally supped first in their own houses with the result that they arrived in uproarious groups, the gentlemen often touselled and dusty from a spill which they would indignantly attribute to the press of carriages on the road, the bad lighting of the streets or their earnest endeavour to make way for a lady driving her own phaeton which had caused them to collide with a tree. Mr. Hickey arrived at a party with all skin scraped off one side of his face which spoiled the effect of his " bright blue silk domino ". This party was a *fête champêtre* given by Mr. Edward Fenwick during the month of May, when the heat of Calcutta is so intense that almost any exertion is exhausting. Mr. Fenwick's guests, in fancy dress and masked, continued dancing till seven in the morning. Perhaps they were inspired by the " many thousand coloured lamps ", by the feats of " an eminent operator in fireworks ", and by the fact that several bands played simultaneously different tunes. This *fête champêtre* was of unusual magnificence ; but even through the hot weather and the rains hardly a week passed without some dance. In rooms without fans, lit by candle light, the exertions required for a cotillion reduced some of the dancers to a sad condition.

> Imagine to yourself [wrote *Asiaticus*] the lovely object of your affections ready to expire with heat, every limb trembling and every feature distorted with fatigue, and her partner, with a muslin handkerchief in each hand, employed in the delightful office of wiping down her face, while the big drops stand impearled upon her forehead.

But few were as fastidious as Asiaticus and when the fiddles struck up the ballrooms were crowded with dancers. The jolliest balls were given by Colonel Gallier, who was devoted to Frenchwomen and danced cotillions with remarkable energy. A constant guest at the Colonel's was Dr. Campbell who was quite startlingly bald and never wore a wig, but who was always to be seen " capering about and gallanting the ladies ".

On Sunday mornings the ladies were carried in palanquins (whose slow progress, however tiresome at other times, was considered appropriate to a solemn occasion) to divine service. There was no church yet in Calcutta and morning prayer was said in the customs office. All the gentlemen of the station, even if racked with bile and indigestion after their Saturday night festivities, rode early to the customs office and waited in a crowd round the door jostling each other in rivalry to escort the ladies to their seats. Etiquette allowed this gallant gesture even among strangers and it was the usual method of introducing oneself to a lady whose acquaintance one wished to make. In consequence there were generally frayed tempers and torn coats among the gentlemen on the first Sunday after the arrival of a ship from England, setting rumours flying round Calcutta of a youthful charmer or an amiable heiress.

There were many more ladies in Calcutta than at the other settlements and much space in the local newspapers was taken up with allusions to prevalent gossip. Two quotations will be sufficient. The first refers to the effect of a Miss Wrangham's charms on a susceptible member of the Government, " Counseller Feeble now constantly drinks a sort of cordial dram which he calls W-g-h eye-water and of which he drinks so freely that he, d'ye see, retires tipsy—he, he ! " " *March 1781—Lost* on the Course, last Monday evening, Buxey Clumsey's heart whilst he stood simpering at the footstep of Hooka Turban's carriage."

The most constant in attendance at the steps of the customs office on Sunday mornings were the senior merchants and officials old enough to be sentimental over fresh English complexions and rich enough to be certain of admiration. As Miss Goldborne exclaimed, " They are chiefly old fellows ! " But it was these old fellows whose courtship was thought especially suitable by the parents or guardians of young ladies ; and income, position in the Government, hopes of further appointments, were the qualities in a suitor most eagerly canvassed in the boudoir. One young lady, however, the niece of Mr. Justice Russel, seemed strangely indifferent to the wealth and position of these elderly gallants. She had been recently come to Calcutta, to

> Those proud halls, for youth unfit
> Where Princes stand and Judges sit,

and she spent most of her time day-dreaming about a young poet called Mr. Landor whom she had met in the Circulating Library at Swansea. But she gave the Calcutta gossips little sport, for soon after her arrival, while still only twenty, she contracted " a most severe bowel complaint, brought on entirely by indulging too much with that mischievous and dangerous fruit, the pineapple " and " at the end of a few days this lovely young girl fell a martyr to the obstinacy of the malady ". Her monument with its dedication, " To the Memory of the Honourable Miss Rose Aylmer " is one of the most striking in Calcutta Cemetery. One of her admirers in Calcutta had been Mr. Ricketts, a cousin of the Earl of Liverpool, and he was so much upset by her death that he " sought comfort for himself in the arms of a vulgar, huge, coarse, Irish slammerkin, Miss Prendergast ".

Having escorted the ladies to their seats the gentlemen lounged against the walls or pillars, whispering and ogling. The local clergy were not such as to inspire respect and attention during the service. " One parson ", notes Mackrabie,[1] " rivals Nimrod in hunting, a second supplies bullocks for the Army, another is a perfect connoisseur in Chinese gardening." And then there was the army chaplain Mr. Blunt.

> This incomprehensible young man [records Hickey] got abominably drunk and in that disgraceful condition exposed himself to both soldiers and sailors, running out stark naked into the midst of them, talking all sort of bawdy and ribaldry, and singing scraps of the most blackguard and indecent songs, so as to render himself a common laughing-stock.

Next morning, however, his remorse was so great that his friends feared for his health and Colonel Wellesley had to

[1] *Diary.*

be requested to deal with the situation. The Colonel " told him that what had passed was not of the least consequence as no one would think the worse of him for the little irregularities committed in a moment of forgetfulness ; that the most correct and cautious men were liable to be led astray by convivial society and no blame ought to be attached to a cursory debauch ". In spite of this advice, however, Mr. Blunt was so depressed by the memory of his escapade that he fretted himself to death within ten days.

In 1787 a new church was consecrated. Some dissatisfaction was caused among the ladies because whereas they formerly sat in a pew in a line with that of the Governor-General, they now could not occupy pews more advanced than those of the Judges. As a wit put it,

> The Ladies on the *Lord* relied
> To dignify their forms divine,
> But now, forsaken by their pride,
> To *court* the praying maidens join.

That all the ladies likely to attend church could be accommodated, as this new regulation suggests, in one pew does not argue a very regular attendance at Matins ; which is confirmed by the popularity of the catch-phrase, " Is it Sunday ? Yes ; for I see the flag is hoisted." The new church was endowed with an altarpiece by Sir John Zoffany representing " The Last Supper " and the chaplain warmly thanked him for " so capital a painting that would adorn the first church in Europe, and should excite in the breasts of its spectators those sentiments of virtue and piety so happily portrayed in the figures ".

There had been a Catholic church in Calcutta since 1700. Its founder was a Mrs. Margaret Trench, but most of its parishioners were Portuguese on whose piety every visitor commented. Perhaps they were inspired by the example of one of the first of their co-religionists to visit the Hooghly. Captured by Mogul forces, he was brought before Shah Jahan who " ordered him to be cast in an arena to a furious Elephant. The Elephant at sight of the friar, lost his native ferocity and gently caressed him with his Proboscis."

There were in Calcutta few unmarried men without a mistress. They often kept Indian women, though modern authors like Mr. Norman Douglas, who congratulate Hickey's contemporaries on their freedom from colour prejudice, overlook Hickey's own admitted " horror at the thoughts of a connection with black women ". On the whole it seems that this prejudice was as pronounced as to-day ; but Hickey's contemporaries were seldom able to find any but Indian or half-caste mistresses in Calcutta ; and being of an " amorous disposition " mistresses they had to have. But if these youths had to overcome a colour-prejudice, they often ended by becoming genuinely attached to their dark mistresses. The latter, however, were generally mercenary and reserved their real affection for men of their own race. Many a youth, after worrying over the extra-ordinary darkness of the children his mistress attributed to him, returned home from office earlier than expected and found the lady sharing his bed with a servant.

That such irregular unions were seldom a secret may be gathered from the account of the birth of *Qui Hi's* son in the satiric poem " The Grand Master ".

> Poor *Gulab* now was in *that* way,
> That those who " love their lords " should be ;
> And in a week, to *Qui Hi's* joy,
> Produced our youth a chopping boy.
> The deuce ! said *Qui Hi* with a curse ;
> It's well, however, it's no worse ;
> For what the d——l could he do,
> If he had manufactur'd two,
> Like other ladies that he knew ?

Our hero now, without pretence,
Thought himself of *some consequence* ;
A child he'd got, and what was curious,
He knew the infant was not spurious ;
For though *Qui Hi* was never tied
By licence to his Indian bride,
Yet he was confident that she
Had acted with fidelity,
But now he finds he must submit
To European damsels' wit.
Wherever *Qui Hi* did appear,
The spinsters titter, chat and jeer.
" O dear, Miss *Pinchback*, have you heard,
La ! what a scandal—on my word."
" What ", (said Miss Pinchback) " prithe say ?
Tell us the scandal of the day ? "
" The fellow ! but we'll send him out
Of our society, no doubt ;
There is sweet Miss *Wabina Stocking*,
She can repeat it—*'tis so shocking* ;
That *Qui Hi*'s creature, it is said,
The other day was brought to bed."
" Oh heaven ! " exclaimed Miss Indigo,
"And could he then have us'd me so ?
And with a *black one* too connected—
A precious precedent's begun,
A mistress first, and then a son."

There were few bachelors as fortunate as Francis who installed his French mistress in a great house at Hooghly to which he would drive out from Calcutta either with a party of friends, or alone for a quiet week-end. There, with his discreet cousin, Baggs, who acted as dragoman, and with the enchanting Madame Grand he would rest after the ardours, intrigues and faction-violence of Calcutta. These pleasant hours could be recorded with brief sighs of satisfaction in his diary. " Sunday. At Hughely. *Ridet hoc inquam Venus ipsa, rident simplices nymphae.*"

The first husband of this lady, the unfortunate Monsieur Grand, was of a Huguenot family with English connections. He was educated at Lausanne and then sent to London where he was apprenticed to Mr. Jones of Lombard Street.

Mr. Jones welcomed him brusquely on his arrival, " and asked me if I had brought him any cheese, which being answered, seemed to work a happy change ". Nevertheless he made Grand sleep in the same bed with a footman and crop his hair in order that " people might not take him for a French monkey ". Luckily his aunt, who had influence at India House, procured for him a cadetship in Bengal. He stayed with Hastings who took some interest in him and despatched him to Chandernagore with a letter of introduction to the French authorities. There he met Mdlle Werlee, whose " fine blue eyes with black eyelashes and brows gave her countenance a most piquant singularity ". He married her and brought her to Calcutta where her beauty caused a sensation. Francis met her at a ball and wrote in his diary : " *Omnia vincit amor*. Job for Wood, the salt agent." A month later Francis tried to break into Mr. Grand's house while the husband was at supper with Mr. Barwell. A servant broke in upon the supper-party and whispered in agitation to Grand that Francis had been caught in his garden apparently trying to break into Madame Grand's bedroom. Grand burst into tears and raced home to find in his garden not Francis as he had expected but Mr. George Shee, a relation of the noble Burke, held down by a posse of servants. The servants explained that while they were holding Francis a rescue party had scaled the wall and set Francis free. They had, however, managed to secure a member of the rescue party.

Francis pretended to be astonished at the uproar that followed. He dismissed his escapade as a " wretched business " as though it was as ordinary a nuisance to find a Member of Council attempting an assault on one's wife as to discover a grass-snake in the bathroom. But Grand was out for blood. He filed a suit against Francis, claiming

1,500,000 sicca rupees [1] as damages. His counsel was Sir John Day, whose knighthood, bestowed by the King shortly before he sailed for India, had inspired George Selwyn to a typical quip. " By God, this is out-heroding Herod. I have long heard of the extraordinary power His Majesty exercised, but until this moment could not have believed that he could turn Day into Knight and make a Lady Day at Michaelmas." Francis was defended by Tilghman, of whom he remarked, enthusiastically, " His principles are truly patriotic, especially when in liquor." But the evidence was black against Francis. Miran, a table-servant, deposed to the discovery of a bamboo-ladder against the house-wall. He called the other servants. While they were talking Francis emerged from the house. He was startled at seeing the servants and said hastily, " I will give you money. I'll make you all great men." They closed round him whereon he began to bluster, " Don't you know that I am Mr. Francis? Why, I am the Great Sahib." But in spite of this they seized him. The servants corroborated each other with remarkable accuracy. Tilghman's cross-examination was singularly feeble. He tried to confuse the servants by searching questions about the exact hour of the offence—a favourite trick of English lawyers in India which, as a matter of fact, never impresses a court favourably, since judges know well enough that Indian witnesses have little sense of time—and often no acquaintance at all with the English hours. Unshaken by Tilghman's inquisition, the servants described the arrival of the rescue party, Francis's escape and their capture of Shee. They nearly captured another rescuer but he managed to free himself. This rescuer turned out to be Ducarel, another of Francis's parasites. Everybody began wondering how he could have

[1] This was then equivalent to £160,000.

escaped while Shee remained prisoner. For Ducarel, a serious-minded person interested in science and in the problem of personal immortality, was a dwarf. He was treated as a jester and buffoon by Francis who once addressed a letter to him beginning "You d——d old fool". So when this unfortunate creature appeared in the witness-box one of the first questions addressed to him was how he escaped. The dwarf drew himself and replied, "Finding myself pressed, I offered, amongst other expedients, three gold mohurs." In other respects, however, he was driven to admit the whole of the prosecution case; and even acknowledged that he had watched Francis creeping down the lane outside Mr. Grand's house, carrying the very same ladder that was found in Mr. Grand's garden and was now produced in court.

During the hearing there occurred the continual wrangles over the spelling of witnesses' names that seem to have been inseparable from the procedure of British courts of that period. There were lengthy discussions on law, for one of the three judges, Sir Robert Chambers, never missed an occasion for eager but largely irrelevant legal disquisitions. He was a sharp-tempered judge and during the hearing of an earlier case had referred to the plaintiff's attorney as "a gentleman probably heated with wine". Whereupon the attorney, as though to prove his sobriety, leapt to his feet and shouted at the judge, "You are a contemptible animal." No such incidents marked the hearing of the Grand case but the interminable discussions, the citing of rulings, the hitches and interruptions, must have been exasperating to Francis who was notorious for his contempt of lawyers, and could hardly utter the word "attorney" without an insolent and wounding sneer. In this he only followed the fashion of the day. For lawyers were perhaps the most unpopular members of the English community in Calcutta, and the papers were full of gibes at them, such as the following " Epitaph " :

God works wonders now and then
Here lies a lawyer and an honest man.

Answered.

This is a mere law quibble, not a wonder,
Here lies a lawyer and his client under.

or this epigram : " The attornies of Calcutta may be said to be to lawyers what apothecaries are to physicians, only that they do not deal in *scruples*." Nor was even the Advocate-General spared ; for when he quarrelled with his assistant and nearly fought a duel, the failure to meet in accordance with the tradition of gentlemen was satirised in this couplet.

If the astonishing account is true,
They met, they talked, they drew—and they withdrew.

The trouble was that while many of them were respectable citizens their numbers were swelled by persons of dubious antecedents, dismissed surgeons or officers convicted of " an error of judgment "—such as the notorious Hall of Madras who, in the war with Hyder Ali was responsible for the loss of 500 men and three guns, which loss caused his commanding officer to succumb to a bilious attack " which prevents me being so explicit as I otherwise should have been ".

The day of the Grand trial, however, the men of law had their revenge on their most violent critic, Francis, for not only did the examination of witnesses drag on and on, but when all the evidence had been heard the judges differed ; which necessitated each giving his separate opinion. Mr. Justice Hyde as junior spoke first and treated the matter as one concerned solely with appreciation of evidence and gave it as his opinion that the plaintiff had established his case.

Sir Robert Chambers then spoke at enormous length, confining himself to the legal aspects of the suit. He was at last interrupted by the Chief Justice, Sir Elijah Impey, who " petulantly observed that he was not prepared to comment upon such a mass of learning in Ecclesiastical Law as had been, he thought unnecessarily and inapplicably, introduced by his brother Chambers, not a particle of which applied to the present case ". He agreed with his brother Hyde and entered judgment for the plaintiff, the suitable damages being, in his opinion, 50,000 rupees. Mr. Justice Hyde had fallen asleep during Sir Robert Chambers' remarks, but as the Chief Justice announced these damages he woke up with a start and said anxiously " Sicca rupees, brother Impey, siccas." " Aye ", said the Chief Justice with relish, " Let them be siccas, brother Hyde."

The Chief Justice's censures on the conduct of Francis and his rescuer Shee inspired a number of pasquinades, of which the following is typical :

> Psha ! what a Fuss, 'twixt SHEE and 'twixt her !
> What abuse of a dear little creature,
> A GRAND and a mighty affair to be sure,
> Just to give a light PHILIP (fillip) to nature.
> How can you, ye prudes, blame a luscious young wench ;
> Who so fond is of Love and romances,
> Whose customs and manners are *tout à fait* French,
> For admiring whatever from FRANCE-IS !

But Madame Grand retired from the curious glances of Calcutta drawing-rooms to Francis's house at Hooghly. After some time, she visited England and stayed at Fitzroy Square with a Mr. Lewin. She had saved a comfortable sum which she invested in English banks ; and when she finally returned to France she was careful to leave her money behind in England. The Revolution thus caused her little concern. But when she learnt of Napoleon's proposed invasion of England she was filled with horror. She visited the Foreign Minister and implored him to promise that the London banks should not be pillaged. M. de Talleyrand was fond of pretty women and presently Francis's mistress became Madame de Talleyrande and Princess of Beneventum. Thereafter she seems to have lived prudently and the only whisper of her former glamour that survived her marriage was Napoleon's confidence that she would seduce the Prince of the Asturias at Valengay.

The chief wealth of the Company and of its servants was drawn from the inland districts then under the Company's control, and it was the ambition of every young civil servant to be appointed Resident at the courts of one or other of the princes of Bengal or Oudh. These rulers, sinking under the burden of their continually increasing obligations to the Company and grown careless of the interests of their decrepit kingdoms, had only one concern, to conciliate and appease every new European who descended on their capitals. And so when Hickey's friend Bob Pott was appointed Resident at the Durbar of the Nawab of Bengal he rejoiced, for not only did "the whole stipend allowed by Government to the Nabob pass through the Resident's hands, in which channel a considerable portion of it always stuck to his fingers", but "he had likewise the further advantage of purchasing and paying for every European article the Nabob wished to have". The Residency was at Afzulbag, four miles from the Nabob's capital, Murshidabad; and in happy anticipation of his future profits Pott spent 30,000 rupees on furnishing this building. Then he invited Hickey and Major Russel to come and stay with him; and they embarked in "a noble pinnace" stored with "abundance of provisions and liquors" and arrived at Afzulbag a week later. They were impressed by the splendour of Pott's surroundings, Hickey being especially pleased with his apartments " of the completest kind, with warm and cold baths belonging exclusively to them and every other luxury of the East ". Next morning Pott suggested a drive in his phaeton. They descended the grand staircase between a double file of servants who bowed like Mogul courtiers at their approach. Grouped round the phaeton in the courtyard was a detachment of light horse, the troopers, gorgeously uniformed, saluting the guests with their drawn sabres. They called on the other Europeans in the neighbourhood and during the following week were invited to a round of dinners. Of these one was at the Nabob's palace and of this entertainment Hickey remarks condescendingly that it was " quite in the English taste ". The Prince was evidently less anglicised in his resources of hospitality than the Nawab of Oudh to whom " an Englishman introduced the elegant European diversion of a race in sacks by old women ". It occurred to very few of the Calcutta gentry, who patronised a local prince by accepting his invitations, what hours of anxiety preceded the despatch of the invitation, what alternating moods of gratitude and panic succeeded its acceptance; what expense to procure the materials of European food from Calcutta, to engage cooks skilled in the mysteries of the European kitchen; what shedding of religious prejudices to provide the guests with beef and wine. Dancing-girls ordered from Lucknow and Delhi—surely Rahema Bibi with her incredibly graceful gestures, surely Zebunissa with her delightful wit and the wonderful memory that enabled her to cap appropriately any Persian quotation—surely these would be to the taste of the scornful strangers, so that they would give a good account of the host to authorities in Calcutta? While in the earlier eighteenth century, many of the English merchants became half-Indianised, enjoyed a nautch and, from the frequent references to " country music " did not dislike Indian music, towards the end of the century, with the increase of wealth, the shorter periods of residence in India, and greater opportunities for enjoying their own varieties of dancing and hearing their own music, few Englishmen would admit to a liking for the " barbarous arts " of the East ; and at these parties the guests generally rewarded their hosts' forethought with sneers at the " horrid screeching ", with requests to terminate " this disgusting caterwauling " and with jokes at the restrained and formalised gestures of the Indian dances—how could they compare with the lively gaiety of a cotillion ? The usual Anglo-Indian reaction to such an entertainment remained fairly constant, and the following verses, though written in the next century, are typical of a guest's impressions :

> The Rajah he bowed and he bowed and he bowed,
> Shaking hands as they came with the whole of the crowd ;
> And he led to a couch the Commissioner's wife,
> And said 'twas the happiest hour of his life.
> Then suddenly sounded a loud-clanging gong,
> And there burst on the eyes of the wondering throng
> A bevy of girls
> Dressed in bangles and pearls
> And other rich gems,
> With fat podgy limbs . . .
> And sang a wild air
> Which affected your hair
> While behind them a circle of men and of boys,
> With tomtoms and pipes, made a terrible noise.

Very few guests were as sympathetic as Mrs. Graham who noted the courtesy and sensitive charm of the host, who " was pleased with the attention the Rajah paid to his guests, whether Hindoos, Christians or Musulmans ; there was not one to whom he did not speak kindly, or pay some compliment on their entrance ; and he walked round the assembly repeatedly to see that all were properly accommodated ".

Nevertheless, in spite of the brusque manners of the English guests there was a greater friendliness between the two races at such parties than there was ever to be during the nineteenth century. They neither understood nor liked each other as a general rule ; but the Indian nobles had learnt their manners in the Mogul court and the English residents or soldiers were men of the world with something of the cynical tolerance and outward polish of that century. Some of the famous breakfasts given by the Nawab of Lucknow, that charming and futile prince, were evidently enjoyed by everyone ; and between the almost endless courses there would be animal-fights or processions of rare beasts such as " a greyish elephant ". But that strange society of Lucknow, with its Europeanised Musulmans and Indianised Europeans was not typical of India. The younger factors met few of the Indian gentry ; their contacts were chiefly with the money-lenders and traders of the capital, whom they would only meet in business hours or at an occasional, inevitable nautch.

If the young factors found little pleasure at these entertainments, their hosts, for all the satisfaction they would at other times have derived from Raji's grace and Kaliani's wit, were too uneasy to enjoy their own party till the guests had gone. Then followed an entertainment of which few English guests were aware. The doors would be shut, and the dancing-girls, excellent mimics like all Indians, would give an imitation of the bored guests who had just left, and the uncomfortable tension of the last hour would be dispelled in bursts of happy laughter. And while the English phaetons clattered home Raji and Kaliani would be dressing up to caricature English costume and executing with indecent exaggeration an Orientalised version of English dances, those minuets and country dances which seemed so innocent and natural to English eyes, so different from the provocative posturing of Indian nautch-girls, but which to Indians appeared utterly scandalous. Maria Graham might be " Sorry I could not go to the nautch the next night, where I hear there was a masquerade when several Pariahs appeared as Europeans and imitated our dances, music and manners ". But her attitude was not general, and Flora Annie Steel's reaction to such a mime was perhaps more typical :

> Two white-masked figures, clasped waist to waist, were waltzing about tipsily. One had a curled flaxen wig, a muslin dress distended by an all-too-visible crinoline giving full play to a pair of prancing brown legs. The other wore an old staff uniform, cocked hat and feather complete. . . . It was a vile travesty.

If the general impression of eighteenth- and early nineteenth-century Calcutta is one of ostentation and extravagance it must be remembered that there were more serious circles than those in which Francis and Hickey moved. Many of Hastings' friends amused themselves by composing Latin verses and translating Tasso and Horace. Hastings was regarded as an arbiter of literary taste and these verses would be sent to him for his approval. He himself made translations from the Indian epics. They were rough-and-ready versions without poetic fire ; he would compose them in his palanquin as he jolted over the plains of Bihar or the steaming paddy-fields of Bengal. He sent them to his wife with a modest little preface. " If you read this with a Composed Mind and admire it only as a Production of mere poetical Merit (for so much I am sure of from the Partiality of your Judgment) burn it ; for it is good for nothing." But if these more solemn poems had little value, there is no doubt that Hastings could turn a skilful epigram when he chose, as his lines on Burke prove.

> Oft have I wonder'd that, on Irish Ground
> No poisonous reptiles ever yet were found :
> Reveal'd the secret stands, of Nature's Work !
> She saved her venom, to create a Burke.

When weary of versifying he would take up a book of extracts from the Mahabharata and the lean disdainful face of the Governor-General would soften with emotion as he read of the old chivalrous heroes of the Hindus, of Arjun the charioteer and Prince Yudishthra who would not enter heaven unless his dog accompanied him. At last he arrived at Benares and the books had to be laid aside. There was always trouble for the Governor-General in that teeming city, whether due to the " clamours of the discontented inhabitants ", the intrigues of the Rajah, or the incompetence of the Resident, Mr. Markham, whom Hastings had appointed to this post at the age of twenty-one to oblige his father, the Archbishop of York. Paternal gratitude moved the Archbishop to become " an active and steady friend " and actually to use " intemperate language in defence of Warren Hastings, which was brought to the notice of Parliament ".[1] The Archbishop did well to be grateful for his son was making £30,000 a year in bribes. But once the situation had been surveyed, the populace quietened or the Rajah relieved of some more treasure, Hastings reverted to intellectual pursuits and his entourage were surprised at the Governor-General's interest in Hindu philosophy, his undignified " Pundit-hunting ". At Benares

[1] *D.N.B.*, quoted in Thompson and Garrett, *Rise and Fulfilment of British Rule in India.*

too, he met Scindia's minister Beneram, and mentioned him in a letter to his wife as one " whom you know I reckon among my first friends ". He studied Persian (which he considered should be promoted to a serious study in English Universities as a companion classical language to Latin) and a Persian lady, Panna Begum, the wife of Colonel Pearse, Hastings' second in the duel with Francis, used to write to him long letters in her own language. Colonel Pearse was now dead and his widow's chief concern was to interest Hastings in her son whom she refers to as " Mr. Tommy ". It is not known whether this was the same son who was afterwards sent to school in England ; but if so he soon shed that Anglicised pet-name, for he was entered at Harrow as " Muhammad ". Hastings' interest in Indian culture led him to an affectionate respect for many Indians such as was uncommon in his time. Perhaps the Indian whom he most esteemed was Ali Ibrahim Khan, Chief Judge of Benares, whom Cornwallis afterwards praised as " a man of great talent and universally respected ". The occasion of Cornwallis's encomium was a request by the Prince of Wales to hand over to the very young son of a gentleman who had financially obliged him [1] the Benares judgeship which as his Royal Highness pointed out was at present only held by " black cann " . . .

Of a part with his studious habits was Hastings' oddly Spartan life. " I eat sparingly," he wrote, " I never sup ; and am generally abed by ten. I breakfast at six ; I bathe with cold water daily." And, in that age most eccentric of all, he practised, " total Abstinence from Wine from which I have already experienced Benefit ". Nor were his clothes appropriate to his station. He only ordered two suits a year and one frock-coat " merely for fashion ".

[1] Basu, *Rise of the Christian Power.*

He was almost happiest when pottering about a garden in the shabbiest of clothes. From his first arrival in India he had been trying to acclimatise English plants, and, as Governor-General, we find him writing to England for seeds of honeysuckle and sweet-brier, to be packed for the voyage "in small bottles with ground-glass stoppers". And on one occasion he records delightedly the arrival of a consignment of "Troffles, Morrelles and Artichoke Bottomes". He bought eagerly rare Asian plants from the Himalaya and the upland frontiers of Burma. He was never tired of experimenting, and was proud of a hybrid grain he had produced which he called "barley-wheat". With animals he was less fortunate; some shawl-goats he had ordered from England died on the way; and he had to content himself with ordinary Indian cattle. It was perhaps from his readings in Hindu literature that he caught an almost Hindu feeling for cows; he describes how they run after him when they hear his voice, and in a letter to Imhoff he confesses his devotion to his cows "on account of their accomplishments and moral virtues".

He found time to interest himself in each new fashion from England. The style of carriages was changing about 1780 and he and his wife were anxious to obtain one of the newest coaches. Mrs. Hastings was excited by an advertisement which appeared in the *Bengal Gazette* of July 16: "Just Imported. A very elegant Crane Neck Coach made entirely in the present taste with a genteel Rutland Rooff, the pannels painted a pleasing Laylock colour, with a handsome Gold Sprig Mosaic." She would have liked to acquire it at once, but the Governor-General pursed his lips and went down alone to inspect the carriage. His report was discouraging. "It is ill shaped, has a Patch in this Form (ovalshaped) behind, and a Crack all across.

I judge it to be old and vamped ; and besides I do not like it." [1]

Mrs. Hastings rising from the uncomfortable situation of a Franconian baroness awaiting divorce to be the wife of the first Governor-General, set a number of problems in etiquette to the ladies of Calcutta. To begin with what was the Governor-General's wife to be called ? The foreigners, for whom in spite of her English marriage she continued to confess so unfortunate a preference, had no difficulties about this ; they called her " milady Hastings " or even " Lady Hastings ". The English seem gradually to have adopted the title of " Lady Governess " whose origin, pleasantly typical of the antiquarianism of that age, is supposed to have been due to some obviously inapposite comparison with Margaret of Parma. Gradually the procedure of etiquette became settled. When the Lady Governess entered a drawing-room she was welcomed by a general cry of greeting from all the ladies. Then each lady set herself to catch the Lady Governess's eye. As Mrs. Jackson told Mrs. Fay, " You must fix your eyes on her and never take them off till she notices you." So they sat round in a circle, staring. The Lady Governess would select one lady and acknowledge her stare with a " complacent glance " to which the lady replied with a " respectful bend ".[2] A brief conversation followed, of almost royal banality ; while the other ladies continued their purposeful stares, each expecting to be the next honoured with notice. But where there were no precedents for such a lofty situation, it was inevitable that Mrs. Hastings, a foreigner, should offend many. Moreover, her every action was spied on and criticised by the faction opposed to her husband. Acceptance of an invitation was sneered at, a refusal caused mortal offence.

[1] Hastings' *Letters to His Wife.* [2] Mrs. Fay.

Even in the Lady Governess's relations with her personal friends the critics insisted on unearthing extravagant motives. Thus when Mrs. Hastings sat talking for some time with Lady Impey, Francis was revolted and scribbled in his diary: " *Vulgo*. Toad-eating." Then Lady Impey invited Mrs. Hastings to supper to meet Mrs. Wheler who had recently arrived from England. Mrs. Hastings, pleading an indisposition, begged to be excused. But no one believed in the indisposition. Mrs. Wheler had brought some new clothes with her from London, in particular a hoop of astounding size concerning which all the drawing-rooms had been agog. It was to be assumed, therefore, that in any ordinary circumstance, Mrs. Hastings would be as anxious as anyone to see Mrs. Wheler's wardrobe. There must be some sinister reason for the letter of refusal. Had she quarrelled with Lady Impey? Francis put it about that she had and exclaimed in his diary that Mrs. Hastings' letter was " an intended slight ".

Probably the real reason, apart from her indisposition, was that Mrs. Hastings was disappointingly uninterested in Calcutta fashions. She dressed to please herself; but her knowledge of Paris styles was far in advance of the Calcutta ladies. She had many correspondents in England and France who regularly reported to her each new fad and fashion. A friend wrote to her that smart women in London " are grown so Young as not only to appear in their Sashes but their Shifts ". And presently the Lady Governess startled Calcutta by the juvenile air of her clothes. Mrs. Fay tittered at this " infantile simplicity " and breathlessly complained of " her whole dress being at variance with our present modes which are certainly not so, perhaps for that reason she has chosen to depart from them ". But when Mrs. Hastings appeared at a ball without powder, her beautiful hair brushed back in artfully calculated disorder like a Greuze milkmaid's, the contrast with the toppling head-dresses of the other guests was so remarkable that Mrs. Fay could only grumble that Mrs. Hastings' "rank sets her above the necessity of studying anything but the whim of the moment".

At Hastings' table there were often foreigners among the guests. Chief among these was the Counte de Boigne, noblest of all the adventurers who hired their swords to Indian princes in that age of anarchy. He had had a varied career. Born in 1751 at Chambery, which was then in the dominions of the King of Sardinia, he had had to escape into France at the age of seventeen to avoid the consequences of having killed a Piedmontese noble in a duel. Arrived at Paris he enlisted in the Clare Regiment of the Irish Brigade. After five years' service, realising that he could never rise beyond the rank of lieutenant in a regiment where Irish nationality was the first qualification for superior rank, he resigned and journeyed to Russia where he became the lover of the Great Catherine. But she tired of him, as she did of all her lovers, made him a captain in her army and despatched him to the Turkish War. He was captured at Tenedos and sold as a slave in Constantinople. Liberated at the end of the war he wandered down to Smyrna where he met some English merchants who had made a fortune in India. His imagination took fire and he set out for Alexandria *en route* to the East. His ship foundered off the coast of Palestine and passengers and crew were captured by Arabs. De Boigne's manners, however, were so pleasant that the Arabs not only released him but paid his passage to Alexandria. There he met a son of the Duke of Northumberland who gave him a letter to Warren Hastings. He stayed for some while at Government House and then

Hastings sent him with letters to the Nawab of Oudh. The Nawab loaded his fascinating guest with gifts, but unfortunately on his return de Boigne was waylaid by Marathas and robbed of all his new acquisitions. Meanwhile the opposition in the Calcutta Council, led by Francis, had got wind of de Boigne's visit to Lucknow and demanded that de Boigne should account for everything he had received from the Nawab. It seemed as if the wretched Frenchman was ruined; for Francis would not have accepted the story that the disappearance of all those valuables was due to a Maratha raid. But when de Boigne arrived in Calcutta, Francis was on his way home and Hastings was supreme. Explanations were waved aside and de Boigne was given letters to another prince, the great Scindia, the effective Regent of the Mogul Empire. Scindia not only greatly admired Hastings and so was glad enough to oblige one of his friends; he was busy building up an army drilled and armed in European style. He was delighted with de Boigne, and gave him command of two battalions of infantry, and presently of ten. These were uniformed like French troops and on their banners shone the white cross of Savoy. At the head of these forces de Boigne destroyed the Rajput armies and made his master the most powerful chieftain in India. He married a Persian princess who became a Catholic and called herself Catherine. He lived in great state at Alighar, and entertained in his palace any Europeans who passed that way. When Mr. Twining stayed with him—

> Dinner was served at four. It was much in the Indian style; pillaws and curries, variously prepared, in abundance; fish, poultry and kid. The dishes were spread over the large table fixed in the middle of the hall, and were, in fact, a banquet for a dozen persons, although there was no one to partake of it but the General and myself.

After dinner de Boigne's hookah was brought in. It was so magnificent that Mr. Twining exclaimed, " What a mean and vulgar thing does the tobacco pipe seem, when compared with this, even in the mouth of its great patron, Dr. Parr ! "

His only rival in local society was the British resident, Colonel Collins, who had an escort which included a brigade of artillery, and " a noble suite of tents which might have served for the Great Mogul ". But whereas de Boigne was a man of fine presence and magnificent physique (his connection with the Empress of Russia offering sufficient evidence for that) Colonel Collins was

> an insignificant, little, odd-looking man, dressed in an old-fashioned military coat, white breeches, sky-blue silk stockings, and large glaring buckles to his shoes, having his highly powdered wig, from which depended a pigtail of no ordinary dimensions, surmounted by a small round black silk hat, ornamented with a single black ostrich feather, looking altogether not unlike a monkey dressed for Bartholomew Fair.

However, there were times when Colonel Collins had the field to himself, for Scindia would quarrel with his great general and then (aware that he would soon be recalled with apologies) de Boigne would retire to Lucknow and stay with his friend General Martin, who was in charge of the Nawab's arsenals. Martin lived in great comfort with four concubines, a number of eunuchs and a host of slaves. His library was famous ; he had collected 4,000 volumes of Latin, French, Italian, English, Persian and Sanskrit works. In his gallery were hung 150 oil-paintings including pictures by Zoffany and Daniel. His house was

> built on the bank of the R. Goomty, and boats passed under the room, in which he dined. He has underground apartments, even with the edge of the water, the most comfortable in the

> world in the hot weather, and the most elegantly decorated. As the water rises he ascends; the lower storey is always flooded in the rains, and the second generally; when the water subsides they are repaired and redecorated. . . . He had a pair of glasses ten feet in length and proportionately wide. It would require a week at least to examine the contents of his house.

He had certain little eccentricities such as interlarding his conversation with explosive cries of "Do you see? Do you see?" But it was difficult not to be eccentric in Lucknow. The court was crowded with raffish adventurers who, wrote Mr. Twining, "lived in a style far exceeding the expense and luxuriousness of Calcutta; they dined alternately with each other and kept a band to play who had learnt English and Scotch airs". And the Nawab himself surpassed all his subjects in eccentricity. He was devoted to a large English dray-horse which he fed on such rich and succulent food that the wretched animal became too fat to move. He liked wearing Western costume, though like most Indians he was "prejudiced against the wigs"; and he would surprise new-comers by appearing dressed as a British admiral or as a clergyman of the Church of England.

From Lucknow de Boigne would travel down to Calcutta to visit his benefactor Hastings; and as he sat at the Governor-General's table, a silent square-headed man with pleasant manners and a prim smile, it must have been difficult to believe he had had so strange a life. He seemed a typical country gentleman of provincial France.

If Calcutta society grumbled at the Hastingses' greater interest in de Boigne's conversation than in that of the richest merchant prince, the tremendous pride, the imperious aloofness of the Marquess Wellesley filled people with a certain awe. He lived, as he described it, "in this magnificent solitude, where I stalk about like a Royal Tiger without even a friendly jackal to soothe the severity of my thoughts ", attributing his reserve to the fact that, " in the evening I have no alternative but the society of my subjects or solitude. The former is so vulgar, ignorant, rude, familiar and stupid as to be disgusting and intolerable; especially the ladies, not one of whom by the eye is even decently good-looking." He consoled himself with an almost Mogul pomp, withdrew from the gaze of the vulgar behind rank upon rank of courtiers and guards. When he went upon the river it was in a boat as magnificent as a Manchu's. Even in the private apartments of his palace he was attended by a troupe of servants as he moved from room to room. As Mr. Hickey noted, with (one feels) a touch of jealousy, " His Lordship's own establishment of servants, equipages, etc., were extravagant in the superlative degree, not only in point of number but splendour of dress, the whole being put to the account of the chaste managers of Leadenhall Street." Moreover, not content with Government House at Calcutta " he commenced a second palace at Barrackpore, almost rivalling in magnificence the Calcutta one . . . the grounds which of themselves were very pretty, he laid out with extraordinary taste and elegance, upon different parts of which he erected a theatre, a riding-house with probably the finest aviary and menagerie in the world ". Distant with Europeans, Wellesley was frankly contemptuous of Indians. As General Palmer wrote to Hastings—

> little or no attention is paid to the Vakils (ministers) of the Native Courts by Lord Wellesley. They are not permitted to pay their respects to him oftener than two or three times a year, which I think is as impolitic as it is ungracious. . . . I observe with great concern the system of depressing them adopted by the present government and imitated in the manners of almost every European. They . . . are treated

> in society with mortifying hauteur and reserve. In fact they have hardly any social intercourse with us.

It was no longer fashionable in Government House circles to profess an interest in Persian poetry or Hindu metaphysics. The deterioration in relations between the two races was very rapid and in 1810 Captain Williamson noted that " Europeans have little connexion with natives of either religion " and in the same year Mrs. Graham regretted that " Every Briton (in Calcutta) appears to pride himself on being outrageously a John Bull ".

Towards the end of the century there was a decline in the general extravagance and licence. Some credit for this must go to Cornwallis. Hickey gives a charming picture of Cornwallis's return.

> Lord Wellesley . . . sent down all his carriages, servants, staff officers, and general establishment to receive his noble supercessor at the waterside. Lord Cornwallis upon landing looked surprised and vexed at the amazing cavalcade that was drawn up, and turning to Mr. George Abercrombie Robinson . . . he said " What ! What ! What is all this, Robinson, hey ? " Mr. Robinson answered " My Lord, the Marquis Wellesley has sent his equipages and attendants as a mark of respect and to accompany your Lordship to the Government House." To this Lord Cornwallis replied, " Too civil, too civil by half. Too many people. I don't want them, I don't want one of them, I have not yet lost the use of my legs, Robinson, hey ? Thank God I can walk, walk very well, Robinson, hey ; don't want a score carriages to convey me a quarter of a mile ; certainly shall not use them ", and he accordingly did walk. . . . Lord Wellesley received the new Governor-General at the foot of the stairs of the Government House, where the two Marquises embraced, then going up hand in hand to the second floor, where a splendid breakfast was set out, Lord Wellesley's band of music playing martial airs, Lord Cornwallis seemed much struck with the magnificence of the apartment, and while walking up to the head of the breakfast table, said, " Upon my word, Wellesley, you have shown much taste

> here, much taste indeed, Wellesley ; it is very handsome, very handsome, indeed, Wellesley."

Later on, however, Cornwallis unburdened himself to Dr. Fleming who asked him if he liked the new place, and Cornwallis replied, " Like it, Fleming ! Not at all ! Not at all ! I shall never be able to find my way about it without a guide, nor can I divest myself of the idea of being in a prison, for if I show my head outside a door, a fellow with a musket and fixed bayonet presents himself before me. I will not have this continued, I won't indeed, Fleming." Even after Wellesley had handed over charge to Cornwallis he continued to drive about Calcutta in a " coach and six, preceded, and followed, by a party of Dragoons and a number of outriders ", while the new Governor-General drove himself " in a phaeton with a pair of steady old jog-trot horses, accompanied by his Secretary, Mr. Robinson, and without a single attendant of any description whatsoever ". But while Cornwallis dropped all Wellesley's new-fangled modes of address to the Governor-General such as " Excellency " and " Most Noble " the pomp of Government House was little affected by his desire that " I will not be pestered, and must have quiet and retirement " ; and his successor, Minto, complained that " the first night I went to bed in Calcutta I was followed by fourteen persons in white muslin gowns into the dressing-room. One might have hoped that some of these were ladies ; but on finding that there were as many turbans and black beards as gowns, I was very desirous that these bearded housemaids should leave me . . . which with some trouble and perseverance I accomplished, and in that one room I enjoy a degree of privacy, but far from perfect."

When Cornwallis succeeded Wellesley he had but a short time to live, but during his first period of office the effect on Calcutta society of his modest and sensible way of life was very noticeable. As an enthusiastic clergyman, named Tennant, wrote, "A reformation, highly commendable, has been effected, partly from necessity, but more by the example of the Governor-General, whose elevated rank and noble birth gave him in a great measure the guidance of fashion." And, his enthusiasm triumphing over his grammar, he added, "Regular hours and sobriety of conduct became as decidedly the test of a man of fashion as they were formerly of irregularity." This was, of course, parsonic hyperbole. Lord Cornwallis was as fond of a bottle of wine as any man of that age. Indeed the two worst offences at his table were to delay passing the bottle and to pass it without replacing the cork. At intervals his voice would rap out, "Pass the wine," or "Fie, fie! Sir, how can you omit to put the cork in the bottle before you pass it?" These two sentences became so regular a feature of a dinner at Government House that when Mr. Auriol (whom Hickey called "a foolish, weak, chattering blockhead", but who, in Zoffany's portrait appears as a staid and stolid paterfamilias) exclaimed, after his first dinner at Government House, that he had liked Cornwallis "vastly indeed. I never saw so well-bred a man in my life. He was exceedingly polite and attentive, and during dinner spoke to me at least thirty times", Auriol's brother-in-law Dashwood said, "Did he? Then I dare conjecture that fifteen of those times were to pass the bottle and fifteen to pass the cork."

Cornwallis's method of reform was simple; to insist on his guests dancing at his dances, instead of only drinking. As Kaye observed, "Before the coming of Cornwallis there had seldom been much if any dancing after supper. The gentlemen-dancers were commonly too far gone in drink to venture upon any experiments of activity demanding the preservation of the perpendicular." But now the local newspapers piqued themselves on reports of the minuets at Government House and their dancers. At the New Year ball of 1788 we read that

> Lady Chambers and Colonel Pearse danced the first minuet, and the succeeding ones continued till about half-after eleven o'clock, when the supper tables presented every requisite to gratify the most refined epicurean. The ladies soon resumed the pleasures of the dance, and knit the rural braid, in emulation of the poet's sister graces, till four in the morning.

When he had no guests Cornwallis preferred to retire early. As he wrote to Lord Brome, " I sit down at nine, with two or three officers of my family, to some fruit and a biscuit, and go to bed soon after the clock strikes ten. I don't think the greatest sap at Eton can lead a duller life than this."

One by one the older generation of Nabobs disappeared from the racecourse and the Assembly-Rooms. They called for their accounts from their *sircars*, and were generally disappointed at what they thought the unexpectedly meagre sum left to them after numerous deductions for commissions, interest on loans and debts to tradesmen. But there was generally enough to their credit to enable them to cut a dash in England, to purchase pocket-boroughs for their nephews, and swagger down Jermyn Street even if people laughed at their " gay India coats " and the tasteless display of jewellery. But first accommodation had to be reserved on a home-going ship ; and the East Indiamen captains, having the common estimate of a Nabob's resources would charge fantastic prices. Colonel Champion had to pay 2,000 rupees for a section of the " great cabin " ; Mrs. Barclay £400 for a passage, and Colonel Wood £1,000, having paid which he died before setting foot on board ship.

Of all the departures that of Mr. Hickey must have most made people realise that an age was ending, for he had been so constant a figure at every party, always on the race-course of an evening in his chariot, the noisiest at every supper, trotting down the law-court corridors every morning, wracked with headache but still bubbling with gossip. And now on December 24, 1807, they read in the *Calcutta Gazette* : " To be sold by public auction by Tullon & Company, on Monday, the 25th January, 1808, at his house adjoining the Supreme Court the truly elegant property of William Hickey, Esq., returning to Europe." His effects included furniture, plate, jewellery, paintings and engravings, books, a billiard table, an organ,

> a full pannel buggy, finished in the finest style with a very handsome steady going good Bay Acheen poney and plated harness ; a very handsome showy fine tempered Bay saddled horse with saddle and bridle. A ditto bay Buggy poney. A ditto bay saddle poney and a grey carriage horse formerly one of a pair and full 14 hands high. A very elegant chair finished in the first style. A fashionable mehanna as good as new.

Most of his pictures he took with him, having entrusted them to Mr. Chinnery to be packed. The latter described his method of packing them thus : " The pictures are rolled on a hollow cylinder, and between each is put a piece of green silk to prevent their sticking to each other. You will be careful to have them gently warmed by a fire as you unroll them." Mr. Hickey kept postponing the time of his departure in spite of the advice of " Doctor Hare, Junior ", who warned him that his " frame was so debilitated from a long residence in a sultry climate that a change was become indispensably requisite ". But it was flattering that the new Governor-General had remarked soon after his arrival that " Mr. Hickey is a gentleman I much want to see, having a message to deliver . . . from Mrs. Burke". And he hated leaving behind his billiard table "which was an excellent one made by the famous Seddons". In fact—

> as the time approached for my departure my spirits became depressed to the greatest degree. . . . I was about to quit a country wherein every wish was in a great measure anticipated, by being gratified before announced, arising from my having a multitude of servants, most of whom had lived with me upwards of twenty years.

He was distressed at the thought of throwing so many of his employees out of work and wished he could afford to pension them all. Even his dog Tiger "seemed to understand that something extraordinary was on foot and appeared as melancholy as myself. . . . During the last three days the animal would never quit my side for a moment. He, in fact, did everything to express his sorrow except speak, and his piteous looks and cries occasioned me many a real pang." It was disappointing that the sale of his effects only realised 18,300 rupees, and some of his pictures fetched almost nothing, although they were "capital performances". But it was a pleasant surprise to find that his friend Peter Speke had sent to await him on board ship "a few dozen of some incomparable Madeira, which will prove very comfortable as a cordial" and also "four beautiful views of the new London docks" which must have been a pleasant adornment to the "little dirty hole of a cabin". But he was still depressed and could not eat anything at his first meal on board and "had recourse to my old remedy Lol Shrob (red wine) though without producing the intended effect. . . . I was restless, uneasy in mind as in body, and completely miserable." His ship set sail on the 18th of February and in the incidents of the voyage he soon forgot his sorrow. It was August when the ship sighted England but Hickey and the Bengali servant, Munnoo, he had brought with him, found the wind disagreeably cold as they were rowed away from the ship in the pilot-boat. But there were comforts at the inn, a feather bed and fresh food, though English cherries and peaches seemed insipid and sour after the luxurious fruits of the East. His luggage had been detained at the Customs, and the Customs officials of those days were as stupid and rude as English Customs officials have always been. They tore his pictures to pieces in their eagerness to unroll them, their curiosity obviously having been excited by the description " foreign pictures ", and having damaged them irretrievably charged him £40 duty on them.

Hickey had been looking forward to his servant's astonishment at the first sight of London, but unfortunately, although it was August, there was a fog when they arrived and so neither of them could see anything. He did not stay long in London but bought a pleasant house at Beaconsfield, where his Indian servant was baptised and his heathen name of Munnoo changed to " William Munnew ". Hickey suffered from liver headaches, and took to " exercise both by riding and walking, to the great surprise of my Indian friends, who knew that in Bengal I took little or no exercise ". The exercise having little effect on his headaches, he followed " the fashion of the time for all those recently returned from the East Indies to take an early trip to Cheltenham, with a view of getting quit of all lurking bile ". It was pleasant to meet a number of Calcutta acquaintances in the Pump Room. They all tried the water, though Hickey did so only once, the taste disgusting him, and his friend Mr. Turner found that so far from curing his rheumatism it gave him a headache which he had never had before. Miss Hickey, on the other hand, " gave it a very fair trial, drinking it regularly, and in proper quantities, but without deriving any advantage ". Still it was pleasant to chat under the palms and complain about the irregularity with which one's dividends arrived from India. He was quite a personage in genteel circles at that watering-place, and *The Cheltenham Chronicle and Gloucestershire General Advertiser* was careful to announce the arrival of " Mr. and Miss Hickey " ; and the third member of the party was sure to be " my faithful Munnew ".

CHAPTER V

THE change that was coming over English society in India was less remarkable in Calcutta than in Bombay. That possession, it will be remembered, had been in a minute of 1825 dismissed as " of little Importance to the Company ". But even when that minute was drafted, Bombay was about to become almost as important to the Company as Calcutta. During the eighteenth century Bombay was a frontier outpost under the menacing shadow of the Maratha power. The fall of the Peshwa and the annexation of the chief territories of the Maratha empire promoted Bombay suddenly to be the capital of a great province. The second stage in Bombay's sudden rise was the opening of the overland route through Egypt. The first steamer sailed from Suez to Bombay in 1830 and thereafter the passage round the Cape went gradually out of fashion.

Passages by the Cape route were much cheaper now; a single passage cost about £120 or for a reserved cabin £150. The cabins were not furnished and passengers were informed that " cabin-furniture and fittings-up shall be procured of the Upholsterers at the East India Docks ". Such fittings-up included " a sofa with mattress, a pillow and a chintz covering for the day-time, a Hanging Lamp, a looking-glass with sliding cover; a swing-tray; a chest of drawers in two pieces; foul-clothes Bag; an oil-cloth or carpet (This merely for the sake of Appearances) ". A travellers' Handbook of 1844 gives an interesting list of articles which a gentleman would need on the voyage to India. Among these were

> six pairs of loose cotton-drawers, for sleeping or bathing in. A couple of brown Holland blouses. A blue camlet jacket. Two pairs of merino, camlet or gambroon trousers. Two dozen pairs of white jean trowsers. Two dozen white jean jackets. Two dozen white jean waistcoats. A hat, in leathern box. A straw hat. A blue cloth forage-cap. Two black silk stocks or cravats. A dozen pairs of white kid gloves. A couple of morning gowns. A boat-cloak of camlet. A bucket and rope (serviceable in drawing up salt water whenever required).

These, as the Handbook repeats, are "*Actual Necessaries*". For amusement it is suggested the gentleman should equip himself with "scientific instruments, telescopes, cards and an outline map of the route", and for his general comfort "water, brandy, lucifer-matches and raspberry vinegar". A lady's "necessaries" would obviously be greater. There was apparently some difficulty about stays, for Mrs. Wise of 31, Saville Row, advertised that she could "assure to lady passengers some invaluable advice and a description of corset of inestimable utility in a relaxing climate". Otherwise the wardrobe recommended for the voyage is much what we might expect, save that in contrast to the number of other dresses, the item "An ordinary gown and common straw bonnet to wear on deck" suggests that most of the day during the voyage was not to be spent on deck. The following necessaries are more interesting: "Quilling-net and piece-net; hair powder; a good supply of papillote paper; hartshorn, aromatic-vinegar, aperients, and a case of Cologne water." The ladies' recreations are dealt with more summarily than the gentlemen's, and they are advised to occupy themselves with "carpet and crochet work, drawing, knitting and netting (For these purposes silver needles are recommended as the moisture of the fingers at a high temperature is calculated to rust the implement), while musical practice will much depend upon the presence of a Piano-forte ". But it was obviously considered unnecessary to offer suggestions for trivial amusements when " there is such perpetual entertainment in tracing the progress of the vessel, in observing the practical use of the compass, in taking lunar and solar observations, marking the changes of the climate, the phenomena of the sea's phosphorescence, the uses of the complex machinery of a ship, etc ".

The increasingly popular overland route cost about the same as the voyage round the Cape. Passengers liked to arrive a few days before the scheduled time at Alexandria so as to see the sights of that place and of Cairo. The only difficulty about this was that it generally meant travelling to Alexandria by a French boat. Lady Falkland found it " by no means agreeable " to have to share a cabin with several other passengers, her maid and the stewardess. When she exclaimed at such discomfort the stewardess pointed out that she, the stewardess, was far more seriously incommoded by the number of passengers as a result of which, " je passerai la nuit à terre ". At Alexandria there were two hotels, the " Orient " and the " Europe ". The former was to be avoided, for in it " the style of living is French and not conducted upon English principles ". Having obtained accommodation, then, at the Europe, one visited Pompey's Pillar, Cleopatra's Needle and the Pasha's palace. On the whole Alexandria was disappointing for those who had looked forward to their first glimpse of the romantic East. Cairo was a different matter altogether. There was the comfortable Shepheard's where, as Mr. Stoequeler remarked,[1] " a bath is an *agrément* which few will deny themselves ". There were one or two details about the hotel baths, however, which needed attention.

[1] Article in the *Asiatic Journal*, entitled " Overland Trip ".

" The soft coir or fibrous matter ", Mr. Stoequeler complained, " which is used instead of flannel or the hair-glove, is not by any means so efficacious as the latter in removing the sodden matter, or *papier maché*, which covers the human cuticle. Then there is neither shampooing, nor joint-cracking, nor moustachio-dying." Nevertheless he was refreshed by his bath and ready for sightseeing. " A journey to the Pyramids ", he observed, " is particularly good fun, apart from the antiquarian enthusiasm which a man insensibly *gets up* on these occasions." On the other hand the Sphinx was disappointing.

> It is certain that age, or that neglect which imparts, in time, a vinegar aspect to the countenance of the most comely belle, has bereft the Sphinx of all her benignity. To my perception the colossal head (all that now remains) very closely resembles, when seen in profile, a cynical doctor of laws, with wig awry, suffering strangulation per tight cravat.

Nor was the Pasha's palace really impressive. Its " rich damask curtains and satin hangings *à la Française* are associated with coarse arabesques and wretched attempts at Perspective by a Greek, and divans and sofas *à la Turque* ", and in the garden " myrtles under severe restraint, box disciplined to represent ships and peacocks, and pavilions built in humble imitation of the Trianons, remind one of the French gardens siècle Louis XIV ".

Mr. Stoequeler does not seem to have penetrated to the Shoobra Kiosk ; but it was as well, for he would have found here the mingling of styles even more outrageous than anywhere in Cairo. The ceilings of its colonnades had been decorated by Italian artists with paintings of Hellenic deities in romantic attitudes ; and in the central courtyard was a large portrait of Mehemet Ali with a double representation of the Virgin Mary on either side of him. In those days, when an Albanian adventurer seemed to have restored some propriety to the name of Egypt's capital (Al Kahira meaning "The Victorious") Egyptians were inclined to be insolent with European visitors. The dragoman at the Shoobra Kiosk would wave a contemptuous hand at the figures of the Virgin and remark, "Look at Joseph's wife whom you Christians worship!" This was especially annoying for English visitors who were at pains to point out that members of the Anglican Church did *not* worship the Virgin, and that it was really rather tiresome to be confused with Papists.

From Cairo the passengers for India were driven to Suez in vans "very strong and capable of bearing, without damage, the violent collisions with lumps of stone and rock". At intervals of ten or twelve miles the horses were changed; and at these stations there were generally inns where you could get "good bottled ale". But after sixteen hours of continuous travelling it was a relief to arrive on board ship again at Suez. There, if you were bound for Madras or Calcutta you embarked on a steamer of nearly 2,000 tons, "with a magnificent saloon or cuddy where eighty persons can dine with comfort in cool weather", and even in hot weather, too, if only the Company had thought of having some port-holes in the saloon instead of "fanciful pictures of the Nile". Passengers for Bombay had, however, to content themselves with the steamers of the East India Company which were "neither so commodious nor so expeditious as those belonging to the Oriental and Peninsular Company".

It was not till 1870 that the first P. & O. steamer passed through the Suez Canal. She was towed by her lascars and tied up at night; and a passenger was heard to observe that it must be a pleasant change for the lascars to go out into the sunlight and have some strengthening exercise.

* * * * *

The social atmosphere of Bombay was almost from the beginning of the century different from that of Calcutta. The latter city in the great days of the Nabobs offers a sufficiently exact comparison to Republican Rome after the acquisition of the Levant; Plassey and Magnesia; Buxar and the fall of Mithridates. A vast territory, long famous both for its wealth and for the unwarlike character of its inhabitants, fell into the hands of an oligarchy of merchant-administrators. Numbers of worthless princelings, without national sentiments or the devotion of subjects to inspire them, conspired with Brutuses and Potts to loot the country on condition of keeping their thrones. The hordes of thievish servants, the tasteless luxury, the legal confusion, the rhetoric and ostentation and furious factions of eighteenth-century Calcutta are reminiscent of the Rome of Clodius. But the territories of which Bombay now became the capital were either barren by nature or ruined by continuous war; the people were sensitive, proud and warlike. There were no courts like those of Benares or Murshidabad where a Company man with influence might be appointed Resident and retire after three years with a fortune. Consequently influential circles in London were not interested in Bombay appointments; here was no place of honourable and profitable exile for the bankrupt son of a bishop or a wild young gentleman on the fringe of political society. Not only therefore were there few men who made fortunes in the Company's service but new arrivals were seldom quite so raffish and unsuitable as those whom Clive proposed to buy out on their first arrival. Fortunes there were, of course, but these were chiefly in shipping and connected enterprises. And in these enterprises Indian firms were early the rivals of the English. The shipbuilding firm of the Wadias soon established a great reputation; in their dockyards was built Codrington's flagship that went into action at Navarino. These Indian merchants were mostly Parsis. And if English visitors found them less attractive than many other Indians (Mrs. Graham described them as "in general a handsome large people but they have a more vulgar air than other natives") there could be no doubt about their industry and energy. Their traditions and way of life offered an extreme contrast to those of rich Indians in Bengal; which province had been regarded by the Mogul authorities as a suitable place of exile for the unscrupulous and rapacious; it was referred to in court circles as "the hell well-stocked with bread"; that is to say, the province whose fearful climate was mitigated by its easily garnered wealth and its opportunities for luxury and debauch.

A foreigner, but not of a European community, was soon to rival the Parsis for application and business acumen. In 1832 a quiet middle-aged man landed in Bombay. He was interested in the China trade and he bought a house, which he used both for office and dwelling, in Tamarind Lane. He never came out of doors till the evening, and then he padded along in the shadows dressed in a long Arab gown. He would hover for a moment near the bandstand or watch the fireworks on days of festival. He had only one friend in Bombay, the missionary, Dr. Wilson, and he was fond of visiting him to discuss a question that greatly interested him, the possibility of reconciling the teachings of Moses and the Prophets with the pantheism of the Sanskrit doctors. Many Indians visited Dr. Wilson, but they were chiefly Parsis in elaborate coaches built from designs of the London Lord Mayor's coach, wearing tall hats and scarlet stockings. The quiet man in the Arab gown would hang about till these grand coaches had gone and then knock gently, standing with arms folded in the wide sleeves of his gown, his head bowed under a big untidy striped turban. His name was Sassoon.

The atmosphere of Bombay, long regarded as a backwater, was hardly changed by a suddenly enhanced prestige, or by the acquisition of wide territories. Most of its English inhabitants continued to be functionaries and officers. They moved in circles not unlike those of a county town in contemporary England. Some of their pastimes would, however, have shocked their friends in England. In 1800, for instance, most of the ladies and gentlemen of the station attended a circus where a wild boar was baited by a leopard. The leopard was nervous of the boar and crouched in a corner. The audience was not to be disappointed and some gentlemen sent their servants to buy squibs and crackers with which they incited the leopard to show a more worthy spirit. The leopard responded by jumping the palisade which separated him from the audience; there was a sad moment of panic and an undignified scramble, during which, as a local newspaper remarked "each waived all ceremony in the order of his going". Fortunately someone had a gun and despatched the savage brute.

In the following year there was an entertaining legal decision which interested all travellers. A new arrival, Mr. Maw, brought an action against the captain of his ship for having permitted those ceremonies known as "Neptune's Rites" which even now have to be submitted to on some English liners by passengers crossing the Line for the first time—ceremonies now sanctified by photographs in the press of Royalty joining in the lathering and ducking with boyish zest. Mr. Maw was evidently a cross-grained creature for he had objected strongly; but the Bombay justices upheld his objections and fined the captain £400. Other suits of interest generally arose out of local quarrels. Tempers were as short as ever in Bombay. The testy English judiciary had already become a subject for Indian caricature and in 1830 the most successful "turn" at an Indian theatre was a burlesque sketch of the High Court during a trial for murder. The judge, red-faced and deaf, shouts and swears in chronic ill-temper. At last a servant enters and whispers that lunch is ready. "Oh," says the judge and springs to his feet. The Clerk of the Court nervously asks, "What is to be done with the prisoner?" "The prisoner!" exclaims the judge in a new transport of rage. "Damn his eyes, hang him."

The English theatre was less topical. Amateurs produced plays that had been successful in London some years before, such as "The Road to Ruin" "The Wheel of Fortune" and most popular of all, "Miss in her Teens and the Padlock". But as the century advanced a new Puritanism frowned on these amusements. The theatre was gradually deserted, on account, said a local journal approvingly, of "the march of morality and the progress of fastidiousness". There were dances but not on the scale of Calcutta, nor so frequent; and it was noticed by the Press as an item of unusual interest that the ball given to welcome General Abercrombie "continued to a late hour, nor did the brilliancy of the scene lose any effect, until the rising sun began to eclipse the minor artificial illumination of the night".

One of the gayest spirits of the Bombay of the Maratha wars had been Malcolm. Corpulent and merry, as famous for his drinking as for his quarrels—so that the term " Malcolm row " passed into Bombay proverb—he had campaigned with the Duke in India, heard him cursing " the cloimate " and met him again in Paris where the Duke said, " Ha ! Delighted to see you ", and told him how at Waterloo it had been " hard pounding on both sides but we pounded the hardest ". And then they went out riding and Malcolm chaffed the Duke in Hindustani, calling him a *lootie-wala*, and they joked about Talleyrand, comparing him to some of the equally crafty diplomats they had met at Maratha courts. And presently Malcolm " became quite fluent in French after a bottle and a half of champagne ". But when he came out to Bombay as Governor in 1825 it was to an India already grown strange to him, an India where civilians and soldiers alike missed the old incentives of excitement, plunder and rapid advancement. They were often bored. And Malcolm was so unlike the old Malcolm that he had become a teetotaller. He missed the earlier amenity of life in Bombay. As the Recorder, Sir James Mackintosh, wrote, " There is a langour and a lethargy in the Society here to which I never elsewhere saw any approach. It is all a cheat. If ever I rise from the dead I shall be very glad to travel for the sake of seeing clever men. . . ." Interests were becoming local and provincial. In the 'forties Lady Falkland was almost in despair for subjects of conversation. She mentioned to an officer " a great event which had lately taken place in Europe. He stared at me and said, ' I know nothing at all about it.' Not discouraged I started another topic connected with public affairs in England when I received a decided check by his answering, ' I take no interest at all in it.' I still hoped to rouse him from such a state of apathy and spoke of the admirable speech of some well-known politician, when to this he calmly replied, 'I know nothing at all about him.'"

The cosmopolitan culture of eighteenth-century Calcutta was in part due to the conditions of service and the connections of many of the Company's servants with political circles in England; they neither desired nor expected to stay long in India; their interests therefore remained those of the richer classes in London. But when fortunes could no longer be picked up in five years and a return to Europe was the final reward of long service, narrowness of outlook and a philistine suspicion of culture became the rule, not only in Bombay but, presently, in Calcutta also. Captain Bellew's Griffin, caught quoting poetry by his seniors, was asked for an explanation of such eccentricity. He stammered out that he supposed that it was his nature to quote poetry. "Huh," said the senior, "philosophising, eh? That is worse still." An interest in religion was preferred to philosophising. The religious revival in England and the eclipse of aristocratic agnosticism was reflected in Anglo-Indian society. Ladies writing to their relations in England referred constantly to their hopes of seeing all India converted. "It is very near," they would prophesy, pointing to the interest of certain Indians in Western education. Stout majors began to discuss the state of their colonel's soul. When Elphinstone became Governor of Bombay his habits awoke suspicion. He never slept in a bed but on the floor, and he rose at 4 a.m. to read Sophocles. It was whispered that he must be "a doubter, sceptic and unbeliever"; which libel continued until Bishop Heber announced that he had stayed with the Governor and found that "on all essential points" his views were "doctrinally correct". Professor Toynbee has found extraordinary the progress of Anglo-Indian character from a Jos Sedley to a

THEATRICALS

Nicholson. The Sedleys have been continuous and many of the attributes of a Nicholson were inherent in earlier characters. Clive could be as ruthless and as complacent; but he had no religious prejudices in the matter of self-reward; and he was not interested in the state of anybody's soul. With Elphinstone we begin to notice what I might call the Mutiny accent. When he had ordered a number of Brahmins whom he suspected of disaffection to be blown from guns, and his friends in some anxiety suggested his applying for an Act of Indemnity he replied, "If I have done wrong I ought to be punished. If I have done right I do not want any Acts of Indemnity." But he was a man of an earlier generation in his scholarship, his knowledge of Persian, Urdu, French, Italian and Latin.

Meanwhile there were evident signs of nineteenth-century progress in Bombay. In 1819 a Scotch kirk had been opened, and the circular inviting worshippers to its service pointed out that the Psalms were rendered in a manner "more plain, smooth and agreeable than any heretofore allowed". Two years later the first dentist was announced. A Mr. Rainitz had set up as an interior decorator. His lady,[1] Clara, describing herself as "of Cairo and Constantinople", advertised her skill in "cleering the teeth and playing them up, extracting and fixing new ones".

A Mr. Schulhof opened a Family Hotel, advertising the attractions of private bathing-places with tents and of a separate bungalow where smoking was allowed. Schulhof's was considered by an approving journal to be a place "where people must stand on their dignity; but if Convenience be preferred above Fashion, there is the New English Hotel in the Fort". But Schulhof's had other attractions besides Fashion. On gala nights the guests

[1] The term "wife" was not used in polite circles till the 'forties.

would be entertained by a comedian " who extracts a yellow handkerchief from his white jacket and sings ".

Cricket had appeared and won immediate popularity, the authorities smiling on the game as " an amusement tending to counteract the effects of this enervating climate by raising the spirits from apathy ". Many of the younger men were fond of jackal-hunting at which Qui Hi, the hero of Quiz's poem " Grand Master ", tried his hand.

Qui Hi, on his *Arab horse*
Sets off to find Byculla Course ;
Where, 'twas determined, ev'ry man
Should meet before the hunt began.
Their breakfast now the sportsmen take,
Merely a " *plug* of malt " and steak,
The bugle's signal now, of course,
Summoned the bobbery to horse ;
They get the word and off they move
In all directions, to Love-Grove.
A jackass, buff'lo or tattoo
The sportsmen anxiously pursue.
A loud " *view-hollo* " now is given
" A dog ! a Paria, by heaven !
Surround him—there he goes, ahead :
Put all your horses to their speed."
But *Qui Hi,* disregarding care,
Fell headlong on a prickly pear.

But was consoled when after the hunt—

" he found the party met
Were all for tiffin sharply set.
What rounds of beef, hampers of beer,
What jumping-powder they had here,
It is impossible to tell—
To *hint at them* will do as well.
It therefore, must suffice to say,
That *Qui Hi* spent a *pleasant day* " and so on.

There were quieter ways of visiting the beautiful country around Bombay than a hunt with the Bobbery Pack. Picnics had been popular during the eighteenth century, when a few hours' riding brought one to the Maratha frontier. At first they were stately, formal affairs, the Governor riding out with a squadron of horse. "Being arrived and alighted a curious cold collation is orderly set forth on large Persian carpets, under the spreading shade of lofty trees where variety of wine and musick exhilerate the spirits to a cherful livelyness and render every object divertive." Even when more ordinary persons made a trip to the country they did so in considerable pomp. Macdonald, that literary footman, describes how his master, Colonel Dow

> set off in a large boat, with sails . . . and a vessel following us with all the necessaries for an empty house, servants, two havaldars or sepoy sergeants, twelve sepoys with their arms, four planakins, with eight men for each, four saddle horses, with their keepers. We had plenty of provisions for us for two days in the boats. I was greatly delighted and thought it was a pleasant thing to live under the East India Company.

As the boat sailed up the wide creek towards Thana, the gentlemen drank punch together while two musicians played French horns. In those quiet backwaters, where an occasional dhow moved softly over the smooth, white water and a warm sea-wind sighed over the reeds stirring the landward-leaning palms and sending the white egrets flapping slowly over the terraced paddy fields, it was delightful to recline on cushions while servants filled and refilled one's glass; the gentlemen's spirits rose and they burst into song; but after a few more rounds of punch they fell asleep. When they reached Bhiwandi the gentlemen drank the waters, dressed, played at cards, and after dinner slept an hour or two; then in the afternoon they rode out on horseback and in the evening played at cards again.

With the turn of the century wines and French horns were less in evidence at picnics and everyone talked of leaving the stuffy city for the rest and refreshment of natural scenery, or the profound reflections inspired by interesting ruins. When Lady West and Mrs. Heber visited Bassein Lady West noted in her journal : " It really fills one with melancholy when one reflects that this once magnificent place is now a perfect desert with not one single inhabitant. . . . We were much pleased with it." People no longer scoffed at " the mouldering antiquities of the Hindoos ". As long as the antiquity was sufficiently mouldering it became an occasion for romantic reverie. Sir James Mackintosh was, in 1808, disappointed to find that the antiquities of Bijapur did not excite in him those interesting emotions that one would have expected.

> I felt nothing of the usual sentiments inspired by ruins in contemplating those of Bijapur. We in general, on such occasions, feel a reverential melancholy and are lifted above the present time and circumstances. But here we see the triumph of force and the buildings of which we behold the ruins were never the scenes of any other qualities than those of debauchery and of war without science.

He could not foresee a time when men would find a charm in the artillery of Bijapur ; in the fantastic cannon executed in the shape of dragons, with jewelled ear-rings and painted tongues that had once been shaded from the dew by purple carpets and from the sun by umbrellas of state. The buildings were too competent, too obstinate in resistance to the ravages of time, the evidence of pride and luxury too painfully clear, to admit of a " reverential melancholy ". One could only feel a sober elation at the doom of that dissolute city. There should be some pathos, a passive decline, a ruin almost unrecognisable in decay. The time should be evening. Young ladies expressed these sentiments in numerous poems beginning " 'Tis Eve ! " or " 'Tis Night the temple-gongs proclaim ! " Added to the fashionable appreciation of nature and of antiquities was a sham Orientalism that, long current in Europe, only spread to Anglo-Indian circles when the Scindias and Tipus were no longer to be feared, had, indeed, become romantic figures of the past. And, of course, every young lady on a picnic had her painting materials with her. There was now no excuse for ignorance of drawing and painting, for in 1822 Signor Constantino Augusto had set up a School of Art for Ladies in Bombay, the proprietor advertising himself as "well versed in the doctrine of the angles of animo-anatomic proportion, and peculiarly correct in his treatment of landscape with chaste colouring and perspective". And it was landscape that every lady wanted to paint. A sketch of quiet river with high banks lined with casuarinas: the jagged and pleasantly "awful" ghats; a temple embowered in mango-grove—the easel would be set up and servants despatched to fetch clean water for the brushes. A tall Brahmin would stroll out of the temple courtyard. Suspicious of all this foreign activity, he would be reassured by smiles and gestures of approbation directed towards the temple and perhaps flattered by a promise to include him also in the picture, that was to give one's friends and relations in England some idea of the wild romantic country that was India. The temple would not be rendered very exactly; in fact those writhing gods and goddesses only spoilt the general grand effect and could safely be omitted. In the end the architecture of the temple seemed, in the picture, to have developed into a blend of Gothic and Grecian; early English arches sprouting from Corinthian columns with just a touch of Egyptian or Chinese decoration. One then darkened the scene considerably to show that it was evening and finished off the picture by adding, in the corner, a tall graceful maiden in white robes drawing water from a well.

Picnics required " arranging " ; servants had to be sent ahead with tents and provisions ; and the weather might turn suddenly hot, making riding fatiguing. So the ladies more often spent the early evenings in their gardens. These were no longer laid out in the formal open manner of earlier taste. Romantic tastes required winding avenues between palms or mango-trees round whose trunks convolvulus, morning-glory, moon-flower and passion-flower were encouraged to creep. There are fewer varieties of song-bird in India than in England ; of these few had yet received their modern titles, and anyway the names were difficult to remember. So one commented on " the *mina*, the *kokeela*, and other birds of song ". Seats of chunam were set at the end of these avenues and having on either side beds of jasmine and tuberose and shrubs of oleander, whose crumpled flowers give a deliciously spicy perfume. The paths were covered with small sea-shells which not only dried quickly after the drenching rain of the monsoon but were supposed to afford an uncomfortable passage to snakes.

Or if the afternoon wind died down, as it so often does in the hot weather in Bombay, at the approach of evening, the garden was too warm for comfort and it was better to recline in a long chair on the veranda. The typical Anglo-Indian bungalow was now being built in Bombay. It was very different from the great mansions of Calcutta which had been constructed with the single hope of imitating and even surpassing the Palladian palaces of the rich at home. These had a façade adorned with heavy Corinthian columns, with a railed balcony behind them far too small for general use. The great windows had to be shuttered most of the day, and the narrow flat roof and the wide expanse of the walls made the buildings, however splendid in appearance, as unsuitable as possible for the Indian climate. The more sensible bungalows of Bombay seemed at first rather humble. One new-comer to India whose " imagination had been excited to a pitch of enthusiasm by English notions of Oriental pomp and magnificence " was bitterly disappointed at the first view of her host's home which was " a long one-storied building, with an overhanging thatched roof, and looking, for all the world, like a comfortable English cow-house ! " However, the interior was much more prepossessing. " We stepped direct, without any intervening hall or passage, into a large and elegant drawing-room, supported on pillars of faultless proportion. A large screen of red silk divided this apartment from a spacious dining-room." And the vast shady veranda, with its palms and ferns, seemed " an agreeable family resort " suitable " for a delightful *reunion* ". On the other hand, after a visitor had seen one bungalow, he had seen all in Bombay, so alike was the furniture and fittings of each room.

> The houses of the richer classes may contain better chairs and couches than those of their less affluent fellow-citizens, mahogany instead of imitative teak, jackwood or blackwood, while the silk or damask of his couches may parade itself somewhat more finely than the chintz of the inferior. The wall-shades, too, may be better by having drops to them,

but these were only details and the dead level of taste was noteworthy.

If the late evening were cooler the ladies would venture out for a drive. Palanquins were still used, but very few people kept their own ; they were hired by the hour. The palanquin-bearers had a bad reputation for insubordination, and for their continual strikes for higher wages. They would put the palanquin down in the middle of the road and scamper off, or crowd round their anxious " fare " shouting and gesticulating. This was annoying enough if one were bound for a dinner-party; but if one were a juror unpunctuality might be visited with a fine or even a conviction for contempt of court. The palanquin-bearers knew this well enough and as soon as they guessed their fare was a juror they were certain to blackmail him for double the ordinary wage. At last the harassed members of a Grand Jury refused to listen to the case until they had uttered a solemn remonstrance in open court, drawing the attention of the authorities to "the ill-regulated condition" of the palanquin trade. Palanquins were not finally ousted by buggies till the 'sixties; and the buggy-drivers inherited all the blackmailing practices of their predecessors. There was no lack of variety in the carriages that succeeded palanquins in popular favour. There were chariots, shigrampos, curricles, sociables, britzkas and clarences; if one could not afford to buy these conveyances one could hire them for £20 a month and in them the ladies, reclining under coloured parasols and gentlemen in dark blue or bottle-green coats drove down the Esplanade. It was interesting to note and comment on the other carriages on the Esplanade.

> There [as Mrs. Postans wrote in 1838] may be seen the English landau fresh from Long-acre; the smart dennet of the military aspirant marked by its high cushions; the roomy buggy of the mercantile Parsee, adorned with green and gold; the richly gilt chariot of a high cast Hindoo, with its silken reins and emblazoned panels.

However smart the carriages, the horses were disappointing after English carriage-horses and Mrs. Postans considered them

> deficient in size, ragged, thin and altogether illproportioned. Neither [she added] is the general effect improved by the

> singular attire of the coloured menials. The coachmen and grooms wear a coarse cloth dress, of whatever colour may have been selected for the family livery, with a cummerband and flat turban of the form of a plate, consisting of entwined folds of orange, blue, or crimson broadcloth, adorned with crossed bands of gold or silver lace. This costume, combined with bare legs and native slippers, appears incongruous.

The warm and unrefreshing sea-wind set the palms rasping and rattling, blew dead leaves in gusty spirals, and bore over the city the regrettable smells of the beach which was used by the fishermen not only for purposes of natural relief but as a convenient dumping ground for the carcases of their buffaloes and the skulls of their ancestors. Every visitor to Bombay commented on the "olfactory horrors" of an evening drive. And behind the boats and mounds of decomposing cattle lurked packs of savage dogs who would rush out to attack anyone who left his carriage for a stroll on the sands. Gradually, however, these inconveniences were mitigated and towards the end of the 'thirties the Esplanade was, during the hot weather, lined with "pretty cool, temporary residences; their chuppered roofs and rustic porches half concealed by the flowering creepers and luxuriant shade . . . and the whole is enclosed with a pretty compound, filled with fine plants, arrayed in tubs, around the trellised verandahs". Their interior decoration was a relief after the heavy crowded furniture of the bigger bungalows with their musty carpets and huge carved sideboards and multitude of tables. "The clean smooth China matting which covers the floors", a few basket chairs, and "a fine-toned piano and a good billiard-table" were sufficient furniture. And as you sat on the veranda you could hear the distant strains of the band and watch the carriages passing down the Esplanade. It was becoming a subject for comment that the gentlemen smoked as they drove, but this roused a great deal of criticism. A hookah after dinner or in the seclusion of a box at the theatre was permitted, but the smoking of cheroots in public provoked a journal to protest angrily against the young men who could be " seen lolling in their buggies, puffing away with the greatest *nonchalance* possible ". Even in 1856 a newspaper critic was disgusted to note that " several young men light their cheroots as soon as the dark of evening is sufficient to prevent a full recognition of their persons and veil their impertinence ". But criticism failed to check this practice. The young men hung round the bandstand at twilight, lurking in the shadows of great mango-trees ; and the more respectable citizens were so incensed at sight of the glowing pinpoints of light that evidenced a group of open-air smokers that there was some demand for police action.

As an alternative to the esplanade, one might visit the menagerie at Colaha. This was not, however, well stocked with animals. But there were " a great many *tame* asses, of the Zebra description, being *mostly striped* or *spotted* ". That they were tame at all was their most remarkable quality, for they were supposed to be quite untamable. Nevertheless, they apparently yielded under the discipline favoured at the menagerie, which was " severe to excess, their noses being generally bored. Many die under the operation ; while others, more restive, are seldom or never brought under restriction. The menagerie was lately under the superintendence of a blacksmith."

Men's dress had undergone a welcome change to greater simplicity, though the tight trousers and heavy rolled collars must have been uncomfortable in the hot weather. Hats still retained an elaborate variety of style. A hatter advertised a new supply of " superfine cocked hats, waterloo shape, trimmed to the Prince Regent's order, bound with black-figured lace, embroidered with silver and cord star loops, rich cockades with very rich bullion tassels, feathers and Saxon plumes complete ", costing £14 each. The last queue was seen in Bombay in 1799; and thereafter a certain manly carelessness in grooming one's tousled hair was fashionable. Men were clean-shaven till Napier, " The Bearded Vision ", brought beards into favour. A relic of the eighteenth century was the fashion still prevailing among men of wearing Musulman trousers in the house on informal occasions. Mr. Stoequeler describes the average young man starting out for his ride before sunrise and returning about eight when " he usually undresses, puts on his loose Turkish trousers, drinks iced soda water, lies down on the couch, novel or newspaper in hand, and in all probability, goes to sleep, in spite of the cawing of crows ". Breakfast was at ten and was as lavish then as now in Anglo-Indian houses. " The said meal ", to quote Mr. Stoequeler again, " consisting at all seasons, of rice, fried fish, eggs, omelette, preserves, tea, coffee, etc., more in the fashion of a Scotch than an English matutinal recreation ". Tiffin, however, seems to have been, for those days, a smallish meal, and Mrs. Postans congratulates the refined taste of her contemporaries in having exchanged the former " hecatombs of slaughtered animals " for " Perigord pies and preserved meats ". While the men went to work the married women either visited each other, or settled down to the traditional Anglo-Indian posture of writing *chits* to each other, which Mr. Stoequeler noticed were " neatly written, neatly folded, on pretty paper, and either sealed with all the discretion of Donna Julia's own, or else so cunningly implicated into cocked hats, twists and other sacred involutions, that to make wax itself *render up its trust* would be far less trouble than the unfolding of such missives by unpractised fingers ". Gentlemen paying informal calls were supposed to visit in the mornings, but they had to content themselves with conversation, for it was " considered an act of glaring impropriety in a lady to invite any gentleman to stay and partake of tiffin who is not either a relative or an intimate friend of the family ".

The ladies generally did their shopping in the mornings. There were a number of Parsi provision shops and grocers' stores. Of these the most favoured was Jangerjee Nasserawanjee ; and there were few things you could not buy there.

> The walls [Mrs. Postans discovered, were] surrounded with glass cases, filled with fine French china, bijouterie, gold lace, sauces, brandied fruits, riding whips. . . . A central avenue is flanked with cases containing jewellery, French clocks, and all descriptions of knicknackery. On the floor have subsided Cheshire and Gruyère cheeses, hams, cases of sardine, salmon and other edibles ; and from the ceiling depend bird cages, lamps, and coloured French lithographs in handsome frames.

If there was no shopping to be done, one could always call on the Governor's Lady (whom Mrs. Postans calls " the Lady President ") between eleven and two " on days advertised for reception ". Government House was at Parell, and after a long drive under the sun of April or May the callers generally arrived too exhausted for much animation. They sat round in a circle and made languid conversation. Lady Falkland complained that the talk " was almost always of illness or the weather ".

It was only in the evenings that the ladies seemed to revive and to show signs of animation, either at some dance in one of those vast Anglo-Indian rooms of which " the floor was covered with a white cloth stretched tight over the boards and rubbed with a kind of steatite or French chalk " or at one of the formal dinners which had superseded the light-hearted suppers of thirty years before. These dinner-parties had already developed a formidable ritual. First came an invitation written by the daughter of the house on dainty rose- or violet-coloured paper, with an appropriate motto—" *qui me néglige me perd* " for instance—on the back of the envelope. The nature of the entertainment would be indicated and *soirées musica es* were coming into favour.[1] The soldiers cut enviable figures in the drawing-room with their " raggies " and " Swiss-jackets " and " Cossack trowsers " ; the civilians had to be content with concentrating on the neat cut of their coats and on the skilful tying of their cravats. The gentlemen stood about in groups, smoothing their moustaches, discussing the ladies' charms (" how lovely Mrs. Brown looks this evening with her tiara of white roses ! "), and exchanging comments on the flirtation going on in the corner between a girl lately arrived from England and an elderly amorous major.—" As dead a case of splice as I ever saw in my life." The hostess addressed each of the ladies in turn, " You both play and sing, do you not ? " and each replied, " Very little," and explained that she had left her music at home and at the moment had a sore throat. Finally one would be persuaded to perform. She sat down at the piano, drew off her long gloves with a flourish and sang " Those Evening Bells " while the other guests sat round and sighed and agreed that Mr. Moore was an incomparable poet and that Erin, for all her faults, was as remarkable for her melancholy yet uplifting melodies as for the humorous anecdotes and comical turns of phrase of her simple sons of toil. Presently the ladies of the house brought refreshments ; sandwiches and

[1] For description of such a *soirée* see Captain Bellew's *Memoirs of a Griffin.*

" acidulous drinks " for the ladies, cake and negus for the gentlemen. The party would break up before eleven. The compliments and thanks of the last guests to leave were generally drowned by the shouts and threats of those who had left earlier and who were now running the gauntlet of the palanquin bearers who always gathered outside any house where there was a party and pestered the home-going guests, refusing to let them pass and even dragging at their elbows. The gentlemen soon exhausted their stock of Hindustani abuse, which was small, so small indeed that from constantly hearing the words repeated the ladies picked up certain indecorous phrases—particularly " Jow Jehannum "[1] . . . which was a favourite expletive with the gentlemen. What could it mean, the ladies sometimes cautiously inquired ; but their curiosity generally remained ungratified ; though on one occasion a hint was thrown out by a languid youth who, pushing back the pomaded curls from his forehead, countered the inquiry by referring darkly to a place " whose vulgar name could hardly be heard with satisfaction by polite ears ".

These parties were generally more animated if the guests included unmarried ladies recently arrived from England. As Lady Falkland noted—

> The arrival of a cargo (if I dare term it so) of young damsels from England is one of the exciting events that mark the advent of the *cold season*. It can be well imagined that their age, height, features, dress, and manners become topics of conversation, and as they bring the latest fashions from Europe, they are objects of interest to their own sex.

While everyone was anxious to inspect, and the gentlemen to make the acquaintance of, the new arrival, acid comments on the mercenary motives of these visitors were

[1] Anglicé, " Go to hell."

already frequent. Hood's verses sum up the general impression of a girl's reasons for a trip to India.

My heart is full—my trunks as well ;
My mind and caps made up,
My corsets shap'd by Mrs. Bell,
Are promised ere I sup ;
With boots and shoes, Rivarta's best,
And dresses by Ducé,
And a special licence in my chest—
I'm going to Bombay !

Though the motives of the trip to India were no longer as honestly announced as in the eighteenth century when " Mrs. Anne Miller ", as a friend wrote to the Governor of Madras, sailed for " your parts to make her fortune ; her father is a Vigntner and an honest man but has many children "—nevertheless the young woman was generally schooled carefully by her parents to concentrate on making a good marriage and therefore to look with scorn on the young and penniless and encourage the advances of the elderly rich. Above all she must set her cap at members of the Civil Service. Thus Miss Arabella Green,[1] asked by her parents to repeat the lessons they had been teaching her before launching her on the Anglo-Indian marriage-market obliged with—

I do believe entirely in
The Civil Service ranks :
The best are worth a deal of tin,
And none exactly blanks.
But I do believe that marrying
An *acting* man is fudge ;
And do not fancy anything
Below a *pucka* Judge.

The civil servants were called " three-hundred-a-year-dead-or-alive men " from the fact that their pay when they joined the service was £300 a year, and if they had put in sufficient

[1] Aliph Cheem, *The Lays of Ind.*

service their widows, on the civilian's death, drew a pension of £300 a year. Unfortunately this was not always understood and one young lady married a civil servant under the impression that she thereby acquired an immediate settlement of £300 a year. When some friends corrected this impression at a dinner-party she shouted indignantly at her husband down the dinner-table, " It's a do after all ! It *is* a *do* ! "[1]

While the girl who married, especially a husband from the ranks of the Civil Service, was envied, those who failed were always derided. Arabella Green in spite of all her efforts never found a husband and her chronicler concludes—

> The passages are booked ;
> They sail ; and other spins are glad
> To see her goose is cooked.

A poem as early as 1813 satirised the frantic efforts of unsuccessful husband-hunters to retain their English freshness and bloom—

> Pale faded stuffs, by time grown faint
> Will brighten up through *art* ;
> A *Britain* gives their faces paint,
> For sale at India's mart.

As this kind of humour has been fairly constant in Anglo-Indian society it will be of interest to compare the way in which a more modern poet deals with this amusing situation of a girl returning to England disappointed. The following verses appeared in the *Illustrated Weekly of India*, December 1936.

> Now sail the chagrined fishing fleet
> Yo ho, my girls, yo ho !
> Back to Putney and Byfleet
> Poor girls, you were too slow !

[1] Lady Falkland's *Cow Chow.*

Your Bond Street beauty sadly worn
Through drinking cocktails night and morn
With moonlight picnics until dawn
What ho ! my girls, what ho !

You scan an old engagement book
Heigh ho, my girls, heigh ho !
Recalling scenes in ballroom nook
" Let go, my girl, let go ! "
When Bill or Harry, Tom or Ray
Did Slap and Tickle with your play
Yet never *never* named the day
No go, my girls, no go !

It was not only young ladies bent on matrimony who realised the superior advantages of the Civil Service. Many soldiers were jealous of the greater salaries and the supposedly higher social standing of the civilians. The authoress of *Letters of a Lady*, describing a dinner at Madras in the 'thirties, relates that an officer turned to her and said, " Now I know very well, Mrs. ——, you despise us all from the bottom of your heart ; you think no one worth speaking to in reality but the Civil Service. Whatever people may really be you just class them all as civil and military—civil and military ; and you know no other distinction. Is it not so ? " With some spirit the lady replied, " No ; I sometimes class them as civil and uncivil." But nevertheless the same authoress had to confess that whatever the men were like, the wives of civil servants were preferable to those of the military.

> The civil ladies are generally very quiet, rather languid, speaking in almost a whisper, simply dressed, almost always lady-like and *comme-il-faut*, not pretty, but pleasant and nice-looking, rather dull, and give one very hard work pumping for conversation. The military ladies, on the contrary, are always noisy, affected, showily dressed, with a great many ornaments, *mauvais ton* chatter incessantly from the moment they enter the house, twist their curls, shake their bustles, and are altogether what you may call " Low Toss ". While they are alone with

> me after dinner they talk about suckling their babies, the disadvantage of scandal, " the officers " and " the Regiment ", and when the gentlemen come into the drawing-room, they invariably flirt with them most furiously.

But if the civil servants had better *ton* their conversation was limited—

> As soon as three or four of them get together they speak about nothing but employment and promotion. Whatever subject may be started they contrive to twist it, drag it, clip it and pinch it, till they bring it round to that and if left to themselves they sit and conjugate the verb " to collect " ! " I am a Collector [1] —He was a Collector—We shall be Collectors—You ought to be a Collector—They would have been Collectors."

They were, on the whole—

> rather grand, dull and silent, tired out with the heat and the office. The houses are greatly infested by mosquitoes, which are in themselves enough to lower one's spirits and stop conversation. People talk a little in a very low voice to those next to them. After dinner the company all sit round in the middle of the great gallery-like room, talk in whispers and scratch their mosquito-bites . . . India is the paradise of middle-aged gentlemen. When they are young they are thought nothing of ; but at about forty when they are " high in the service ", rather yellow and somewhat grey, they begin to be taken notice of and called " young men ". These respectable persons do all the flirtation too in a solemn sort of way, while the young ones sit by, looking on.

It is further to be assumed that the young men had no great desire to flirt : for all visitors to Bombay refer, almost with awe, to the good morals of the young. Partly this was due, no doubt, to the very public manner of life in Bombay and to the lack of opportunity for dissipation. As Mr. Stoequeler pointed out—

> In our Oriental city there are none of those lures and haunts which prove so attractive and fatal to the young Londoner.

[1] Head of a District.

> His Indian contemporary almost *must* spend his evenings in a decorous manner, for not only would he soon become marked if he frequented such scenes of debauchery as there are, which are of the very lowest description, and where common soldiers, sailors and such absolute blackguards resort; but there is not that field for *lark* which tempts the spruce London apprentice, and youths of higher degree, to take to the streets in search of such adventures. Drinking, too, is a practice not at all encouraged or countenanced in the Anglo-Indian community. It used to be so, but its pernicious day has long gone by, and the very, very few who are still victims to its brutifying power are looked upon with mingled pity and contempt by all other classes of their fellow citizens.

As a result Bombay Society, if neither intellectual nor quick-witted, was at least excessively refined. And a visitor was pleased to note

> the absence of all approach to broad vulgarity in the circles of an Indian salon. Startling as this fact may appear it is clearly deducible from, firstly, the circumstance that we have neither *Parvenus* nor *nouveaux riches* among us to shock one with their upstart airs; and secondly, that with very few exceptions no one comes to this country without having either laid the foundation, or completed the accomplishment, of a gentleman's education. . . . The man of cultivated mind will perhaps meet with less to shock his fastidious tastes than in the necessarily mixed society of England.

CHAPTER VI

ANGLO-INDIAN life in the inland towns had changed considerably from the days of Hickey, when Company's servants were mostly Residents of the courts of native princes who were still responsible for the main administration of the country. Now, over half of India it was the Company's servants who administered. Before the fall of the Maratha Empire, a voyage inland from Bombay was a considerable adventure. It was not uncommon to travel up to Poona while Elphinstone was Resident there. But the visitors were pleasantly thrilled to compare the security and comfort of the Resident's " bunglo ",[1] with the uneasy murmur of the Indian city, then in its last agony of anarchy and sedition. One heard wild tales of intrigue and cruelty : one was aware of a mounting frenzy that must some time break out in open war ; and yet when one met the Peshwa, the last head of the old Maratha federation, Bajirao II, it was difficult not to believe that Poona city was as tranquil as a suburb of Bombay, so extraordinary was the charm of that prince (Malcolm considered him the most charming ruler in India or Europe), so plausible his manner. Still it was a relief to return to the Residency, with its wide veranda overlooking the junction of the rivers Mula and Muta, the garden descending on both sides of the house in terraces to the edge of the water, the groves of mango trees on the far bank and in the distance the violet-shadowed hills. The Residency itself was comfortable enough. Elphinstone himself described it as " a tiled palace on wooden posts

[1] Mrs. Graham.

twelve feet high " ; but he added that to equip it for entertainments he had only " six plated dishes ; six dozen silver spoons ; two little union flags carried by the gardeners on high days or holidays ". But he was less interested in the traditional magnificence of a Resident than in his hobbies and studies ; and after reading a page of his diary one wonders that he had any time at all to devote to his guests.

> April 4th. Read three hundred lines of the " Antigone ". Breakfasted. Put my papers in order. Set off in my palanquin for the Hall. On the way, finished Mackintosh. He is eloquent and acute, but inexperienced and enthusiastic. Also read some of Page. At the Hall ordered repairs. Read an Idyll of Theocritus and Jenkins read aloud almost the whole fifth book of Homer. At five rode back. Dined. In bed, read Locke on Liberty and Necessity. April 5th. Finished " Antigone ". I perceive this to be a very affecting play.

He was also engaged on his work *Account of the Kingdom of Canbue.* Nevertheless he found time to play " round games of cards " with his guests. One such party was in progress when Mr. Briggs arrived with news of the Peshwa's decision to attack the English. Elphinstone had long been afraid of this and guessed that Briggs brought bad news, but he continued the game without apparent concern, " handed the last lady of the party into her palanquin " and sauntered up to Briggs " rubbing his hands, and said, ' Well, what is it ? ' "[1] Although he knew that the Residency was incapable of defence he refused to leave it until shortly before the Maratha attack so " that we had only time to leave with the clothes on our backs ", abandoning the Residency to destruction.[2] In spite of the danger he could not resist turning, once he had crossed the river, and watching the Maratha forces advancing from the city.

[1] Colebrook's *Memoir.*
[2] It was subsequently rebuilt and is now the Judge's bungalow.

It was towards the afternoon of a very sultry day, there was a dead calm, and no sound was heard except the rushing, the trampling, and the neighing of horses and the rumbling of gun-wheels. The effect was heightened by seeing the peaceful peasantry flying from their work in the fields, the bullocks breaking from their yoke, the wild antelopes, startled from sleep, bounding off, and then turning for a moment to gaze on this tremendous inundation which swept all before it, levelled the hedges and standing corn and completely overwhelmed every ordinary barrier as it moved.[1]

The whole thing reminded Elphinstone of the battles in Vergil ; he quoted " *quadrupedante putrem sonitu* " and called for some tea and bread and butter.

The English abandonment of Poona did not last long : the Peshwa collapsed, and Poona, famous for so long as a centre of Hindu orthodoxy and the capital of the Maratha confederacy, became in an extraordinarily short time the Poona of Anglo-Indian saga. Six years after the conquest Lady West found " the city of Poona much in decay since we have had it, and the Peshwa's Palaces miserable Places. We saw his Pagodas and were allowed a peep at his Gods Vishnu etc. to Christians a most disgusting spectacle." She was staying with Sir Lionel Smith whom she considered " a very gentlemanlike, agreeable Man " but for others in Poona she had little praise.

The Society here [she noted in her journal] is very formal, and the Ladies very self-sufficient and consequential, thinking of little but their fine pearls and *local* rank. . . . We are terribly observed, and of course I doubt not pulled to pieces, but thank God we are still quite English, and domestic taking our walk together every evening, our tea and bath afterwards, none of the indolence and finery of an Indian Lady.

In the rains a number of visitors arrived and presently

[1] Grant Duff.

there were dances given by the Governor at Dapoore, to which the guests drove in their buggies for eight miles, often in monsoon storms and gales. There were other discomforts, too ; the Poona blister-flies which often arrived in swarms and quite spoilt a ball. Lady Falkland related how

> some of these little tormentors climbed up into flannels, hid themselves in folds of net, visited the mysterious recesses of complicated trimmings ; some crept up gentlemen's sleeves, others conceived themselves in a jungle of a whisker. One heard little else all evening but " Allow me, Sir, to take off this blister-fly that is disappearing into your neckcloth " or " Permit me, Ma'am, to remove this one from your arm."

Even after the pacification of the Deccan, travelling was troublesome to a degree. The usual conveyance for a long journey was the palanquin or later " palkee-garry . . . with its two wretched ponies, rope harness, nearly naked driver, and wheels whose sinuous motions impress one with the idea that they must come off at the next revolution ". The journey could not be begun without a considerable correspondence with the postmasters of the various stages where the traveller proposed to halt. Everything could be provided for him provided that he was prepared both to wait and to pay ; at even the most remote villages beer could, by previous arrangement, be bought, but at a price relative to the honesty of the postmaster and the urgency of the traveller's need. It was useless to complain of discomfort, of damage and loss, of the desertion of one's servants and the theft of one's money, for the Government had expressly announced that " neither Government nor any of their officers are responsible for the misfortunes and disappointments which are inseparable from dak travelling ". English District officers were still comparatively few. Isolated by vast tracts of country they lived alone in half-Oriental state.

At Sholapur ruled Meadows Taylor, enormous and benign, relishing the devotion and gratitude of a province and the various pleasures of a well-stocked harem. He sat at his ease in a great cane chair, puffing at his hookah, fanned by chowries and thought of Lady Blessington's salon and the evening when he met that odd Louis Napoleon and Nesselrode was so impressed to hear of the efficiency of the Sepoy Army.[1] He enjoyed his visits to England, he liked gratifying the ladies with new and ever-stranger stories of India, and he was flattered by the astonishment and awe with which his white topi hung with gold braid was greeted in the streets of Europe. But he was happy to be back again in his kingdom, surrounded by his subjects and his girls, all rivals for his favour. When my grandfather stayed with him the old gentleman was particularly satisfied with the newest recruit to his household, a fifteen-year-old Maratha girl who was uncommonly skilful at " mulling " his eyebrows.

In districts less remote than Sholapur then was, the traditional Anglo-Indian " Stations " were springing up. The lordly mansions of eighteenth-century Bengal were but faintly recalled by the square white bungalows with high thatched roof; the unrailed verandah, white unornamented pillars, the doorways hung with screens of khus-khus grass (and presently curtains of jingling coloured beads); and the low white wall enclosing the compound. This curious word, compound, supposedly derived from the Malay *Kampong*, had come into early use to denote any walled place; though no one knew its origin and new-comers were puzzled by it as one of the oddest words in the new vocabulary with which they had to familiarise themselves. As a poet complained,

[1] *Memoirs.*

THE COFFEE-SHOP

In common usage here a *chit*
Serves for our business or our wit.
Bankshal's a place to lodge our ropes,
And Mango orchards all are *Topes.*
Godown usurps the warehouse place,
Compound denotes each walled space.

While formerly applied as commonly to a factory or square, the word was now generally used to denote the enclosed courtyard of a bungalow. Of this the garden formed but a small part. But that garden was the pride of each bungalow-owner. Water was drawn from a step-well in some corner of the compound, and all day long the yoked bullocks trudged up and down an inclined path drawing up from the dark abyss of the well a skinful of water which was caught by an under-gardener, the contents emptied into a channel leading to the flower-beds, the skin released, and the bullocks stumbled slowly backwards up towards the well-wall again. The bullocks were urged, expostulated with, beaten and sung to, by a wrinkled peasant in red turban and grey loincloth, and if the lords of the bungalow woke hours before dawn they heard his melancholy chant begin, " Ah-ee-oh-ay ", followed by the rattle of the pulley, and the creaking of the ropes. It was unfortunate that the trees had to be mostly palm and plantain, which gave rather a wild and unhomelike aspect to the garden, but you could always grow roses which, arrayed in big silver bowls, gave an English touch to the desolate drawing-room. The water from the well, led by narrow channels to every part of the garden, served each flower-bed by a series of little sluice-gates of mud, patted into place by the nimble fingers of the gardener, removed when more water was required or raised a few inches higher when the bed had been sufficiently watered and might rest under its square soaking sheet of muddy water, a convenient breeding-place for mosquitoes.

The larger part of the compound, however, offered no opportunities for the gardener. An expanse of grey earth, little mounds of stones, an occasional deciduous oleander-tree, and the inevitable dumps of rubbish thrust against the wall and awaiting the sweeper's attention. And then along the back-wall, the " servants' quarters ", flat-roofed white-washed buildings of baked mud in which the servants swarmed—the senior ones with a whole room to themselves in which their dozen or so children might have proper room, the juniors herded together, not only with other servants but with distant connections, friends and acquaintances of the senior servants, who for a tiny monthly rental were allowed to enjoy the protection of a roof and the prestige of a good address. Long before daybreak the servants' quarters would be astir, for the Sahib had to be awakened for his morning ride. Exercise was already a fetish and the early hours of the morning were, in the hot weather, the only time when riding was not unpleasant. The head-servant—butler, bearer or boy according to your province—advanced towards the bungalow, stalked along the veranda where the punkah coolies squatted, reclining against a pillar and pulling the punkah-rope with drowsy jerks or lying flat on their backs, the punkah-rope tied to their big toe, while with one leg they made the kicking motions as of a man learning to swim. They relieved each other at intervals and those whose turn was over or had not yet come lay about on the veranda in touselled groups. The butler reached the doorway of his master's bedroom and looked into the gloom. There were basket-chairs, woven in the bazaar, ranged round the walls. Tin boxes (which could resist both white ant and moth) contained his master's wardrobe. There was no carpet, for during the heat of the day it would be necessary to splash cool water over the floor.

The bed was an Indian "string-cot" (the Anglo-Indian word cot for a bed was used as early as the seventeenth century when Fryer wrote "There did sit the King in State on a Cot or Bed"), and since a mattress would not only be unpleasantly hot but might breed fleas, a couple of cotton carpets were stretched over the knotted ropes. There with the flapping fringe of the punkah but a foot or so off his face lay the master of the house, exhausted by a tiring night during which he had had continuously to shout at the punkah-coolies, who, falling asleep, had let go of the punkah-rope. Then, to quote Edwarde's account of the ritual of his rising in the 'forties,

> A black rascal makes an oration by my bed every morning. I wake, and see him salaaming with a cup of hot coffee in his hand. I sit on a chair and wash the teaspoon till the spoon is hot and the fluid cold (others less delicate, or perhaps disdaining even so trifling an effort, would hand the cup to the butler who blew vigorously on it till the coffee was cool enough to drink) while he introduces me gradually into an ambush of pantaloons and wellingtons. I am shut up in a red coat and a glazed lid set upon my head, and thus, carefully packed, exhibit my reluctance to what I am going to do—to wit, my *duty*—by *riding*.

A number of servants gathered round the porch to watch him mount his pony. He swore at them in duty bound—for did not every Anglo-Indian do so? Was it not a pleasure in Lahore to watch John Lawrence emerge from morning prayer at the new church and, refreshed by his devotions, fall with furious blows upon the servants awaiting him at the church door? And then he trotted down the straight wide roads of the station, the grey dust rising under the horse's roofs, past dozens of whitewashed bungalows, looking sadly alike—for all Mrs. Forsyth's much advertised garden and the major's vine terrace—past the church with its dignified white façade, pillars, square windows, like a London parish church—but there were some fanatics who talked of pulling it down and building a church in the new-fangled Gothic style, all fidgety decoration and red-and-yellow brick. Luckily the padre had set his face against any innovation. He liked the services short, did the padre, and always had a servant with a cigar and a glass of beer ready for him in the vestry to refresh him immediately after the service.

While the gentlemen rode, the ladies began their day more quietly. A long day ahead, it was good to take one's ease, to recline in a long basket-chair while the ayah brushed one's hair endlessly—it was pleasantly soothing that brushing, and one's hair stiff from the dry heat crackled excitingly under the hard bristles. It was the ayah's duty to provide all the gossip of the station. It was particularly important to know what was eaten or said at dinner-parties at which one had not been present. There were some houses which, owing to distinctions of rank it was impossible to visit ; but it was all the more important to know if the scandalous stories one heard of Mrs. X could be true, and whether Mrs. Y really got all those flashy dresses from Europe as she pretended—and if so, how could her husband afford it, for one knew what his pay was ?—and if not was it true, as one had all along suspected, she had fashion-plates copied by the bazaar dressmaker ? All these things the ayah was expected to find out. She also had to flatter her lady, exclaim with clasped hands and upturned eyes over a new dress or water-colour sketch of the military cemetery with its shady trees and with crowned tombs. When at last she was dressed the lady of the house would review the provision-cupboards to forestall the servants' pilfering, would inspect the pencil-strokes she had drawn on her husband's bottles after dinner to mark last night's level of brandy, would visit the various rooms of the bungalow to see that they were dusted, the silver cleaned, the paper, pencils, pens ready on the drawing-room table for her morning letters to her friends in England—those immense letters with long accounts of local feuds, of Hindu customs and Indian plant-life, of the sickness of pets and the daily perils from snakes, of the number of recent conversions and the wickedness of the Government in not supporting the missionaries more strongly—for the women then as now were the fiercest advocates of Strong Measures on all political occasions. The books too would be generally arranged on the thick, carpet-like tablecloth of the drawing-room's blackwood centre-table ; if left in a bookshelf the servants did not dust them properly and those odious little " fish-insects " crept in between the leaves. In any case there were few in the station who owned many books. They were expensive. A novel (but there were three volumes to it) cost a guinea. Collections of sermons and Lives of Bishops were popular ; they were full of elevating sentiments and thoughtful passages. The change in taste is noteworthy. We seldom hear now of Theocritus or Euripides. While Elphinstone would discuss with Jenkins the ethical problems of the *Antigone*, Nicholson was now writing, " I am just finishing a most interesting work, which, if you have not already read, I strongly recommend you to do so ; it is Faber's *Fulfilment of the Scriptural Prophecies*." Henry Lawrence, hearing that a colleague had taken offence at some action of his, copied out from the *Memoirs of Bishop Sandford* this passage, which he despatched to his colleague as a rebuke for harbouring vengeful thoughts : " My fears for those who retain a spirit of unforgiveness are overpowering. I will sincerely declare to you that I could not myself pray to God, or ask His

Pardon for my many transgressions, before I go to bed at night, with any comfort, or with any hope of being heard unless I were conscious that I did from my heart forgive as I ask to be forgiven." The brooding in lonely places over obscure texts of the Old Testament and even obscurer commentaries thereon, the ever-present sense of sin, the consciousness that one was a member of the elect and that all round were millions of doomed heathen led to a strange tension in the minds of these men, so that even in their most heroic moments is evident a mental condition that seems occasionally unbalanced and almost hysterical. Tears and groans, terrible outbursts of anger and sad moods of remorse, the temper of seventeenth-century covenanters (and it is to be remarked, how many of that generation came from North Ireland) alternating with a more modern sensibility were common at a crisis. It is impossible to read of the long death-agony of Henry Lawrence without being moved ; but the atmosphere is oddly rarefied and remote. He called all the garrison to his bedside and begged them to forgive him and to kiss him ; he spoke of his wife and burst into tears and when he mentioned his daughter his weeping became uncontrollable for some time ; he urged each of the soldiers to read their Bibles and at once " those seemingly hard rough men were sobbing like children ". He died " with the most beautiful expression of calm joy on his face ".

If books of commentaries and sermons were read by the men, there would also be in most drawing-rooms a book or two of poetry, and a book of pressed wild flowers—though Indian wild flowers were so different from those of English hedgerows, they were often so large and unwieldy, the magnolia, for instance, and the leathery petals of the yellow champak. There might even be a case or two of " insects ". Collections of coleoptera were quite fashionable for a time, and several ladies, finding on their arrival in India that their fellow Anglo-Indians could not tell them the names of any beetles or butterflies and that Indians (putting on enormous spectacles, pursing their lips, tilting their heads to one side as though really interested in the problem) asserted that this was a particularly rare species till now unnamed, formed sudden resolves to be naturalists. But the making of a collection was always a difficulty; for one could not go hunting beetles oneself—one's husband would have been sadly distressed at such undignified conduct—which meant that one had to delegate this duty to servants; who, in spite of professing enthusiastic interest in their mistress's hobby were dreadfully stupid, continually producing with an air of triumph cockroaches and other horrors, instead of the beautiful winged insects, metallic-glistening and many-coloured, that whirred past one's lamp in the evening.

Lacking other occupation the ladies amused themselves by writing each other endless *chits* in which they excused themselves for not calling in person but the heat or a headache made rest essential for that day. If they dropped a handkerchief they would "just lower their voices and say 'Boy'!' in a very gentle tone and then creeps in some wizened, skinny brownie looking like a superannuated thread-paper who twiddles after them for a little while and then creeps out again as softly as a black cat".

Of course the drawing-room and the books had often to be left when the official had to tour in the districts; and the women of that age seem, on occasions of duty, to have been as physically hardy as indifferent to discomfort and danger. The admirable Honoria Lawrence accompanied her husband on his most trying journeys. As Revenue Surveyor he had once to visit

a dense jungle at the foot of the Nepaul hills, intersected with

> belts of forest trees—a famous tiger tract. The dews were so heavy, that my bed under a small tent was wet through. Fires were kept constantly lighted to keep off the tigers and wild elephants, which gave an unmistakable indication of their proximity, and it was not till eleven or twelve o'clock that the fog cleared sufficiently to permit our laying of a theodolite. It was in such a tract that, after three or four days, we[1] connected our survey, and when we met, to my surprise I found Mrs. Lawrence with him. She was seated on the bank of a nullah, her feet overhanging the den of some wild animal. While she, with a portfolio in her lap, was writing overland letters, her husband, at no great distance, was laying his theodolite.

And after hours in the sun Mrs. Lawrence had no quiet bungalow to return to. They lived in one tent under a mango-tree.

> The tent was of the ordinary size prescribed for a subaltern with a marching regiment, about twelve feet square ; but it is not so easy to describe the interior. A charpoy in one corner, an iron stove in another, a couple of tables and three or four chairs, but every superficial inch of each was taken up with papers, plans or maps.

Some of those Spartan women found real pleasure in the wild scenery amid which they journeyed. They were serious-minded and reflective and their emotions before noble landscapes were appropriately religious. Their letters home often contain as many verses as sketches and Mrs. Edwardes, though bitterly disappointed at her husband's transfer from comparatively civilised Jullundur to savage Hazara on the North-West Frontier, was consoled by the gloomy magnificence of the views at their new station. The River Nynsook inspired her to composition :

> Well may the stranger, shudd'ring, look
> Down on the torrent of Nynsook.
> Yet should it be his mood to find
> A moral in each whispering wind,

[1] The story is told by an unnamed fellow-Surveyor of Lawrence's quoted in Kaye's *Lives of Indian Officers*.

An angel-face in every gleam
Which lights the earth, in every stream
A nook which overflows with love
To men below from Heaven above—
Then will he view Nynsook aright,
And own 'tis well called Eye's Delight.

But for others in less remote districts it was a pleasure and relief to return to the house which one had spent so much trouble over. It is pathetic to read of Mrs. Lushington's joy at seeing her and her husband's books lying under a lamp on the centre-table when they returned from a visit to a strange bazaar and a walk round the local temple. The temple alone was exhausting enough, for Mrs. Lushington had never been inside one before, and the whole experience affected her like some wild dream. Even the witty Miss Eden confessed, " I shall always respect marching for making me like Calcutta, and making me feel the advantage of a quiet room, with books and tables and chairs all clean and in the same place every day." In spite of the absence of so many amenities they soon became attached not only to their houses but to the even monotonous life of the " station " ; indeed, when they visited England they felt as though they were in an unfamiliar country in which they found much to criticise and little to approve. As Lady Lawrence wrote to John Nicholson who was then on furlough—

> I must not forget to say that we were *delighted* with your verdict on the Opera. In like manner, when we were in town, we went *once*, and, like you, said, " We have nothing so bad in India ! " Did not London fill you with the bewildering sight of such luxury and profusion as we in the jungles had forgotten could exist, and of vice and misery which unless in a year of war or famine, could not be equalled here ?

It was only those who were temporary residents in India

who now regarded India with the irritation and nostalgia of Miss Eden who scribbled acidly—

> Miss Fane is again laid up with mosquito-bites. Mrs. Fane and Mrs. Beresford were part of Sir Henry's party, and the most conversable of the ladies we have seen—a slight tinge of London topics about them, or at least of London readiness to talk. After dinner all the ladies sit in a complete circle round the room, and the gentlemen stand at the farther end of it. I do not suppose they would have anything to say if they met but it would look better. . . . There are five long years before us.

The days passed uneventfully. After their morning ride the gentlemen usually gathered at the station "Coffee Shop". There in their gaiters and topis of fanciful and varied design, with their dogs and their servants, they sat round at bare deal tables and between steaming cups of coffee discussed the gossip of the station. They would tell each other, with many guffaws—

> that Nicaldo, the itinerant dentist, had arrived and that Mrs. McGhee, whose teeth, numerically as well as positively, had dwindled to their shortest span, had had the balance summarily extracted, and that Nicaldo is engaged to supply new ones, which have already been designated "Mother McGhee's new dinner-set". This circumstance naturally led to the extravagance of the lady implicated, inasmuch as old McGhee had been seen that morning at the auction-sale of poor Sergeant Trail, and that he purchased for the sum of two rupees eleven annas, three flannel waistcoats, five pair of socks, and an old toothbrush—all of which he carried home in his hat; and that he frowned so hard at the bugler boys that they were afraid to bid against him—sufficiently proving his character is favourable to economy. Then we hear the opinions that are expressed relative to the last night's "feed" at the Gander's; how the ham, professedly a "prime York" had been distinctly traced as having had its origin in the ravine that skirts the lovely Kabob; and that fellow Garlic insists upon it that he saw, with his own naked eye, the native vendor of swine disposing of his produce to Mrs. Gander in her verandah. More-

> over, we discover that the turkey was the leanest old bird in creation, and that its breast was puffed out by the ingenious introduction of a tough old fowl, but which the keen eye of Pullow detected. Then we are told of the hop last night at the Guddurs', which was pronounced to be " deadly lively " ; that the heat was so great that Mrs. Chunam, who, as it is declared, has eleven pence out of the shilling of Hindoo blood floating in her veins, and who delights to veneer as much of herself as is exposed to public view, for the purpose of the whitening of her otherwise shady complexion—the heat, we understand, was so great that the veneer cracked and peeled off in flakes ; and further, that her dress happening to subside from off her shoulders, a lovely olive rim, where the veneer had not been applied, became visible, for the general edification. Guddur then relates his adventure in the dance with Barbara, who travelled about the room like a paviour's rammer, to the detriment of his feet and knees ; and we also ascertain that Miss Goley favoured the company with a song all about " a bonnie coo "—which Guddur declares was a hymn, or at any rate a roundelay, while Pullow bets him a new hat that it was a Caledonian melody of an agricultural character.

These dinners were usually even more animated when a stranger, probably an official passing through on his way to a new appointment, passed a few nights in the station. If the visitor were someone of rank there would be brisk competition for the honour of entertaining him between the District Magistrate and the Judge ; for each of them

> delighted in welcoming within his portals the great ones of the land ; he (the District Magistrate) has ensnared several mighty men of renown. A Governor was once entrapped in his snare, to his unlimited satisfaction ; while last year, he skilfully made capture of a bishop, but for whose appropriation popular rumour avows that he betokened symptoms of repentance.

Sometimes it would only be a party of common soldiers passing through. They would spend the night under some trees, and the District Magistrate would visit them to inquire if they had their Bibles with them. One party, thus interrogated by Mr. Lushington, had the presence of mind to say that of course they had their Bibles but they valued them so much that they did not want to expose them to the ravages of the climate as they travelled, and that therefore they had kept them neatly and carefully wrapped up at the bottom of their trunks. The Magistrate was so much impressed by these noble sentiments coming from rough privates that he not only gave them some cheap Bibles to use on the way, but some tracts as well. There was, indeed, a very general preoccupation with the morals of poorer Europeans. A Governor-General, Lord Auckland, spoke very seriously to some sailors and advised them not to drink more than was good for them. Lord Dalhousie wrung his hands over the soldiers' taste for beer. A chaplain refused to visit soldiers in the Calcutta Hospital suffering from diseases aggravated by alcohol; the very fact that they were ill was evidence of divine displeasure at their conduct and it was not for him to endanger his salvation by consorting with those lost souls. Even the indulgence of soldiers in theatricals was viewed with suspicion; and when a party of the Cameronians acted a play to raise money for the European Orphan Asylum (to which were despatched the children of their fallen comrades) the money was refused on the grounds that it had been gained in so "unchristian a manner" as theatricals, which must "hurt the feelings and principles" of the orphans.

Generally the visitors to the station would be young officers and there would be some competition to secure their presence at dinner-parties. A letter would arrive: "My dear Captain Quiz—*Do* induce your newly arrived friend to accompany you to-night and give us the pleasure of his company at dinner; we shall be *so* delighted to see him.

Believe me always *very* sincerely yours, Isabella Byle." At dinner,

> the host and hostess occupy their respective centres of the table, while the top and bottom, with their appalling concomitant consequences of turkey and ham to carve, are studiously shunned, and become the refuge for the Griff (most junior officer present) who in this sphere of action imbibes his earliest lessons in carving. He dissects the turkey, but consigns a pound and a half of stuffing into the velvet lap of the adjoining Mrs. Koofter ; the flounce of the punkah becomes partly disengaged, and, after flapping about remorselessly like an unreefed sail in a gale of wind, succeeds in whisking off the protecting wire-gauze top of the lamp, and launching it on the apex of Miss Goley's head, occasioning the blowing-out of the lamp, and the consequent oleaginous effluvium that proceeds from the expiring wick, to the general discomposure of the nasal organs. Then the punkah has to be stopped to undergo reparation; and frantic and awful is the heat that is engendered thereby. Then, after an interregnum of considerable duration, the second course is produced, succeeded by a pause " more fearful than before ". The sweets have vanished and at last the dessert, indicative of a concluding climax ; the decanters are circulated, and the fair hostess telegraphs to the " Burra Beebee " the signal for departure. . . . Then the gentlemen are doomed to a further session, which terminates in the production of coffee, when the gong tells its tale of midnight. The piano is heard in the adjoining room ; some faint voice warbles a doleful strain, the " Burra Beebee " rises and a general dispersion ensues.

Such dinners were, however, a treat and generally the day closed with the husband reading alone and the wife sewing.

Such a régime may not seem exciting ; but it did not differ greatly from that of the Governor-General and his ladies in their palace at Calcutta. This is how Miss Eden describes her day—

> We breakfast at nine. . . . I throw a great deal of sentiment into my eating, always having watercresses for breakfast,

> because they are so English. . . . We dawdle about the hall for a quarter of an hour, reading the papers, and doing a little civility to the household ; then Fanny and I go to the drawing-room and work and write till twelve, when I go up to my own room, and read and write till two. Fanny stays downstairs, as she likes it better than her own room. I do my shopping, too, at this hour : the natives come with work, and silks, and anything they think they have a chance of selling, and sometimes one picks up a tempting article in the way of work. At two we all meet for luncheon and George (Lord Auckland) brings with him anybody who may happen to be doing business with him at the time. Then I go up to my own room, and have three hours and a half comfortably by myself. I draw a great amount, and was making a lovely set of costumes, but my own pursuits have been cut in upon by other people. One person wants a picture of a sister she has lost touched up, and in fact renewed, as the damp has utterly destroyed it. There are no professional artists in Calcutta, except one who paints a second-rate sort of sign-post, and though I cannot make much of all these likenesses, yet it feels like a duty to help anybody to a likeness of a friend at home, and it is one of the very few good-natured things it is possible to do here, so I have been very busy the last ten days making copies of these pictures. To finish our day : at six we go out. George and I ride every day now ; Fanny about once in three days. At 7.30 we dress ; dine at night, and at ten go off to bed.

Miss Eden's chief hobby was her menagerie. The inmates of this included—

> a goat that is too handsome—an immense creature with white silk hair half a yard and more long. It stalks upstairs and into my room and is a nice good-humoured animal ; two young bears, two fawns and a very young mouse-deer. One fawn died but the other and the mouse-deer I am trying to rear by means of a teapot and some milk.

Miss Eden found some amusement in the foibles and oddities of the people she met in Calcutta ; and in a small station, the characteristics of the officials and their wives were not very different from those of residents in the capital.

The figures of each local hierarchy emerge with recognisable regularity from the verses of satirists.

> There's McCaul the Collector our biggest gun
> A capital hand at whist.
> And passable company, when he's done
> Prosing over "The List".[1]
> And Jones, his clever conceited sub.,
> The "competition-elect".
> A youth into whom I should like to rub
> A lineament of respect.
> There's Tomkins, our Civil and Sessions Judge,
> A pompous, ponderous Beak,
> Who sneers at McCaul's decisions as fudge—
> *We* know it's professional pique.
> There's little Sharp, the Surgeon, in charge
> Of the Central Sudder Jail,
> He's a habit of taking very large
> Potions of Bass's Ale.
> There's the padre, the Reverend Michael Whine.
> The sorrowfullest of men,
> Who tells you he's crushed with his children nine,
> And What'll he do with ten?

And so on.

If there were a regiment at the station the social round would be more varied. Amateur theatricals (in spite of the frowns of the pious) were popular among the young subalterns. Performances would be given in the local assembly room where there was usually some old scenery which had done duty in countless earlier dramas.

> The back scenes are a corresponding trio, that roll up—one a wood for the romantic and the perpetration of horrible murders with a circular cut in a dab of sky for the addition of a gentle moon when requisite. Then we have an interior, which by a judicious arrangement of properties, duly set in order by the momentary introduction of a John, whose livery consists of a strip of yellow paper tucked to his collar and cuffs, can equally represent the boudoir for interviews with unfavouring papas

---

[1] The Civil List; Bible of all those interested in promotion, then as now.

> or the drawing-room where scenes in connection with bended knees are enacted. Lastly, we have a dungeon, for the express benefit of enchained gentlemen who have got solos to communicate. Great, however, as is the artistic excellence of these scenes, the drop is incomparably superb. Some ambitious individual, overflowing with perspective on a novel design, has poured it forth on canvas in the shape of columns ingeniously receding to the front and approaching to the rear.

There was a natural rivalry for the chief parts : and three short plays were generally given to accommodate all the officers and their ladies, the privates forming the audience, and an occasional sergeant being allowed to sing a comic song in the intervals while the better-bred performers tittered, as they changed for the next play, at the way the sergeant " exasperates his *h*'s and is apt to hear futsteps a comin' when he will be hoff to claim the 'ands of his Hevelina for his bride ! " Edwardes, whose later letters are so regrettably burdened with references to the favour of the Almighty and the villainy of Asiatics, was as a junior anxious to acquaint his friends in England with his success and popularity as an amateur actor.

> They may talk [he wrote to Cowley Fowles] of Lord Grey's exertions, but think of a small ensign being slapped on the back with a side-scene, and desired to rise up Grand Duke Alexander brother of the Emperor ! Oh, dear me ! this is a bad time of the year to have honour thrust upon me ! Already has one letter informed you of my theatrical triumphs in the asthmatic and crutch-line as Sir Anthony Absolute ; and now while I stand upright, I unroll the seven and twenty towels which gave people to understand that there is gout in the neighbourhood, take off servitude in fact and don the iron youth of a *Russian Autocrat* !

Not content with acting Edwardes painted some new scenery (as he was careful to explain " for the amusement of the men ") and on one occasion " stood six hours a day depicting cottage scenes and lordly castles of the land we still call

MISERIES OF THE FIRST OF THE MONTH

after Rowlandson

'home' on immense sheets of canvas". Unfortunately the effort exhausted him; he fell ill and had to take a holiday at Simla. This depressed him and on the journey he wrote some verses on a popular Anglo-Indian theme, that of exile.

And are my days all happy now?
Youth's dream is life's reality?
Are there no clouds upon my brow
Because there are none in the sky?

And do I love the matin screen
Of gaudy parrots in the glade?
Or nightly mingling in my dream
The little bul-bul's serenade?

Sing not to me thou merry bird;
Thy song is but an Eastern tale,
I'd give it for the simplest word
Of England's gentle nightingale.

And as he journeyed he was displeased at the Hindu ritual of cremation. "These disgusting obsequies" he exclaimed, "I have watched them with my glass throughout the whole process and seldom indeed have I seen anything which betrayed that sort of love which *we* feel for the dead, which shrinks from familiarity with the object."

The increase of Puritan intolerance of other religions and contempt for their followers, the middle-class suspicion of foreigners and their customs, had an inevitable effect on the relations between Englishmen and Indians. When Mrs. Lushington asked a senior lady what she had seen of the country and its people since her first coming to India, the latter replied, "Oh nothing, thank goodness. I know nothing at all about them, nor I don't wish to. Really I think the less one knows of them the better." But each station had its pet Raja or Nawab, and there was some cordiality between them and the senior officials. A Collector would even dine with a big landowner ; after all there would be plenty of champagne, even if there was some confusion in the service and in the order of the dishes so that " Lobsters and tart fruits commingle, while truffled sausages and sugared almonds share mutually the same dish. Nor is it for want of cookery as dishes and plates, and vessels even of the most domestic character, grace the board, side by side with silver plate and glittering ormolu, to the unsmotherable amusement of the guests." [1] And the Collector's wife would pay little compliments to the Rani and send her " twopenny handkerchiefs with alphabets and pictures on them " [2] and even herself paint for them Christmas cards with views of Vesuvius in eruption and underneath, in Gothic lettering, an appropriate quotation from Lord Byron illustrating the impressive effect of wild natural scenery. The Collector and his wife would be invited to tea at the Raja's house and as they wandered through the rooms of their host's palace, they smiled at the lumber in each room, the " pianos by the dozen ; harps, babies' cots, four-post bedsteads, ladies' wardrobes, marble-topped round tables ; billiard-tables, with caverns for pockets, and a prevailing irregularity of surface, engendered by the curling up of the wood ". These rooms were thus furnished to display the Raja's attachment to Western taste. In some recess of the building would be a few rooms reserved for himself and his family furnished in the traditional Indian manner ; and from these he would bring, with an apologetic smile, the old pictures that court-artists had painted for his ancestors a century or so ago. The modern taste for Mogul or Rajput art was still undreamt of, and the Raja would listen, agreeing politely, while the Collector's wife pointed out how sadly lacking in all knowledge of Per-

[1] Atkinson. [2] Mrs. Lushington.

spective and Anatomy those old painters were. Indeed, on one occasion, a Collector's wife was good enough to send for her paint-box and with a few skilful brush-strokes restored certain patches where damp or rough usage had smudged the original paint ; then, warming to the good work, she spread over the surface of all her host's pictures a thin wash of vandyke brown, so that the horrid glaring colours were subdued to an even tone and the whole effect was now that of a respectable Old Master.

Sometimes there would be not only pictures to show, but also old letters or documents of historic interest ; and when Lady Falkland visited the widow of Nana Farnavis she was shown some letters from the Duke of Wellington. The widow was now an old woman, but once she had been a great lady, the wife of the Indian Metternich. Lord Valentia had noted that she was " really a very pretty girl, fair, round-faced ", and the Duke, then plain Arthur Wellesley, called on her and offered her his escort, finding her to be " very fair and very handsome ". Now Lady Falkland

> beheld, sitting in the small doorway, and as if in a frame, a little old woman ; there she remained motionless, reminding me somewhat of one of the Hindu deities in its shrine. She was covered from head to foot with a large red shawl. When I advanced to her, she gave me her hand, and was very silent at first, so I had time to observe her. She is very old, but still traces of great beauty are visible, the features small and delicate, and her eyes large and bright for her age ; her little naked feet peeped out from under the folds of her shawl, and I remarked her hands were well formed.

But if there still remained traces of former beauty, there were no traces of former splendour. " Between the pillars hung very shabby curtains : an old bit of carpet and two ricketty-looking chairs were all the furniture of the apartment."

There was, however, one prince whose wealth, hospitality and pleasant manners extorted a certain envious admiration from the residents of an Upper India station. This was Dhondu Pant. He was born in obscurity and poverty and concerning the manner, place and date of his death nothing is known. But for a brief period he was to the English the best known and best hated of Indian princes. He passed his childhood in Venegaon, a small village near the Bhor Ghat between Bombay and Poona. His father was the local priest. The village has scarcely changed and one may still see the old earth-brown temple shaded by a giant peepul-tree whose silvery leaves keep up a busy whispering and trinkling through the quiet of morning and the hush of noon. Under its shadow Dhondu played or watched his father enter and leave the shrine with trays of offerings and tall brass lamps. Then one day the child left his humble village and was taken north to be adopted by the last of the Peshwas, Bajirao II, who lived in luxurious exile at Bithur near Cawnpore, and who, more than all his riches, desired a son. As in all Hindu families of rank, the boy had now to take a " household title " and he chose that of Nana Sahib in imitation of the greatest of the Peshwas. The adoptive father died and the Government refused to continue paying to Nana Sahib the liberal pension that had been granted to the deposed Peshwa. But, if he smarted under the implied refusal to recognise his succession as titular Peshwa, he was wealthy enough even without the pension. He apparently enjoyed the society of Europeans and officers of the Cawnpore garrison were often at his table. One of the guests described dinner in the palace :

> I sat down to a table twenty feet long (it had originally been the mess-table of a cavalry-regiment) which was covered with a damask tablecloth of European manufacture, but instead of

> a dinner napkin there was a bedroom towel. The soup—for the steward had everything ready—was served up in a trifle-dish which had formed part of a dessert service belonging to the Ninth Lancers—at all events the arms of that regiment were upon it ; but the plate into which I ladled it with a broken tea-cup was of the old willow pattern. The pilau which followed the soup was served upon a huge plated dish, but the plate from which I ate it was of the very commonest description. . . . The cool claret I drank out of a richly cut champagne glass, and the beer out of an American tumbler of the very worst quality.

As time went on the Nana's parties became more sophisticated. He had sent to England to argue his case his secretary Azimullah Khan, a plausible Musulman, who having been footman in an Anglo-Indian household had acquired a mastery of English. This person was lionised in Mayfair, voted charming and witty and, though he failed to impress the directors in Leadenhall Street, continued to correspond with titled ladies even after his return to India. Indeed, if we may believe his own account, personal experience of the easy morals of ladies in the great houses of London confirmed his opinion of the wisdom of the veil and the eunuch-guarded harems of the East. " They are all the same," he said to Mr. Russel. " Like moths in candlelight they will fly and get burned." In any case, he now knew enough of the West to advise his master in English etiquette and the balls given by Nana Sahib were the talk of Cawnpore. Everyone in the station hoped to be asked. The host was self-assured and his manners charming. He " inquired after the health of the Major's lady ; congratulated the judge on his rumoured promotion to the Sudder Court ; joked the assistant magistrate about his last mishap in the hunting-field ; and complimented the belle of the evening on the colour she had brought down from Simla ". He " played billiards admirably while he was yet slim enough to bend over the table without inconvenience ". The officers and their wives flattered him, gaped at his carriages and his jewellery, and when their envious hints led him to offer them whatever they had especially admired they made no difficulty about accepting jewels, silks and shawls, or using his carriages as their own. He had the added fascination of a reputation for secret orgies on a Neronian scale. While the ladies of the station strolled through the Westernised reception rooms in Nana Sahib's palace they whispered together about the secret inner apartments whose walls were covered by European artists with paintings that were " vicious with deeper than Parisian immorality ".

Save for the intriguing figure of the Nana Cawnpore was much like any other station with its carefully regulated hierarchy, its formal dinners, its evening parade of carriages in the Mall. " Whose buggy is that ", asks Mr. Russel, " preceded by two native troopers and followed by five or six armed natives running on foot ? " " That is the magistrate and collector."—" What does he do ? "—" He is the burra Sahib or big man of the station."—" Who is in the smart gharry with servants in livery ? "—" That is the chaplain of the station who marries and baptises and performs service for the Europeans."—" Does he go among the natives ? "—" Not he ; he leaves that to the missionaries. . . ."—" Well ; and who comes next along the drive, in that very smart buggy with the bay mare ? "—" That is the doctor of the station. He attends the sick Europeans. He also gets, under certain circumstances, head-money for every native soldier in garrison."—" Does he attend them ? " —" I should think not."—" But why is he paid for them ? " —" Ah, that is another matter. You must understand our system better before you can comprehend things of this sort." "And who is this jolly-looking fellow on the grey Arab?"—"That is the judge of the station; a very good fellow. All judges are rather slow coaches, you know." At that time of the evening they would all be bound for the Bandstand and later for the Assembly Rooms, for the Cawnpore Assembly Rooms were the gayest in North India; a handsome building with "pillars of the Roman Doric order".

There were more lavish parties than ever at the Nana's palace as 1856 drew to a close. There seemed to be more money in Cawnpore than in most up-country stations and a visitor noted with approval that "many of the Cawnpore houses are now handsomely furnished, the chairs, tables, and sofas, being of valuable wood, richly carved, with cushions and coverings of damask, or of Bareilly manufacture, black, with gold flowers, resembling the japanned chairs, fashionable in England forty years ago". The gardens, too, were a fine sight that winter in Cawnpore; and though there was some complaint that the broad beans had not done well, the grapes and peaches were unusually "luxuriant". It was in most stations a pleasant cold weather. In Calcutta an amusing play "Cockneys in California" drew crowded houses. In the newspapers there was an unusually brisk exchange of letters from civilians and soldiers each accusing the other's service of a tendency to snobbery and to "giving themselves airs". The races in Calcutta were well attended, though people grumbled that the Municipal Board would not water the course sufficiently. The following spring was unexpectedly cool and in the Punjab no punkahs were used before May. At Sialkot a new church was consecrated, "the most chaste and beautiful structure of Modern Gothic in India", and the *Englishman's* correspondent, after describing the consecration ceremony, added, " The future historian will love to dwell upon a picture like the present—a few score strangers dedicating their churches to be set apart from all profane uses for ever with such fixity of purpose—and this in the midst of millions distinct from them in race, religion and feeling." There were a few odd rumours of unrest among these " millions " but there had been such rumours before and no one paid much attention to a story that from January maize-cakes had been circulating in the villages, had been passed from hand to hand with the whisper " All shall become red ". More interesting to most stations was the extraordinarily fine crop of strawberries that year. At Lucknow, in May, they were " having large plates of strawberries every morning ". In Delhi everyone was talking about the quarrel at a dance between the colonel and a conceited young civilian. The latter refused to apologise whereon the colonel (whose regiment had provided the music) not only left the dance himself but ordered the band to follow him, thus bringing the dance to a sudden end. People felt that the colonel, though no doubt justified in feeling some irritation, ought not to have incommoded all the guests on account of the fault of one guest; hasty, they said, and thoughtless. A Delhi newspaper intrigued its readers by a paragraph in the gossip column. " A wedding is talked of as likely to take place soon, but the names of the aspirants to hymeneal bliss I will refrain from mentioning just yet, lest anything should occur to lesson [*sic*] their affection for each other before the knot is tied." Alas, this arch allusiveness was wasted. A few days later the " aspirants to hymeneal bliss ", the writer of the paragraph and most of its readers were dead. The wind of revolt was blowing down the Ganges valley. The ladies who had shuddered deliciously at gossip of the Nana's sensual pleasures were now to find a far more sinister side to his character.

The last letter that left Cawnpore was one from Miss Ewart.

> My dear child is looking very delicate. My prayer is that she may be spared much suffering . . . My companion, Mrs. Hillersdon, is delightful. Poor young thing, she has such a gentle spirit, so unmurmuring, so desirous to meet the trial rightly, unselfish and sweet in every way. . . . If these are my last words to you, you will remember them lovingly and always bear in mind that your affection and the love we have ever had for each other is an ingredient of comfort in these bitter times.

The horrors that followed are summarised most poignantly by the last entries in Miss Lindray's diary: "May 21. Entered the barracks. June 5th. Cavalry left. June 6th. First shot fired. June 17th. Aunt Lilly died. June 18th. Uncle Willy died. June 22nd. Left barracks. George died. July 9th. Alice died. July 12th. Mamma died", and there the diary ends, for Miss Lindray herself perished in the final revolting massacre. Another book found in the débris was a Bible with this entry on the flyleaf "For darling Mamma, from her affectionate daughter Isabella Bell. 27th June. Went to the boats. 29th. Taken out of the boats. 30th. Taken to Sevadah Kottri. Fatal day." And there was a prayer-book open at the Litany, the pages stained with blood.

The story of Lucknow is as well known as that of Cawnpore and there is no need here to describe the extraordinary heroism and endurance of the besieged. But it is interesting to recall that even at the most perilous moment of the siege the etiquette of Anglo-Indian life remained as rigid as in time of peace. People still referred to the "upper ten" and the rules of visiting and speaking were not relaxed for a day. Presumably if class-distinctions were divinely ordered, no situation could justify abandoning them. According to *The Times*' special correspondent,[1] " whilst some (of the garrison) were starving, half-fed on unwholesome food, and drinking the most unpleasant beverages, others were living on the good things of the land and were drinking Champagne and Moselle, which were stored up in such profusion that there were cart-loads remaining when the garrison marched out." But, I suppose, the lower ranks would themselves have thought it strange to be invited to share the champagne of the " upper ten ".

The reaction in Calcutta clubs to the news of the outbreaks and disasters up-country was remarkable. The most peaceful and charitable gentlemen fell into convulsions of race-hatred. Everywhere retributive torture was advocated. Subalterns sat on billiard-tables discussing till the early hours of the morning suitable punishments of rebel leaders. The walls of Mess dining-rooms were covered with charcoal drawings of a crowd of torturers applying their skill to the prostrate body of Nana Sahib, and with a series of vengeful verses in which " wife and daughter " rhymed meritably with " slaughter ". The English Press discussed the situation with a ferocious hysteria compared to which General Goering's most unbalanced outbursts would seem polite commonplaces. Hymns of Hate usurped the Poet's Corner of the *Englishman.*

> Barring [cried one poet] humanity-pretenders,
> To hell of none are we the willing senders.
> But, if to Sepoys entrance must be given,
> Locate them, Lord, in the back-slums of Heaven.

Smiles went out of fashion, even in portraiture. The

[1] W. H. Russel. See *My Diary of India*, p. 119.

noblest expression for a "sitter" was a cold ferocity. Art criticism followed the fashion and a journal drew favourable attention to the

> Portrait of Captain Hazlewood which may be seen in Thacker and Spink's Gallery. The friends of the gallant officer will at once recognise the likeness, and feel confident that no undue lenity on his part will be shown to the murderers of women and children, for he has a stern expression of countenance as if he had just given an order to hang them and their favourers.

Favourers, here, means the small minority, chiefly civil servants, who, though advocating tremendous reprisals, were yet suggesting that it might be as well to avoid indiscriminate massacres, in which a far greater number of innocent than guilty must obviously suffer. This point of view seemed so wrong, so unmanly and unhealthy, that those who held it were denounced as agents of Nana Sahib and there were serious proposals that a number of European officials should be executed as a warning to the others.

Troops were pouring into Calcutta, but, while the ardour of the soldiers was inflamed by numerous and often untrue atrocity-stories, no one seems to have thought it necessary to tell the soldiers that the war was against certain rebels and not against the population of India. In consequence of this omission there were some regrettable incidents in the streets of the capital. A soldier had just landed when "I seed two Moors talking in a cart. Presently I heard one of 'em say 'Cawnpore'. I knowed what that meant; so I fetched Tom Walker, and he heard 'em say 'Cawnpore', and he knowed what that meant. So we polished 'em both off." On the other hand the arrival for the first time in a strange country of so many British troops gave rise to as many jokes among the civilian population as in the early months of the last war. Foremost among the heroes of these amusing stories was, of course, the Irish soldier, or " worthy son of Erin ", who is shocked to find in the Indians a race as loquacious as his own. At last in exasperation he addresses the crowded street, " with an unmistakable Hibernian Brogue ; ' Silence ! silence there, boys ! Don't have so much *tarlking* wid ye. Bedad ! When a man opens his mouth, sure half his strength just pops out of it.' " And the cream of the joke, of course, was " that this apophthegm (a piece of barrack-yard chaff), uttered as it was in the vernacular, fell unappreciated upon the ears of his present audience ". But the strangeness of a foreign country soon passed off and officers were alarmed to see how quickly their hardy privates adopted Asiatic comforts. They were particularly annoyed at the way the soldiers would pay a few annas to the regimental sweepers to help them keep their kit clean. This was felt to be bad for the soldier's moral fibre, and Lieutenant Majendie exclaimed, " It is not, it cannot be necessary or judicious to pamper him as though he were some indolent rajah, and to *wink at* his procuring natives to clean his boots or appointments." But worse was to follow. When the troops were marching over the Gangetic plain in the fantastic heat of Indian summer—

> as regards the appearance of the troops, the less said the better. Under any circumstances, the wicker helmet used by the men is by no means a becoming head-dress, giving an appearance to the wearer of being extinguished ; but to this is added that the greater part of the troops marched . . . actually in their shirt-sleeves like a lot of insurrectionary haymakers !

In command of soldiers so informally attired Havelock was advancing on Cawnpore. The ramshackle kingdom of Nana Sahib collapsed without serious resistance, for it had little support in the town. Nanekchand, a Cawnpore lawyer, had noted in his diary, "The shopkeepers and the citizens curse the mutineers from morning till evening. The people and the workmen starve, and widows cry in their huts." Some days later he

> was sitting in an orchard when I observed a shopkeeper running up. He came, and seated himself under a tree near me and told me he was hastening to pack up his wife and children, as the Europeans would arrive shortly and would spare nobody. I thought to myself this must be true, and the gentlemen must be very savage. I returned to the city and saw several villagers with their dresses changed coming along the banks of the Ganges and I joined them. The terror in the hearts of all was so great that they asked each other no questions.

The terror was justified, for the wretched inhabitants who would gladly have welcomed back their former rulers were indiscriminately massacred here, as at Delhi, where, as a Bombay newspaper exulted, "All the city people found within the walls when our troops entered were bayoneted on the spot; and the number was considerable, as you may suppose when I tell you that in some houses forty or fifty persons were hiding",[1] and at Lucknow where Lieutenant Majendie noticed hundreds of pariah dogs gorging themselves on the slain and cracked a neat pun over it. "A sort of cannibalism. For no one can dispute my right (with the assistance of a little *dog*-latin) to designate the taste as *cani*-balic."

There were wild scenes at the plunder of the palaces. In the Kaiserbag at Lucknow Russel saw

> lying amid the orange-groves dead and dying sepoys; and the white statues are reddened with blood. Leaning against a

[1] It is worth noting that when the Nawab of Farukabad, who happened to be innocent of any seditious activity, was put to death in a "most disgusting" manner a chaplain was among the interested spectators.

> Venus is a British soldier shot through the neck. . . . From the broken portals issue soldiers laden with loot or plunder. The men are wild with fury and lust of gold—literally drunk with plunder. Some come out with china vases or mirrors, dash them to pieces on the ground and return to seek more valuable booty. Some swathe their bodies in stuffs crusted with precious metals and gems.

Mr. Russel, with more refined taste, went in search of the priceless porcelain known to be stored in the palace.

> Stewart and myself and one or two other officers, selected a few pieces and put them aside near the well. It was well we did so, for, just as we had put them aside, the shadow of a man fell across the court from the gateway; a bayonet was advanced cautiously, raised evidently to the level of the eye, then came the Enfield, and finally the head of a British soldier. "None here but friends," shouted he. "Come along, Bill, there's only some officers, and here's a lot of places no one has bin to!" Enter three or four banditti of H.M.'s Regiment. Faces black with powder; cross belts specked with blood; coats stuffed out with all sorts of valuables. And now commenced the work of plunder under our very eyes. . . . One fellow, having burst open a leaden-looking lid, which was in reality of solid silver, drew out an armlet of emeralds, diamonds and pearls . . . "What will your honour give me for these?" said he. "I'll take a hundred rupees on chance!" Oh, wretched fate! I had not a penny in my pocket.

He promised to send the money that same night. But the soldier was a fatalist. "Oh! faith an your honour how do I know where I'd be this blissed night? It's may be dead I'd be, wid a bullet in the body. I'll take two gold mores and a bottle of rum on the spot. But shure it's not safe to have any but reddy money transactions these times." But Mr. Russel had no bottle of rum on him at the moment and so, as he sighed, "I saw my fortune vanish."

The typhoon left a vast desolation in its track. All along the main roads of the north "bungalows, police stations, tehseels, were all burned down, blackened and in ruins".

When *The Times* correspondent entered Delhi, he found himself

> in the ruined streets of a deserted city, in which every house bore the marks of cannon, or musket-shell, or the traces of the hand of the spoiler. . . . As the gharry rattled along at the foot of the huge red wall, not a creature was to be seen, except a hungry pariah, or an impudent cow. . . . To some of the houses doors of matting and rude jalousies were put up and chubby-faced English children looked out of the glassless windows as the gharry drove by. A few natives of the lower order slunk through the wide street.

But the new English commissioner was already installed in " a fine mansion, with turrets and clock-towers, something like a French chateau of the last century. . . . The comfort and luxury of the house itself were a positive gratification to the senses. Large lofty rooms—soft carpets, sofas, easy-chairs, books, pictures." There were two breakfasts, one at 8, the other at 3 o'clock. As an evening amusement the commissioner would take his guests to see the captive Mogul Emperor.

> In a dingy, dark passage, leading from the open court or terrace in which we stood to a darker room beyond, there sat, crouched on his haunches, a diminutive, attenuated old man, dressed in an ordinary and rather dirty muslin tunic, his small lean feet bare, his head covered by a small thin cambric skull-cap. It was the descendant of Tamurlane.

The day of Mr. Russel's visit the Emperor was ill. " With bent body he seemed nearly prostrate over a brass basin, into which he was retching violently." It was really quite a relief to return to the commissioner's bungalow and enjoy " a civilised evening. Mr. Egerton, the magistrate of the city, came in, and several other gentlemen, who, with the guests, formed a large and agreeable party, not unmusical or unvocal either, and not so much given to piano and song as to be tiresome."

The ravages of the siege were soon repaired ; and when Lieutenant Majendie visited it a few months later he was pleasantly surprised by the " clusters of bungalows ", and an English hotel known as " Lewis' " had already opened. It was disappointing as an hotel, for one would have thought that as nothing can have survived the siege, the furniture and provisions of the hotel would be fairly new. But it is interesting to find that even in such promising circumstances Lewis' Hotel was from the moment of its opening faithful to the traditional appearance of an up-country " European " hotel in India. In the Coffee-Room was

> a dingy appearance of chaos, more singular than pleasing, furniture new and old and not a small quantity antediluvian ; potted meats and treatises on astronomy ; faded neckties and bloater-paste ; preserved soup and books without backs ; glass lamp-shades and rusty knives ; rakish old chairs on three legs, making love to young book-cases with no books in them.

So Lieutenant Majendie was glad to leave the Coffee-Room after toying with " altogether exceedingly uninviting a display of *eatables*, . . . tasting unpleasantly strong of the smell of a *cow*-house ", and wander amid the splendours of the Mogul palace where, reflecting on fallen might, he ejaculated (will you be surprised to hear it ?) " *Sic transit gloria mundi !* "

MISERIES IN INDIA

after Rowlandson

CHAPTER VII

THE effect of the Mutiny on Anglo-India can hardly be exaggerated. It is difficult to see why such terrible bitterness should have been roused among the English at the first news of revolt. The war was to some extent a civil war and as such inevitably bitter. But this does not explain the strange outburst of racial hatred among the secure civilian population of Calcutta. No one is likely to palliate the Cawnpore horror (though the cry for vengeance had broken out before the tragedy of the well was known) but the slaughter of the women was not the work of rebel soldiers and it is even doubtful whether Nana Sahib ordered it. The atrocity gossips enjoyed themselves with salacious and untrue details, but these were easily disproved. The Black Hole of Calcutta would seem to have been an equally repulsive crime but though Suraj-ud-dowla had to be defeated and driven back to his territories, no one seems to have held him in particular horror (indeed Clive and many other English officers accepted handsome presents from him at the conclusion of peace), much less to have blamed his crime on all his followers. Similarly, Tipu, far more purposefully cruel than either Nana Sahib or Suraj-ud-dowla, was never hated with any personal hatred ; " that mad barbarian " never lacked admirers even among his enemies. There was nothing to admire in Nana Sahib or in most of the rebel leaders, and it is possible to excuse the massacres and sacks of the " justly infuriated " (to quote the *Oxford History*) loyalist troops. But once the rising was over and every " guilty city " had been visited with fearful vengeance it might have been hoped that the victors would soon abandon an attitude of hostile tension. This did not happen. Long after the last rebel had laid down his arms, been hanged or vanished into the jungles the Calcutta Press continued its ferocious tirades. The non-official population was encouraged to believe in a maudlin Government, pro-rebel in sympathy, unpatriotic and radical. When for five years this chorus of abuse and these cries for blood had continued, a European called Rudd was so unfortunate as to be arrested for murdering one of his Indian employees. The murder was attested by a number of witnesses and there was no doubt at all about his guilt. He was duly convicted and sentenced. There was an awful pause ; and then the Press burst into a deafening scream. The *Bengal Hurkaru* which had distinguished itself among other Anglo-Indian papers as an advocate of extermination, now printed leaders, dilating on the wickedness of capital punishment and organised processions and mass meetings of Europeans " to achieve the gain of a human life, an existence which is forfeit to the *public strangler* ". The Government refused to yield to the clamour, whereon the Press suggested that several senior officials were secret devotees of the Hindu goddess of destruction, Kali, and desired the life of the wretched Rudd as a human sacrifice to that deity ; as for the rest of the members of Government they had long been known to be crypto-Hindus who had now come out in their true colours.

Eighteen years later, the Ilbert Bill controversy provoked a similar explosion. Unfortunately there was now an Indian Press to reply in kind. And Hartington, warned by Maine, wrote to the Viceroy : " I am afraid that if the English Press takes up the discussion of the proposed measure (the Ilbert Bill) the Native Press will probably reply . . . which may not be altogether convenient." That opposition would come was certain. Everything Ripon did roused some opposition and the Government of Bombay had already achieved the distinction of publicly attacking the Viceroy's Local Self-government policy ; but then in that presidency certain works of the seditious author Macaulay were still (in 1882) banned. The extent of the opposition to the Ilbert Bill was, however, unexpected, in spite of past lessons. A monster meeting of Europeans took place at the Calcutta Town Hall, at which " the speeches were of an intemperance beyond all limits of decency ". An Anglo-Indian Defence Association was formed ; the Volunteers were urged to resign ; and attempts were made to seduce the loyalty of the Army. Gangs of planters were brought down to Calcutta to insult the Viceroy in the streets. The wife of the Chief Justice got up a " Ladies' Petition " against the Bill. Day after day the *Englishman* printed letters from furious correspondents, of whom *Britannicus* deserves to be remembered for his opening paragraph. " The only people who have any right to India are the British ; the SO-CALLED Indians have no right whatever." Much of the agitation was openly financed by the European capitalists in Calcutta who owned plantations and tea-gardens up-country and were afraid of any diminution in the power and prestige of their local agents. As the head of the Criminal Investigation Department reported to the Viceroy's private secretary : " To make their grievance a general one they raised the cry of danger to European women." Faithful to this policy, the editor of the *Friend of India* exclaimed, " Would you like to live in a country where at any moment your wife would be liable to be sentenced on a false charge, the Magistrate being a copper-coloured Pagan ? " Attempts were made to stir up opinion in England by lurid pictures of the nightmare existence facing poor Europeans in lonely districts. A person called Atkins was equipped with funds and sent to England to address working-class audiences. He was not, however, a successful emissary, and " at his most important meeting in Edinburgh, a motion was carried unanimously against him ".[1]

The extent of the tumult was such that *Punch* printed a cartoon showing an elephant with Ripon as its mahout and a number of Europeans leaning out of the howdah to attack him ; the title being " The Anglo-Indian Mutiny (A bad example to the elephant) ". This was no exaggerated picture. There was already talk of Direct Action by the malcontents ; there were only seventy Europeans in the Bengal Police and the Viceroy felt that " to employ European soldiers against Europeans in this country would be a step of the gravest kind ". Finally a compromise of a kind was arrived at, which the English Press in Calcutta announced as a victory for Anglo-Indian agitation and printed incorrect accounts of the so-called " concordat " to establish this claim.

These remarkable manifestations were only symptoms of the self-conscious isolation of the English community in India, which continued with little change for more than half a century after the Mutiny. Even Ripon himself seems to have had no contact, other than official, with Indians. And it is curious to compare the letters of Lady Dufferin with those of Miss Eden or with Lady Falkland's journal. Miss Eden had all a Whig's disdain for those poorer or less well-educated than oneself ; and most of her comments on the people she met, whether Indian or English, in India are faintly acid ; nevertheless when she describes an Indian like Ranjit Singh the man stands out as a real character who

[1] Northbrook to Lord Ripon.

impressed her for all her well-bred titters at his odd customs. Lady Falkland was deeply interested in the Maratha gentry she met, in their families and beliefs, and she clearly expected her readers to be equally interested. In the letters of Lady Dufferin (a good and vivid correspondent and a vicereine who is remembered still with gratitude in India) Indians are only rarely mentioned and then in the briefest and most formal phrases. She met the Nizam's great minister Salar Jung and comments, " He is quite a giant ", and passes on to describe his uniform which " though not very Eastern is handsome ". There was " a really magnificent " dinner with the Nizam ; and then the Viceregal party passed on to Mysore, whose Maharaja " dresses beautifully. When he came to the station he had a sort of loose kincob coat and turban." They had tea with him " and then we saw his sitting-room with its more modern arrangements, writing-table, etc.". Prince after prince appears for a moment. There are notes on his turban, his jewels, the respectful way he talked to the Viceroy, the illuminations to greet the vice-regal party, the expensive dinners, the Prince's nervous children in their amusing clothes. One passes an encampment of Indian troops and the viceregal party comment on the bravery of Indian soldiers in Egypt ; it was satisfactory to note that the men " looked very fine and soldier-like ". The Vicereine began learning Hindustani, in which language she was able to read " a series of tracts and little moral stories ". She did not, however, apparently learn enough to interpret for her husband and Lord Dufferin was, on occasion, ill-served by his interpreter. He remarked to an Indian guest that he liked Indian music, especially for its melodies in the minor key. The translation was that what His Excellency really liked about Indian music was that it possessed a small key (of a box). Occasionally there are references to the odd superstitions of the Hindus. Mr. Broughton, Administrator-General, while discoursing on local topics, mentioned casually that he was trustee for an idol, to which he paid 250 rupees a month. " This idol is a sacred stone and can perhaps scarcely be dignified with the title of god." But it was more interesting to revert to the costume of the Maharaja of Jaipur who had just called and who wore " a pink moiré frock-coat . . . white satin waist-coat, diamond and emerald necklace, and a turban made of red silk cord. . . . His manners were quite as beautiful as my own and he made his exit most gracefully." There is a note of pleased surprise if a prince can speak English or a princess wears English shoes. It is difficult to realise that the Indian National Congress had already held its first meeting. There were other things of greater immediate moment. The punkahs, for instance :

> Our bonnets were perpetually swept by the punkahs. They are dreadful things, I think. There is a sort of confusion which is bewildering. Some swing across you, and some to and fro from you, and they are pulled by different men, who keep different time, and one feels as if one never could get accustomed to the unsteady appearance of everything overhead.

But sometimes the sermon compensated for these hardships. On one Sunday there were two sermons by the Archdeacon, of which everyone was talking.

> The first was upon the observance of Sunday and the second upon our lives of dissipation. It is quite true that the atmosphere of the place is one of pleasure-seeking. As the Archdeacon said . . . He speaks so very well and earnestly, without any exaggeration or want of liberality, that his exhortations ought to do good.

Anglo-Indians of the eighteenth, and even of the first two decades of the nineteenth, century could hardly escape a close, often an uncomfortably close, acquaintance with the

Indian world. A factor or cadet in Madras could not until 1799 be absolutely certain that he would end his life as a subject of King George and not of Tipu Sultan. During the first half of the nineteenth century while there was no longer any doubt about English hegemony, there were still many survivals of an earlier age. There was, for instance, still a titular Emperor, regarded by many as the rightful ruler of India. Though harassed at intervals by the Company, he maintained till the Mutiny the traditional pomp of his station. The ceremony of the Mogul court was almost unchanged. Contests of poetry between the two most famous of Urdu poets were the theme of popular talk. The Imperial elephants were exercised almost daily amid the acclamation of the people. The Chandni Chowk was a tree-shaded boulevard down which the nobles rode at evening, dressed as though for a durbar of Akbar. And when the Emperor himself appeared, often in order to recite his own verses, he was greeted with the obeisances due to a reigning monarch.[1] Till 1849 there was to the north-west the formidable kingdom of the Sikhs, iron-braceleted, long-haired fanatics possessed of admirable artillery and commanded by Europeans who had seen service under Napoleon. You might disapprove of Ranjit Singh's low humour and his habit of misconducting himself in public on an elephant, but you could not ignore him. And then there was, as always, a regrettable Nawab at Lucknow. This ruler was now dignified with the title of King of Oudh, but the increased honour never inspired him to greater dignity. Though the territories of Oudh were large there was no administration worth the name, and taxes were collected by cavalry employed as gangsters. The chief

[1] But after the capture of Delhi he was tried for rebellion and sentenced to life exile in Burma.

interest of the ruling family was in animals and in the parks "elephants in scores, tigers, rhinoceroses, antelopes, cheetahs or hunting-leopards, lynxes, Persian cats, Chinese dogs, might all be seen sunning themselves, either in their cages, or stretched listlessly on the grass, as commonly as sheep and cows in an English meadow". The king was an unassuming man, whose only wish was to become "the best drum-beater, dancer, and poet of the day". This was, perhaps, better than a predecessor's unnatural devotion to a barber which must have been inexpressibly distasteful to a generation of Anglo-Indians who were horrified at Monsieur de Jacquemont's confession that he made use of an enema in preference to pills.

But in the second half of the century all these survivals of an older India had vanished, lingering only in the sad memory of Indians who, as Henry Lawrence noted, seemed to have been much happier under the governance of their crazy kings than under the careful and conscientious rule of English Commissioners. The deposed King of Oudh still lived on and on,

> utterly devoid of every moral sense. He never does any good to anybody, and he spends his monthly lac of rupees in keeping 25,000 pigeons . . . who fly in flocks and are pretty, and there are whole fleets of pelicans sailing about on tanks, and long-legged birds with decidedly light fantastic toes who hop about ridiculously, and peacocks perching in the trees.

The Government did not mind his keeping so many birds, but the consciences of senior officials were worried about the numbers of his women. They sent him finally an order to reduce his household to decent proportions. Instead of submitting to this reasonable demand, the king, with a levity that one can only regret, not only tore up the letter but added ninety more women to his harem that same day.

QUI HI ARRIVES AT THE BUNDER HEAD

after Rowlandson

This intransigent old man was, however, forgotten even by most Indians. And to Anglo-Indians Lucknow was thought of as the city of the heroic siege and not as the capital of one of the oddest of Indian kingdoms.

The general feeling in the districts where the Mutiny struggle had raged most fiercely was first an immense relief when the storm had passed, and then a curious reaction of regret for the excitement and glamour of battle. Alfred Lyall was writing home in 1859, " Life in India is just now very dull. There is a sort of reaction after the excitement of the last two years." And a year later, " I sit alone in the evening and long for something to happen. The whole country is hopelessly quiet ; there is not even a murder or a highway robbery. . . . Life in peace times is completely stagnant." While the Press was fulminating ceaselessly against the late rebels, Lyall, like many who had actually been under fire, had a certain respect for the fighting qualities of the enemy. He had sympathised with Indian emotion over the annexation of Oudh, complaining to his mother about " the scandalous cant with which we tried to whitewash " that transaction ; and now he confessed to sympathy for the medieval world that had gone down in the ruin of the rebel cause and writes with appreciative humour of one of the Barons of Oudh who escaped with his life as " a sturdy rebel, who has now surrendered, received back his lands, and dwells sulkily in a small town about five miles off, no doubt cursing the Feringhis night and morning ".

The new generation that arrived in India after the Mutiny, the " Competition-Wallahs " as they were at first called by the old hands who had had to undergo no such humiliating experiences as a competitive examination, had no such equivocal sympathies. They knew nothing of pre-Mutiny life and they were already imbued with a busy imperialism.

In 1862 a new recruit to the civil service wrote to his fiancée on his first voyage out—

> The political value of Aden is not to be underrated. It is one of the keys of our Indian Empire. . . . You understand our position in the Mediterranean? The French have Toulon, with divers other fortified harbours on their coast. . . . Now for the *points d'appui* of England. Gibraltar, Malta and Corfu, at the entrance, middle and extreme east of the Mediterranean —these are our strategic points.

Their training and an increasing competition strengthened the sense of caste. Young William Hunter was writing:

> It is easy to be a Company-man and yet to be superior to the common run in an intellectual aspect but it is impossible to be first-class—I mean the very first, one of a set of men picked out from the whole country for their talents, and fritter your evenings away in walking quadrilles and consuming ices. I aspire to a circle far above the circle of fashion. I mean the circle of Power. . . . Until I can earn a position in that circle I do not choose to waste my time filling up a lady's drawing-room or eating people's corner-dishes.

Let us follow for a while the opening stages of this promising young man's career. The competition, he knew, was severe. But this did not alarm him; he had accustomed himself to a discipline of study which was certain to produce good results. "Whenever I read up a subject I become so interested in it that I go into the minutest points rather as if I intended to write a book than to stand a general examination. Never do I attack a subject without writing what would make a bulky pamphlet."

His diligence was rewarded and on July 16, 1861, he was able to congratulate his examiners. "I have found the papers rational, well considered, and easily enough answered if you have read extensively, and above all, thought carefully over what you have read." Not all of the 207 candidates were so well prepared and in that long fusty hall of old Burlington House with its feather-padded, red morocco seats, its sad green walls hung with 150 portraits of half-forgotten statesmen, there were many anxious faces bent over the desks. Some of them " turn black in the face as soon as they see the questions, and vanish, others sit looking suicidal for half an hour and then disappear also ". Some of them could hardly afford to fail ; they were " the sons of clergymen who have staked a long and expensive education on the chance of success : younger sons of country gentlemen who have fallen into decay and just succeeded in giving their lads two or three years at Oxford, and then a 15-guinea-a-month cram with some private coach ". As a rule, however—

> it is comforting to find the candidates seem wealthy swells, always coming in a cab and sojourning at Morley's at a daily expense of two or three guineas. It is wonderful to see with what resignation even twenty-two-year-old fellows, who have been plucked last year and have this as a last chance, take their discomfiture. After eyeing their papers with a blank, dreary gaze, they slowly take out a cigar case, examine its contents, smell its Russia delicacy, extract a cigar, put on their hats and march out. ' Cabby, drive to Morley's.' And this is repeated twice daily ; meanwhile they eat like prize fighters to support the waste of the body and of the mind.

Hunter was naturally one of the last to leave and when he stepped out of Burlington House it was not to drive round to Morley's but to journey to 11 Maismore Square, Peckham. He passed out first in the final examination and sailed for India, leaving as a farewell present to Miss Murray, to whom he had proposed, six books including Prior's *Life of Burke* in two volumes and splendidly bound in " peach-coloured calf " and also his " gold Albert chain " which, as he told Miss Murray, " will make a nice chain for you, or you can have the key taken off, and use it with a locket of my hair as a bracelet or necklace ".

He found Calcutta in the 'sixties a decidedly pleasant place after Peckham. " Imagine everything that is glorious in nature combined with all that is beautiful in architecture, and you can faintly picture to yourself what Calcutta is ". But here again he had to criticise the irregular lives led by some of his contemporaries.

> This morning half-a-dozen of my set had a more or less severe attack of dysentery. They are all cursing the climate, and no doubt will write home by this mail saying that they feel so horribly seedy in this city that they are going up-country immediately. Now what is the plain English of all this ? Simply that after a tiffin, consisting of soup, two or three kinds of meat with an immense heap of curry, no end of fruit, with beer and sherry *ad lib*, they went to the cricket ground and played for three hours in the burning sun. Dinner lasted from 7·30 till nearly midnight—ice-pudding with champagne. Then, till 2 a.m. they played a wild game of loo.

He settled down in a boarding-house in Midleton Street and started to study languages ; but

> three days a week I drive out to make calls at 11-30 and return at one. No one is received after two o'clock ; people have tiffin at that hour and are invisible till they appear on the Course between five and six. All my friends live in and around Chowringhee, and our house is in the very centre of that fashionable quarter, so that with the aid of my quick-paced mare I can make six or eight visits in one and a half hours.

His prospects seemed fair enough ; for, as he wrote to Miss Murray, " If God gives us health and long life together we shall be rich, very rich, before we are fifty. I mean three or four thousand a year from our savings and my pension. Let us be thankful to Heaven for its mercies." And the more he saw of India the prouder he became of his own caste.

> Here we Englishmen stand on the face of the broad earth, a scanty pale-faced band in the midst of three hundred millions

of unfriendly vassals. On their side is a congenial climate and all the advantages which home and birthplace can give ; on ours long years of exile, a burning sun which dries up the Saxon energies, home sickenings, thankless labour, disease and oftentimes death far from wife, child, friend or kinsman. How is it that these pale-cheeked exiles give security to a race of another hue, other tongues, other religions which rulers of their own people have ever failed to give ? Dearest, there are unseen moral causes which I need not point out. . . .

Towards the end of his first cold weather he was invited to a State Ball at Government House. It was an elaborate affair.

As four to five months' notice had been given most people got their fancy-dresses from London, Paris or Madrid. Some came from Rome, one from Petersburg and several from America. . . . For some time past Calcutta has been a big milliner's shop, and all the ladies have been little else than modistes. It is quite unsafe for a man to enter female society unless he was able to tell whether green looked well upon purple, or whether in " our " quadrille the ladies were to go in powder or not.

He had chosen as his fancy dress the costume of " a Spanish courtier of high rank ", though of what century does not appear, but one can be pretty confident that there were no anachronisms for " Major Burke looked me over and saw that all was *Comme il faut* ". He arrived at Government House in good time and

at a quarter to ten the band played " God save the Queen ", the drawing-room doors were thrown open, a procession was formed, and we all filed in at one door, passing Lord and Lady Elgin on their dais, each one making the bow suitable to his costume and out by the other door. . . . Of all the Calcutta ladies [he adds rather abruptly] I admire Mrs. O. most. She is by far the most intellectual woman I know here, and has that strong, confiding ambition for her husband which is the chief charm of a high-bred English lady. . . . I was leaning over her chair, and apropos of some satirical remark she had made about mature matrons of five-and-forty still insisting upon dancing, I was asking her to prescribe some lotion for my arm

> which I had a moment ago sprained in whirling a particularly plump and aged partner round the room when suddenly I saw her face become grave. She rose majestically, and, raising my head, I saw that His Excellency had come up and was shaking hands with her. I fell back a pace or two and stood respectfully silent till the interview was over.

The Viceroy was in a good temper and began " making such surmises about the mosquitoes coming in at the window and eating up the ladies at supper ", and added, as a capital joke, that " Lady Elgin got so fearfully bitten that even on the morning of the ball she did not know if she could appear ". Young Hunter listened with admiring attention to these pleasantries and noted how the Viceroy was " smiling from ear to ear at something funny he has just said ", and wondering if perhaps it was quite in keeping that the " ruler of the most extensive Empire that ever obeyed one man " should so far unbend, when the interview was suddenly over. " There—he has made his bow, the stars and decorations turn away, Mrs. O. sits down, the lancers strike up, and she and I hurry to the next room before our *vis-à-vis* gets into despair and takes in a new couple. Then there is that most charming of all dances—the fifth set." Meanwhile the Viceroy had pottered off and cornered another lady and began " talking again about the mosquitoes coming in at the open windows ".

But after recounting the dissipations of this great ball he felt it wise to sound a warning note to Miss Murray. " Why do not the various Secretaries do something lasting? Because they are married, my dear. The lady is tired of the long day's idleness, and her husband must amuse her by conversation or backgammon all the evening. . . . It is a dreadful fate—that of a woman who takes away her husband's chance of greatness." Such greatness could be achieved only by avoidance of conversation and backgammon and by unremitting study. He was continually buying new books. " It is useless talking of the poverty of a country's literature unless you do your best to encourage men of letters by buying their works. I have impressed this on my chum, Gribble."

Next year Miss Murray was to sail to join him in India and the last letter she received before embarking contained much advice as to her conduct on board ship. " When you hear anything said, any story told, any word approaching a scoff at religion, or the least attempt at indelicate wit or allusion, show by your manner that you are not pleased." They were married in Calcutta Cathedral and Hunter was posted as Assistant Collector of Suri. The cold weather passed in furnishing their new bungalow, which cost £140, and in bearing " their full share of station hospitalities ". Suri, like most of the smaller Indian stations, had its Mutton Club, managed by an honorary secretary, who kept a sufficient stock of sheep, bought at less than two shillings a head, and fattened them for the table on a diet of pulse. One was killed every week, and the meat divided among the five members. The hostess on whom devolved the succulent saddle was expected to ask the other members to dinner, followed generally by a modest game at loo, and such music as her much-tried piano afforded. But the short cold weather of Bengal was soon over and then

> the hot winds set in like a consuming fire. The large double-doors which form the windows of an Anglo-Indian house stood open at night and were shut up tight in early morning. The public offices opened at seven and closed for the day at noon. Then each man drove swiftly through the furnace of shimmering air to his darkened and silent home. A lingering bath and a languid breakfast brought the hot hours to one o'clock. The slow combustion of the suffocating afternoon was endured somehow under the punkah. . . . About six we all met at

the racket court whose high wall by that time cast a sufficient shadow. A couple of four-handed games (the doctor was too stout to play) left us steaming at every pore and making at each step a damp foot-print through our white canvas shoes on the pavement. Then the delicious plunge in the swimming bath in the Judge's garden—the one moment of freshness looked forward to throughout the exhausting day. A cheroot and an iced drink as we lay fanned by the servants on long chairs . . . and the blinding glare of day gave place to the stifling stillness of night.

The heat, the bouts of malaria, snakes and noxious insects—all these are a recurring theme in Anglo-Indian letters and reminiscences. But there were many compensations. The native population was submissive and devoted to their masters. Their ways were not, of course, Western ways; and many a memsahib echoed the *cri de cœur* of Miss Mabel Hunter, " Oh ! They are queer kittle-kattle, these natives, their depth past finding out." But a kick or cuff often helped them to better, wiser standards of conduct, though, as Miss Hunter hurriedly added, " Let not the idea take root that castigation is the common lot of the native—the safety-valve of the Englishman, and least of all, of a little Miss Sahib, howsoever tempted. You do want to break the law and the prophets, and the native would much rather have a kick or cuff than an angry word, but that kick must come from the Sahib." In fact, " it is best to treat them all like children who know no better, but . . . they are proud of their lies and the innate goodness of the European is not understood by them."

And if there was a military cantonment near, life was cheerful enough, for the young officers were determined to enjoy themselves in spite of the rigour of the climate. The ladies enjoyed their unsophisticated flatteries at the big dinner-parties and would confide in each other how pleasant their " rights " and " lefts " at dinner had been. For the men too it was always pleasant to be asked to dine at the Mess. On these guest-nights the traditional decorum of the Anglo-Indian was laid aside. Lord Baden Powell, recounting his Indian experiences, confesses with a chuckle, " we were capable of being pretty frivolous ". And he gives some interesting examples of the military amusements of those days. Chief among this was the ragging of one officer by all the rest. This " breaks the monotony of existence, especially for the victim. A fellow ", he adds, " seldom gets ragged without having given some cause for it ; either he is dirty and wants washing, or he has got some characteristic which needs toning down." A favourite form of ragging was known as the Fire Alarm. The raggers were divided into two parties, of which one went outside the Mess building and waited, while the other hung about inside the Mess until the victim was " comfortably settled down to whist ". They then raised a cry of " Fire ! " followed by shouts of " Smith (or whatever the victim's name was) is afire ! " They rushed at him, tore him from the card-table and threw him out of the window to be caught by the other band of raggers, stationed there to break his fall. Sometimes, however, an amusing mistake in the plans occurred and the victim would be thrown out of the wrong window. Another game was known as " The Bounding Brothers of the Bosphorus ". This had been introduced by the Colonel's brother, " a quiet harmless planter from Behar ". They piled all the furniture in the middle of the room with the writing-desk in front of this pyramid. Each member of the Mess in turn then clapped his hands three times, " three times " insists the Chief Scout, " that was the etiquette of the game ", rushed forward shouting " I am a bounding brother of the Bosphorus ", turned head over heels on the writing-desk and landed on his back on the upturned legs of the chairs and tables, which hurt a good deal.

But, alas, the military were not always there to enliven the station. Wars broke out and there would be a grand send-off as the regiment left for Afghanistan or South Africa. The ladies clustered round the officers and asked them if they were not full of "joyous ardour" and they would reply, "Oh ! it is grand to be a soldier !" and the band would strike up "Home, dearie Home" or "When the boys come marching home again" (if it were a Sepoy regiment the band would play "We don't want to fight but, by Jingo, if we do", which tune had been found to appeal to native troops and so long continued to be played by their bands), and remembering the bishop's stirring address on the glories of rest after victory the men marched off with heads held high, while handkerchiefs fluttered and the pretty new parasols and flowered hats of the ladies, ordered down from Calcutta especially for this exciting occasion, made a bright pattern against the whitewashed walls of the cantonment.

Everyone missed the brave fellows. Dinner-parties were seldom so successful now. And young bachelors found that Christmas without the festivities in the Mess was a melancholy occasion. As a poet wrote,

> One feels, now one hasn't a regular Mess
> It's a bore to go out and a nuisance to dress ;
> And a feed at the commandant's bungalow
> Is a dreary attempt at Christmas, you know.
> The punkah, instead of the Christmas fire !
> The colonel, instead of the dear old squire !
> The lizard and withering noon-day glow
> Instead of the robin and frost and snow !

And letters from home but added to the melancholy of the whiskered and moustachio'd administrator as he leant back in his long basket-chair so that the light from the smoky oil-lamp (set as far from his chair as possible because of its attraction for night-flies and other insects) might dimly illumine the slanting handwriting, crossing and recrossing the thin grey note paper.

> My mother's writing ! my hide is tough,
> And the road of life has been somewhat rough.
> The fount of my tears, one would think, was dry,
> But it always brings a tear to my eye.

* * * * *

Meanwhile the news from the war areas was often more than disappointing. Lord Lytton's Afghan war, undertaken in order to dissuade the Amir from an " alliance with the ambitious, energetic, not over-scrupulous Government of such a military empire as Russia, rather than in alliance with a Power so essentially pacific and sensitively scrupulous as our own ", was particularly inglorious. But while the apostles of the forward school were disappointed, there was a sub-current of satisfaction in certain Anglo-Indian circles at Lytton's failure. His strange appearance, as of a well-groomed conjurer in a society drawing-room, his exaggerated manners and mannerisms (an apocryphal story went the round of the clubs that he had embraced a Persian envoy on the grounds that he, too, was a poet) and the undoubted fact that he had literary tastes did not endear him to the " heavies " in backwater stations. Nor could Lytton's scheme for an Indian Peerage and Heralds' College for the Princes seriously commend itself to less baroque imaginations. The Viceroy had even caused coats-of-arms to be designed for each of the Princes by a Mr. Robert Taylor, " a Bengal civilian who possessed some heraldic knowledge, and who travelled round the country and invented for each Chief an escutcheon with supporters and a motto in the most approved Heralds' College style ". With great pomp and solemnity they had been presented to each Chief " being brought in (they were very top-heavy) by stalwart Highlanders and conferred by Lord Lytton with a suitable exhortation. Since then they have reposed in the Durbar rooms or Treasuries, where I (Lord Curzon) have sometimes come across them during my tours, dusty, faded and torn ". Moreover, he earned a certain unpopularity by censuring the Judge of Agra, Mr. Leeds, for passing a nominal sentence on an English lawyer named Fuller who had killed his servant. A civilian wit circulated the following poetic comment on this incident :

> Robert Lord Lytton
> Had little to sit on,
> Being slender of body and limb,
> Till he heard of the deeds
> Of the lenient Leeds,
> And proceeded to sit upon him.

The whole case excited much bitter comment in the United Provinces, the Local Government and the High Court taking opposite sides. But when, some time after, the Viceroy visited the capital of the United Provinces the still-lingering dispute was forgotten in the solemnity of the occasion. For Lytton had come to open the Memorial Hall at Allahabad, erected to the memory of a previous Viceroy, Lord Mayo. An enormous crowd had gathered for the occasion. " An amateur chorus of all the best and most cultivated gentlemen and lady singers of that part of India . . . accompanied by an admirably touched organ [1] sang to the tune of " Dal tuo stellato soglio " from *Mose in Egitto*, the following ode to the murdered Viceroy :

[1] H. C. Keene, *A Servant of John Company.*

On thee, great Shade! we call—
Unseen, though still at hand—
To consecrate this Hall
In Thine adopted land:
Long may that honoured name
Bestow its favouring fame,
Mayo!

While Jumna's water pours
Her tribute to the sea,
Still may these votive towers
Proclaim our love for thee;
Thy noble life laid low
By treason's felon blow,
Mayo!

For thou wert of the few
Who conquer Destiny;
Brave, merciful and true,
All that a chief should be.
Hail to the mighty dead
Whose life for us was sped,
Mayo!

A viceregal visit was a rare excitement in up-country stations. To see the Viceroy and Vicereine in person, to shake hands with them and perhaps even exchange a few comments on the uncommonly hot weather for the time of year—what more could one desire? If the dutiful official revered the Viceroy as the head of the administration, the unofficials were excited by contact with a peer and peeress.

> I flatter myself [wrote one lady, recalling, in the melancholy of retirement, such a glamorous occasion] that intercourse with my fellow-men is good for them as it is for me; and when, as in India, it was my happy lot to revel with our English lords and ladies of high degree, so unapproachable in this dull, cold, cheerless country, with military celebrities as well and, oh! best of all, Royal Princes and Princesses the Most Gracious—God bless them—then was my cup of happiness quite full.

She recalls in particular a viceregal visit to her little station in Assam and relates that

> Crowds had assembled to welcome the Lord and the Lady.

> Every honour possible had been prepared for their reception. The station band was playing its best. A fine bodyguard of Volunteers was in attendance under (en passant) an old Eton boy's command. . . . There was the great hum of native chatter ; but how one always misses the British cheer ! There was the little group of English ladies in their pretty frocks, topees and sunshades, all white, so symmetrical and pleasing, a characteristic of the Indian plains . . . with picturesque effect and dignity unimpaired, the Queen's proud representative landed, followed by his suite in glittering array. It was a better setting they wanted than rough sand banks and bare shadeless country ; yet was ever scene more impressive, more loyal and quaintly grand ! and was ever the National Anthem played with greater effect !

There would be a round of entertainments. Viceroy and Vicereine would express interest in the jail and hospital, and the turn-out of the Volunteers. An eminent Indian landowner, or a Raja if the district could raise one, would give a dinner ; and the local monuments would be visited ceremoniously. Most of those monuments were subsiding into drab decay before the advent of Curzon ; but his interest in ancient buildings made his viceregal visits uncomfortable work for the local officials, for he dealt severely with the philistines among them. But an earlier Viceroy had favoured the dismemberment of the Taj Mahal and the use of its fine marble for the adornment of Government House.

* * * * *

If Viceroys came but rarely, a Lieutenant-Governor might be expected to visit the station every now and then. There followed the same round of festivities though perhaps on not quite so regal a scale. Every hostess in the station hoped to be able to entertain the august visitor. Nevertheless there were agonising moments at these dinners. Questions of precedence became increasingly intricate. They were nothing then to the inextricable maze that they have since become. Only members of the Imperial Services had any precedence at all; and engineers and such-like were not even considered. My grandfather resigned from his club when he heard of a proposal to admit engineers and forest-officers. Nor did the Civil List in those days envisage such difficult questions as the status of a Nominated Member of the Council of State *vis-à-vis* an Army dentist holding the rank of captain; or whether the sister of a Bishop preceded the wife of an M.B.E., or whether an Honorary A.D.C. to the Nizam would sit on the right or the left of the hostess when the Siamese consul had also been invited; or what on earth one did with all these cold-weather tourists who had no conceivable status and yet hated being sent in to dinner after a black Jesuit physiologist. Nevertheless even in the last century questions of precedence were baffling enough. A single instance will show how vitally these questions affected people's lives.

The Lieutenant-Governor of the United Province visited a certain station in his province. The chaplain held rehearsals of the welcoming service in the station church, the choir consisting of the Collector's wife and the Judge's wife and a few nonentities. There was great rivalry between these two leading ladies of the station. The former, Mrs. Crawford, could claim that her husband was a "pukka collector" while the wretched Hamilton was only "officiating". This was no comfort to Mrs. Hamilton. Mrs. Crawford was High Church and wanted an anthem to be sung during the Governor's service. Mrs. Hamilton was Low Church, and was even against hymns. However, she consented to sing "From Greenland's Icy Mountains", to which, it being a missionary hymn, she had less objection than to any other kind of hymn—though the wits of the station said that her weakness for this hymn was by way of a hint to her husband who would not let her go up to Simla sufficiently often or for sufficiently long. The service went off without a hitch and, after it, the whole station had been invited to dine with the Governor. The occasion was as solemn as was fitting. A local barrister, Mr. Ilterdus Prichard, describes how when he arrived—

> the ladies were sitting in a semi-circle, the gentlemen standing about in groups, no one saying a word. His Honour was standing with his back to a stove, conversing slowly, as if anxious not to exhaust the subject too rapidly, upon the weather, with Colonel Surgeon. No one else spoke a word. . . . It was a great relief when dinner was announced. But I doubt whether if an earthquake had set all the tables and chairs dancing, there would have been as much consternation as now took possession of the Budgepore monde. For His Honour, on dinner being announced, walked slowly and with dignified mien up to where the ladies were sitting, passed quite close to Mrs. Hamilton and offering his arm to Mrs. Crawford, led her off. Then thousand thunders ! . . . For a whole month after that, whenever any two of the residents of Budgepore met together, that event formed the sole topic of discourse. Every conceivable motive and many inconceivable motives were ascribed to the Lieutenant-Governor.

The honour of the judiciary was at stake and the Hamiltons were determined not to let the matter rest. That summer Mrs. Crawford went to Mussoorie to escape the heat, and the Hamiltons followed her. They watched Mrs. Crawford carefully and wrote long letters to all their friends in Budgepore, relating fearful tales of her debauched conduct. These stories "reached Crawford's ear and he was exceedingly indignant. He refused all explanation, he would not ask for any. His wife, conscious of her innocence, resented his unworthy suspicions, and an angry altercation ensued between husband and wife, who had hitherto lived together on the most affectionate terms." Their letters became more and more violent. Mrs. Crawford refused to return to Budgepore and went straight down from Mussoorie to Calcutta, sailed for England and never met her husband again. He, a promising officer, though " lacking in religious principle ", consoled himself for her loss by heavy drinking, became a dipsomaniac and exceedingly unchaste.

As there was no Collector's wife in the station when the Lieutenant-Governor next paid a visit Mrs. Hamilton did not again have cause for complaint.

In the larger stations matins on Sunday mornings was the chief weekly reunion of the European community. A typical service is described by the journalist Knighton :

> In all directions the large fans, called punkahs, were hanging by ropes from the lofty roof, and were pulled rigorously to and fro by natives who attended church for that purpose. With the turbans on, and bare feet—*their* symbols of respect—they moved noiselessly over the vacant spaces by the sides of the rows of pews, each holding the end of a rope in his hand, and as the large canvas fan fixed on a wooden frame swung from him he followed it a few steps, and then, with a rigorous tug and a few steps backward, brought it back again to the side. A long line of natives so employed stretched down either side of the sacred edifice, whilst similar functionaries lined the galleries above, all busily and noiselessly plying their vocation, their ordinary every-day vocation on this day of rest, in the very House of God. It looked strange, but, as Mr. Lollipops (the chaplain) assured me, it was absolutely necessary ; the heat would be otherwise intolerable, and people would not go to church ; and besides, they were heathen, those punkah-pullers, and might possibly be improved by some word in season by their attendance—which, as I found they were ignorant of English, did not appear to me to be very probable. A similar fan moved over the head of the junior chaplain in the reading desk, as he read the prayers, another over the venerable Mr. Lollipops at the communion table. . . . What with watching . . . the angry looks cast by indignant elderly gentlemen, at the unfortunate punkah-pullers when they relaxed in

> the slightest degree from the orthodox strength with which the punkah *should* be pulled, I found it utterly impossible to give my usual attention to the service. . . . At length, Mr. Lollipops mounted the pulpit stairs, and, with a bland, benignant aspect, surveyed the congregation beneath him. . . . He was one of those men who, without being fluent, insist on preaching ex tempore. He explained to us that light and darkness were opposed to each other, that the one was considered the contrary to the other. He was proceeding to enforce the truth that darkness was symbolical of evil, light of good, when my attention was directed from him by a low smothered sound, like bare wet feet pattering over a slippery pavement, which was evident in my immediate vicinity. . . .

It appeared that the senior I.C.S. official Mr. Ducklet had fallen asleep and was beginning to snore.

> a rustling of stiff muslins and ribands convinced me that Mrs. Ducklet's elbow was making its way forcibly into her husband's side . . . the rumblings and rattlings of the offending nasal organ ceased at once, and turning towards his better half abruptly, Mr. Ducklet sharply asked, " What are you about ? "
>
> " Hush ! " said the lady, fixing her eyes on the preacher, " you have been snoring."
>
> " What's that you say ? " asked Ducklet, louder than was consistent with the place and time.
>
> " You were snoring—snoring," said Mrs. Ducklet, tartly, in his ear.
>
> " I wasn't snoring," said Ducklet pertinaciously. " I wasn't snoring. You shouldn't poke a man in that sort of style."
>
> As the clergyman closed the large Bible and squared it before him, a signal that his remarks were at length coming to a conclusion, there was a general rustling amongst the congregation, that indicated preparation for the finale. . . . A general buzz of preparation for departure pervaded the congregation —active ladies who had slept comfortably with one eye partially open, proceeded to urge their children and spouses to wakefulness and alertness by kicks, pushes and nudges—only gentlemen, who had been dreaming of inflicting summary vengeance on offending punkah-pullers, rubbed their heads energetically with their handkerchiefs, and then slightly fanned themselves in the hope of aiding the punkah—while fast young men who had come to church to please their uncles or their

inamoratas, seized their hats, and brushed from them imaginary particles of dust.[1]

Outside, on the veranda of the church there would be a babel of conversation, the ladies discussing the sermon, complimenting each other on their children and enjoying each other's dresses. The well-to-do would pretend that they ordered everything "out from home", even their parasols and the trimmings of their hats; but the less prosperous could always refer to "a wonderful little man I know in the bazaar. Quite a genius in his own way. This skirt, for instance, with the violet flounces, he ran it up with no assistance from me; just by copying a fashion plate which I had received from my cousin Agatha who is always up to all the latest fashions. Yes, I found him myself, but I could send him along to your bungalow if you liked." And the bandy-legged little tailor would turn up next day with his chit, bowing and smiling and ready for the terrific bargaining at which memsahibs were so expert; and he would sit cross-legged behind a screen on the veranda, his spectacles far down his thin nose, while the memsahib pounced on him at intervals to see if he was working or to give him another length of stuff to be worked into the dress.

While the ladies smiled and nodded together on the church veranda, the gentlemen stood apart in more serious groups. They wore morning coats and grey trousers, curiously domed white topis and heavy gold watch-chains. They would talk shop in a vague disguised manner or discuss the news from Europe as revealed in the last mail's batch of newspapers, a weighty speech in Parliament, the Russian menace, or the perennial impudence of the French. But one part of the congregation—the Eurasians—took little

[1] Knighton, *Tropical Sketches.*

share in this almost family-gathering. Their menfolk would appear as smart as any, perhaps smarter with their large signet rings and gold-headed canes. The women's dresses were, however, rather *outré*. They had started well enough in the current fashion but their wearers could not resist an extra rose here, another purple bow there, a love-knot, several gold chains and two or three huge brooches. But these little solecisms were not the cause of the constraint which fell on other members of the congregation when they appeared, of the almost masochistic obsequiousness of the Eurasian men or of the nervous giggles and gawky bows of the Eurasian women. They were as painfully aware of their colour as of their whiter neighbours' disdain, which they, hating as they did all even darker than themselves with pathological ferocity, could not but acknowledge in their heart of hearts to be justified. They bowed, giggled and grinned their way past the True Whites and settled themselves in overflowing numbers in shabby carriages whose coachmen were attired in compensatory glory and drove off to their houses furnished in unconscious caricature of English taste, with even more occasional tables, silk cushions, brassware and potted ferns than in the bungalow of the Collector. In the crowded drawing-room an occasional blushing subaltern, having met one of the daughters at a dance, would be entertained with stifling hospitality, while the rest of the station sneered and quoted Mr. Kipling's apt description of the wiles of such people and the snares that they set for the young unmarried officer. . . . One by one the carriages drove under the porch. There were elaborate good-byes, for some would not meet again till the same place next Sunday, the ladies smiling and bowing, clutching children or manipulating parasols, the gentlemen monosyllabic and gruff. The carriages left in strict order of precedence, and inside each carriage there was a sudden liveliness, a return to natural behaviour after the stilted dialogues on the church veranda where, in front of the whole European community one had to be so guarded —and Indians standing about in the sun, too, watching and listening, and so many of them able to speak English, what with the missionaries and all this education. For missionaries were not as popular as before, even among earnest officials' wives. They spoilt the servants and put about subversive egalitarian ideas.

And now as the carriages rattled down the Mall in the blinding sunshine, red-coated peons majestic on the box, a cloud of white dust springing up under the wheels, the ladies eagerly criticised Mrs. Brown's extraordinary hat and the very unbecoming colours which Mrs. Smith saw fit to wear at her age. And the gentlemen sat back and thought with pleasure of a bottle of iced beer and the Sunday lunch of roast beef and Yorkshire pudding, horse-radish sauce and baked potatoes, and a long sleep afterwards with the heavy punkah stirring overhead, the glare of Indian noon shut out by bamboo-splinter curtains.

When they arrived at the bungalow there would be a barking of dogs to welcome them. For no Anglo-Indian household was complete without fox terriers, bull-terriers or spaniels. Bull-terriers were perhaps more popular with young army officers, for they were not the modern neat slim breed but great gross animals afraid of nothing and difficult to tame. Their masters would sometimes pit them against pariah-dogs from the bazaar. You could not call it fighting, for the pariahs were almost helpless against practised gladiators ; but it kept the bull-terriers in fighting trim. The dogs would be looked after by dog-boys, the sons probably of some of the other servants ; and of an evening when the family had gone out for a carriage drive the Mall would be full of dog-boys gossiping together while their dogs panted or rolled in the dust or growled at each other—a sight still typical of an Indian station, though it is in Bombay that the sight is commonest, for almost every anglicised Indian family has followed this practice, save that there the dogs are generally dingier but the dog-boys much more smartly uniformed in smart tight white coats with brass buttons.

It was pleasant to step out of the dusty carriage into the cool of the veranda with its geraniums and lobelias in pots and maidenhair ferns in wire baskets hanging from the roof. And pleasanter still, while peons held the coloured glass-bead curtains aside, to come into the darkened drawing-room ; a real English room ; comfortable chairs with coloured cushions, numerous brass tables with flowers or flowering-plants in brass bowls ; a china cupboard and on the shelves a collection of the quaint brass gods and goddesses that were such useful presents for people " at home " ; a rug before the fireplace, a brass fire-guard and brass fire-irons and a pot of ferns in the empty fireplace ; a piece of pretty Chinese cloth hanging in careful folds from the mantelpiece on which were more brass ornaments and flowers. On the floor tiger-skins or panther-skins and heads on the walls, (" Yes, I got that brute year before last. Did a lot of damage in the villages round and the villagers came in a deputation asking me to kill the brute. Had to wait up night after night. When I got him the villagers had a dance, regular Irish reel." But those were days when tigers were shot in circumstances of great danger, not as in more recent times when the more notable shoots are carefully staged for the amusement of eminent visitors) and in between the heads some of cousin Ada's water-colours of the

Nile or of bluebells in an English woodland or hollyhocks against a sunny wall.

Lunch on Sundays always began with mulligatawny soup. In every Anglo-Indian household this was an unalterable rite, a rite that has continued to be observed for over sixty years. There would be more desultory conversation about the church service and feeling references to the heat. " It will soon ", the master of the house would say, " be time to think of the hills." For though he himself would seldom be able to get away for long, he would like to send his wife and children (" get back the English roses to their cheeks ") for a holiday in the hills. Which hill-station, then ? Simla, if one could afford it. But rents were high there, and lodgings expensive. And if one were a district officer, one often felt out of it, not knowing anyone in the exclusive " Simla set ". As *Vanity Fair* put it—

> The Collector never ventures to approach Simla when on leave. At Simla people would stare and raise their eyebrows if they heard that a Collector was on the hill. . . . So the clodhopping Collector goes to Nainital or Darjiling, where he is known either as Ellenborough Higgins, or Higgins of Gharitpur in territorial fashion. Here he is understood. Here he can babble of his Bandobast, his Balbacha and his Bawarchi khana ; and here he can speak in familiar accents of his neighbours, Dalhousie Smith and Cornwallis Jones. All day long he strides up and down the club veranda with his old Haileybury chum, Teignmouth Tompkins ; and they compare experiences of the hunting-field and office, and denounce in unmeasured terms of Oriental vituperation the new sort of civilian who moves about with the Penal Code under his arm and measures his authority by statute, clause and section.

It cannot be denied that the ambitious youth aimed generally at a Secretariat career. But while no one now knows who was secretary of what department in any given year, the names of the district officers of that generation have lived on in Indian memories. Through the mist of time the figures of earlier administrators loom in almost Homeric grandeur. The racial exclusiveness which in their successors was resented is in them viewed by Indians as the natural reserve of royalty; the higher scale of European living, in recent years the subject of so many diatribes, in former administrators seems but the pleasing display of megalopsychic qualities. " He lived like a raja " you hear Indians in reminiscent mood say with smiling approval. Almost every district has one such traditional figure of an Administrator. Collectors remained for a long period in one station. They regarded themselves as fathers of their people and were so regarded by the people. They planted trees, endowed schools, knew the language well and many of their subjects by names. Parents drew the attention of small awestruck children to the tall lean figure in riding breeches, Norfolk jacket and Terai hat discussing the state of the crops with a cultivator or the need of a new site for a cemetery with the village Mullah. As a recent Anglo-Indian poet expressed it—

When Thomson ruled in Thomsonpore,
Somewhere round eighteen eighty,
From end to end his District wore
An aspect warmly matey.
No deep division severed then
The Powers that Be from other men;
But all was friendly to the core
When Thomson ruled in Thomsonpore.

When out on tour, a word or jest
He'd have for every ryot,
And oft by kindly souls be pressed
To taste their humble diet;
Or Mrs. T, with playful spank,
Would bathe the children in the tank
And all would laugh with merry roar—
When Thomson ruled in Thomsonpore.

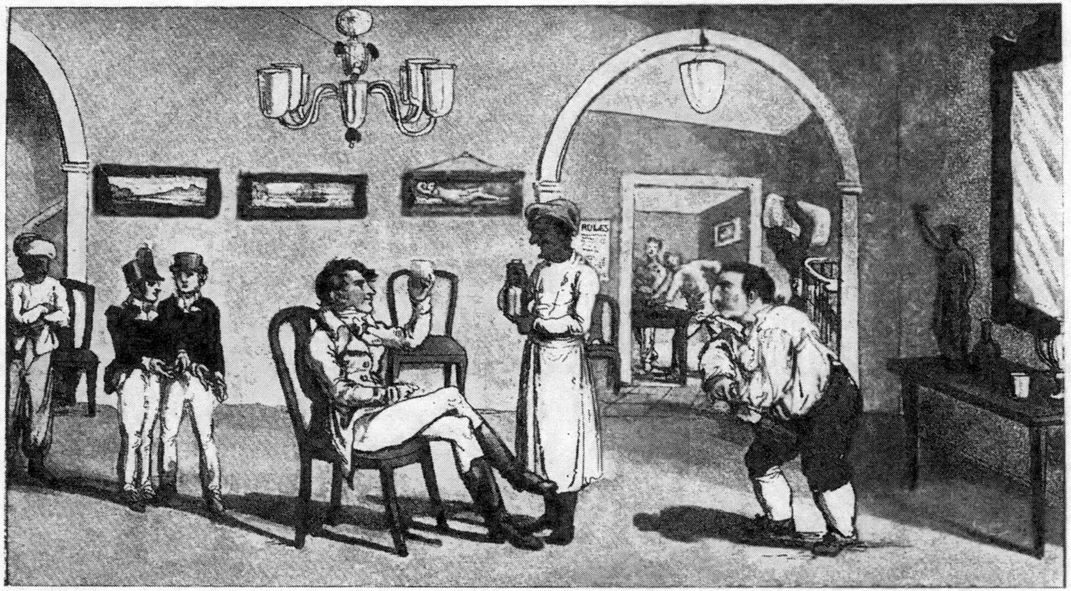

THE BOMBAY TAVERN

after Rowlandson.

CHAPTER VIII

IN 1827 Lord Amherst had started the summer move to Simla. In spite of the difficulties of transport Simla soon became popular. Twenty years later Miss Eden on her arrival there wrote—

> Well, it really is worth all the trouble—such a beautiful place—and our house, only wanting all the good furniture and carpets we have brought to be quite perfection. . . . Our sitting-rooms are small, but that is all the better in this climate, and the two principal rooms are very fine. . . . It has been an immense labour to furnish properly. We did not bring half chintz enough from Calcutta, and Simla grows rhododendron and pine and violets, but nothing else—no damask, no glazed cotton for lining, nothing. There is a sort of country cloth made here—wretched stuff in fact, though the colours are beautiful—but I ingeniously devised tearing up whole pieces of red and of white into narrow strips, and then sewing them together, and the effect for the dining-room is lovely, when supported by the scarlet border painted all round the cornice, the doors, windows, etc. and now everybody is adopting the fashion. . . . We brought carpets and chandeliers and wall-shades (the great staple commodity of Indian furniture) from Calcutta, and I have got a native painter into the house, and cut out patterns in paper, which he then paints in borders all round the doors and windows and it makes up for the want of cornices and breaks the eternal white walls of these houses. Altogether it is very like a cheerful middle-sized English country house and extremely enjoyable.

On a second visit Miss Eden was even more pleased with Simla.

> It is a jewel of a little house and my own room is quite *overcoming*; so light and cheerful, and then all the little curiosities I have collected on my travels have a sweet effect. . . . I have just been writing to C. E. for a few Chinese articles, a

> cabinet, and a table or so. . . . I have an armchair and a book case concocted at Singapore and a sort of table with shelves of my own devising that is being built at Bareilly under the Magistrate there. That, I think, may prove a failure, but I have a portfolio and inkstand on the stocks that will be really good articles. I got some beautiful polished pebbles from Banda.

And one evening when "we dined at six, then had fire-works, and coffee, and then all danced till twelve", Miss Eden began to reflect that

> twenty years ago no European had been here, and there we were with the band playing the *Puritani* and *Massaniello* and eating salmon from Scotland and sardines from the Mediter-raneon, and observing that St. Cloup's *potage à la Julienne* was perhaps better than his other soups, and that some of the ladies' sleeves were too tight according to the overland fashions for March.

And Miss Eden enjoyed the little theatre. Generally the female parts had to be taken "by artillery men and clerks" but sometimes Mrs. C. would act and she was a great change. "She really acts as if she had done nothing else all her life. But then she has been brought up in France." But some-times the performances had to be postponed owing to quarrels among the cast.

> One man took a fit of low spirits, and another who acted women's parts well would not cut off his moustachios and another went off to shoot bears near the snowy range. That man has been punished for his shilly-shallying; the snow blinded him and he was brought back rolled up in a blanket.

As the century advanced and methods of transport im-proved Simla became increasingly crowded with summer visitors, with Secretaries and with those who hoped to be Secretaries. Many of the ablest civilians were bored by the routine of district life and aspired to the higher sphere of the Central Government. But how to become a Secretary?

The Secretary was usually marked out for Secretariat employment from his earliest years. Let us turn again to *Vanity Fair* for a satirical impression of a Secretary to Government in the 'eighties.

> He has always been clever. He was the clever man of his year. He was so clever when he first came out that he would never learn to ride, or speak the language, and had to be translated to the Provincial Secretariat. But though he could never speak an intelligible sentence in the language, he had such a practical and useful knowledge of it, in half-a-dozen of its dialects, that he could pass examinations in it with the highest credit, netting immense rewards. He thus became not only more and more clever, but more and more solvent ; until he was an object of wonder to his contemporaries, of admiration to the Lieutenant-Governor, and of desire to several Barri Mem Sahibs with daughters. It is about this time that he is supposed to have written an article published in some English periodical. It was said to be an article of a solemn description, and report magnified the periodical into the *Quarterly Review.* So he became one who wrote for the English Press. It was felt that he was a man of letters ; it was assumed that he was on terms of familiar correspondence with all the chief literary men of the day. With so conspicuous a reputation, he felt it necessary to do something in religion. So he gave up religion, and allowed it to be understood that he was a man of advanced views ; a Positivist, a Buddhist or something equally occult. Thus he became ripe for the highest employment, and was placed necessarily on a number of Special Commissions. He enquired into everything ; he wrote hundredweights of reports ; he proved himself to have the true paralytic ink flux, precisely the kind of wordy discharge or brain hæmorrhage required of a high official in India. He would write ten pages where a clodhopping collector would write a sentence. He could say the same thing over and over again in a hundred different ways. The feeble forms of official satire were at his command. He desired exceedingly to be thought supercilious, and he thus became almost necessary to the Government of India, was canonised, and caught up to Simla. The Indian papers chanted little anthems, the Services said " Amen ", and the apotheosis was felt to be a success. On reaching Simla he was found to be familiar with the two local jokes. One of

these jokes is about everything in India having its peculiar smell, except a flower ; the second is some inanity about the Indian Government of being a despotism of despatch-boxes tempered by the loss of the keys. He often emitted these mournful jokes until he was declared to be an acquisition to Simla society. . . . I have said that the Secretary is clever, scornful, jocose, imperfectly sinful, and nimble with his pen. I shall only add that he has succeeded in catching the tone of the Imperial Bumbledom. This tone is an affectation of æsthetic literary sympathies, combined with a proud disdain of everything Indian and Anglo-Indian. The flotsam and jetsam of advanced European thought are eagerly sought and treasured up. *The New Republic* and *The Epic of Hades* are on every drawing-room table. One must speak of nothing but the latest doings at the Gaiety, the pictures of the last Academy, the ripest outcome of scepticism in the *Nineteenth Century*, or the aftermath in the *Fortnightly*.

It was not to be expected that Secretariat circles approved of that new writer, Kipling. *Plain Tales from the Hills* caused the utmost irritation by its hints (which corroborated the propaganda of disgruntled missionaries) of loose living among the highest circles in Simla.

Mrs. Hauksbee was an outrageous caricature and though one might admire the way Kipling caught the spirit of Simla gâiety as in

Eyes of blue—the Simla Hills
Silvered with the moonlight hoar ;
Pleading of the waltz that thrills,
Dies and echoes round Benmore.

"*Mabel*", "*Officers*", "*Goodbye*",
Glamour, wine and witchery—
On my soul's sincerity,
Love like ours can never die!

Yet the continual refrain that these romances of the hills were only the distractions of bored wives separated from hard-working husbands left on the burning plains was very offensive.

> Woman, behold our ancient state
> Has clean departed ; and we see
> 'Twas idleness we took for Fate
> That bound light bonds on you and me.
>
> Amen ! here ends the comedy
> Where it began in all good will,
> Since Love and Leave together flee
> As driven mist on Jakko Hill !

Nor were his continual references to intrigues in high places in any better taste. The poem about Delilah's alliance with Ulysses Gunne,

> . . . Perhaps the wine was red—
> Perhaps an aged Councillor had lost his aged head—
> Perhaps Delilah's eyes were bright—Delilah's whispers sweet
> The aged member told her what 'twere treason to repeat. . . .

Or the rapid rise of Ahasuerus Jenkins of the *Operatic Own* who was a poor soldier but had a nice voice ; so

> He took two months at Simla when the year was at the spring,
> And underneath the deodars eternally did sing.
> He warbled like a bul-bul, but particularly at
> Cornelia Agrippina, who was musical and fat.

She " controlled a humble husband, who, in turn, controlled a Department " and so Ahasuerus Jenkins was removed to Simla and rose rapidly.

> Now, ever after dinner, when the coffee-cups are brought,
> Ahasuerus waileth o'er the grand pianoforte ;
> And, thanks to fair Cornelia, his fame has waxen great,
> And Ahasuerus Jenkins is a power in the State !

It was not that Simla circles did not enjoy a number of jokes about each other's intrigues. The joke that you cannot sleep at night at Simla for the noise of the grinding of axes must be almost as old as the hill-station itself. But those jokes were very different from the gibes of a journalist. Consequently when the Bard of Empire's public rapidly grew, hard-bitten administrators in remote districts melting into unwonted admiration for a poet under the rain of his bouquets and romantic young Imperialists finding in his verses a Message, Simla remained cold. The fellow was clearly a bounder ; his stories of life in the Hills were informed by the natural envy of a cad who had sought and been refused an entrée to Simla society. Till her death in 1933 my grandmother continued to speak of Kipling as a subversive pamphleteer given to criticise his betters.

Not that Secretariat circles formed more than a small proportion of Simla society. There were a great many summer visitors from military cantonments and even from the rich business circles of Calcutta. There were even permanent residents who had bought house property and settled down there. The well-known brewing family of Dyer had long ago settled there in a house called Ladyhill, " built on English lines with a big garden full of English fruits and flowers ". Bishop Cotton had founded at Simla a school to be run on English lines so that it was hardly necessary to send one's children home for their education, though many of the Simla residents liked to have their children's education completed in England. Mr. Dyer's brewery was at Solon near Murree, but he preferred to live at Simla ; for as his son's biographer records he was " the Ganymedes of an Indian Olympus whose gods were the major deities of the Government of India and the minor deities of the Punjab administration, and whose nectar was bottled beer ". His son Rex was sent to Bishop Cotton's school. He stammered a little and this exposed him to " the derision of his schoolfellows ". But as he was " hot tempered and pugnacious " he was able to take revenge on his tormentors and " frequently came home with the scars of battle on his face ". He showed considerable personal courage on more than one occasion. Thus he was sent to bring his sisters home from school and was returning when

> he came full face upon a hyena, which stood motionless in the narrow hill path, barring his way. Rex, remembering what he had been told about animals fearing the human eye, advanced slowly, staring steadily at the horrid jowl, turned as he passed the animal, and, still staring, walked backwards until it was out of his sight. Thus [adds his biographer],[1] early in life he thrilled with the man's instinct to protect his womenkind.

Shortly after this the boy had an unfortunate experience in the Simla forests. He had gone out with his gun. Aiming at a bird he had brought down a monkey and the pathetic spectacle of the dying creature, its fur bespattered with blood, so distressed him that he gave up shooting.

* * * * *

New houses continued to spring up, new shops and new hotels. In the 'eighties and 'nineties Peliti's was the fashionable hotel. " The comfortable sitting-room invites him (the visitor) to read and dream in the great chairs, and the well-ordered café is of never-failing interest, for here in the groups of laughing, faultlessly dressed English men and women he finds the true Anglo-Indian." It was here that Mrs. Hauksbee had tiffin with Mr. Bremmil while Mrs. Bremmil remained at home and wept into an empty cradle. And that Kipling considered it the centre of fast life is evident from his lines put in the mouth of a virtuous monkey who boasted

> never in my life
> Have I flirted at Peliti's with another *Bandar's* wife.

Above Peliti's was the Mall down which most of the characters in *Plain Tales from the Hills* made their way at one time or another ; Strickland (responsible for how many unworthy epigoni in modern adventure fiction) with Miss

[1] Ian Colvin.

Youghal's horse, Pluffles the Subaltern, Young Cubbon, Peythroppe and the Cusack-Bremmils. And here Sweet Seventeen's rival held her daily review of admirers.

> She rides with half a dozen men
> (She calls them " boys " and " mashes ",)
> I trot along the Mall alone ;
> My prettiest frocks and sashes
> Don't help to fill my programme-card,
> And vainly I repine
> From ten to two a.m. Ah me !
> Would I were forty-nine.

And here Young Gayerson and subsequently Very Young Gayerson rode with the " Anglo-Indian deity Venus Annodomini ".

At the top of the Mall rises Christchurch's noble Gothic structure. It was as certain a rendezvous on Sunday mornings as any church in the plains. But they emerged more sedately from under the Tudor porch with its crenellated roof. Topis were hardly necessary, and though some of the gentlemen wore those odd honeycomb-shaped topis others preferred less tropical headgear. None of the ladies wore topis. Here at last they could sport their wide-brimmed straw hats with banks of flowers and ostrich feathers ; and it was comforting to be able to wear a wide lace collar or even a feather boa without feeling too hot. There was no veranda here, for everything about Christchurch had to be as English as possible. You came out on to a little terrace with a fence round it and a wide view over Simla. There was of course no parade of carriages, for no one but the Viceroy, the Governor of the Punjab and the Commander-in-Chief might use a carriage in Simla ; but the rickshaws waited for their passengers, two *jhampanis*, very smart in white tunics and tall and tapering turbans, stationed by each rickshaw.

There would be hardly likely such opportunity for criticising the sermon as after a service in the plains, for the clergy in Simla were chosen for their ability. An Archdeacon of Simla stood as high above an ordinary cantonment chaplain as a Secretary above a " clodhopping collector ". For a contemporary description of such an Archdeacon let us return once more to *Vanity Fair.*

> He is the recognised guardian of public morality, and the hill captains and semi-detached wives lead him a rare life. There is no junketing at Goldstein's, no picnic at the waterfalls, no games at Annandale, no rehearsals at Herr Felix von Battin's, no choir practice at the church even, from which he can safely absent himself. A word, a kiss, some matrimonial charm dissolved—these electric disturbances of society must be averted. The Archdeacon is the lightning conductor ; where he is, the levin of naughtiness passes to the ground, and society is not shocked. . . . I like the recognised relations between the Archdeacon and women. They are more than avuncular and less than cousinly ; they are tender without being romantic and confiding without being burdensome. He has the private *entrée* at choti hazree or early breakfast ; he has private *entrée* at five o'clock tea and hears plans for the evening campaign openly discussed. He is quite behind the scenes. . . . With the inferior clergy the Archdeacon is not at his ease. He cannot respect the little gingerbread gods of doctrine they make for themselves ; their hocus-pocus and their crystallised phraseology falls dissonantly upon his ear ; their talk of chasubles and stoles, eastern attitude, and all the rest of it, is to him as a tale by an idiot signifying nothing. Of course the Archdeacon may be very much mistaken in all this ; and it is this generous consciousness of fallibility which gives the singular charm to his religious attitude. He can take off his religious spectacles and perceive that he may be in the wrong like other men.

As the rickshaws went jolting down the steep path from the church a cold wind would, in spite of the noon sun, blow from the snowy peaks. Perhaps it blew from the bleak plateaus of Tibet, a country which to those who had " taken up " theosophy was regarded as the last refuge of the mysteries of an older world. There were Mahatmas there who spoke in broken English, and revealed the secrets of life and of death. They would control vast resources of power ; and it was considered rash of Colonel Younghusband to invade their country. At Adyar miracles had already been performed and the discovery by the commission of the Psychical Research Society, that Madame Blavatsky's Mahatma was a Bengali graduate in disguise, was attributed by the faithful to the machinations of the Bishop of Madras. Who could doubt the powers of the followers of the Ancient Wisdom after that picnic in the hills where it was found that the party were a cup and saucer short and a miracle (resembling closely that of the marriage at Cana) saved the hosts from embarrassment, for a cup and saucer, even of the required size and pattern, were found buried in the earth? The wind ruffled the feather boas of the ladies and stirred the ragged clothes of the uncouth hill-tribesmen who wandered along the Mall, and the heavy red coats of the Government orderlies everywhere apparent as they hurried to and fro with important despatches or invitations to tea ; it bent the pines and deodars along all the winding roads of Simla ; and, in the gardens of innumerable little cottages with gabled roofs of corrugated iron and windows hung with lace curtains, it tossed the white and scarlet fuchsias in their wire baskets and the hollyhocks along the sheltered wall. It blew over Annandale where the famous Annandale roses grew and the ladies held their archery competitions. And it blew up towards Observatory Hill whereon rose the new Viceregal Lodge. The old Viceregal Lodge, which Mr. Montagu thought so charming—" it really is an awfully nice half-timbered house with a glorious garden and a beautiful panelled hall and dining room ", had proved too small for the always increasing entourage of the Viceroy and the Dufferins had moved into the new Viceregal Lodge. Lady Dufferin complained of the great size of their new summer-house and wondered how she would ever be able to furnish it, but by the time of Lady Minto it seemed so small that it was necessary to add a new wing. It was an imposing edifice, though as Mr. Montagu remarked, it had the air of a Scotch hydro, " the same sort of appearance, the same sort of architecture, the same sort of equipment of tennis lawns and sticky courts, and so forth. Inside it is comfortable, with suites of apartments comparable to those of the Carlton or the Ritz." A more usual and decorous way of describing the place was " the stately summer house of the Viceroy, set well back in beautiful grounds. The various Vicereines have tried to make their Simla house as English as possible, and it might be England but for the presence of the grinning little Gurkhas, the Viceroy's Guard of Honour."

* * * * *

Most Vicereines were enchanted with Simla and found Viceregal Lodge a pleasant change after the oppressive magnificence of Government House in Calcutta. But Lady Curzon was an exception. " The first view of Simla ", she wrote to her husband whom she had left behind in Calcutta, " amused me so—the houses slipping off the hills and clinging like barnacles to the hill-tops—and then our house ! I kept trying not to be disappointed." If the outside was uninspiring, " the inside is nothing fine but nice ; and Oh ! Lincrusta you will turn us grey ! It looks at you with pomegranate and pineapple eyes from every wall." But there was no denying that the situation was unusually fine. As she observed with feeling, " A Minneapolis millionaire would revel in this, and we shall love it and make up our minds not to be fastidious. . . . A look out of the window makes up for all, and I can live on views for five years ", and when they went on an expedition to the Bagchi forest she found the trees to be " as fine and as immense as the tall pines in California ". In spite of the beauty of the scenery, however, she found those expeditions in the hill forests rather taxing and in her diary are many entries such as " At 8.30 we went shooting, first riding and then clambering, climbing, sitting and sliding, and making every effort possible to slay two coveys of partridges. After walking five hours our bag consisted of five head of game and after a break-bone climb we got into camp for a four o'clock lunch."

For different reasons Lord Curzon disliked Simla. " I congratulate you heartily ", he exclaimed to Sir Walter Lawrence, " on one thing—on leaving Simla so soon. How I hate the place ! " So far from being oppressed by the size of Government House at Calcutta he loved to remember that it had been built in imitation of Kedleston. And while in Calcutta he enjoyed his long evening drives while he meditated upon imperial problems and surveyed benignly the teeming anonymous crowds of his subjects, here in Simla he could only drive slowly down winding lanes where the very officials whom he had been seeing all day would recognise him and raise their hats. The festivities of Simla meant nothing to him. When he had a ball he liked it to be of suitable magnificence such as the " big Fancy Dress Ball of the Wellesley period " which he gave in 1903 to celebrate the centenary of Government House, Calcutta, when he appeared as Lord Wellesley and as a guest enthusiastically wrote : " We became our grandparents again, imitating in spirit, language and dress the high-waisted ladies and stately men who danced in these very halls a century ago." But of the ordinary round of entertainments in Simla society he was almost unaware. He sat almost all day and half the night in his office, the handsome aloof face bent above the continually increasing files. He might cry out in irritation, " The real tyranny that is to be feared in India is not the tyranny of executive authority but that of the pen ", but he himself was a more determined penman than all his secretaries. The pen hovered for a moment, the pale lips were pursed, and then with a sigh he began to write again in his clear sloping handwriting an admirably phrased minute pointing out clearly, very clearly (for really some of his correspondents seemed unnecessarily obtuse) that the auditorium for the durbar should provide " for a combination of Oriental outlines with European features, such as striped canvas, streamers and flags ", or that the new telegraph office opened by Colonel Younghusband in Tibet was *not*, as was claimed, the highest in the world, for there was a higher one in the Andes. Sometimes there were moments of depression when he could write, " grind, grind, grind, with never a word of encouragement ; on, on, on, till the collar breaks and the poor beast stumbles and dies. I suppose it is all right and it doesn't matter. But sometimes when I think of myself spending my heart's blood here and no one caring one little damn, the spirit goes out of me and I feel like giving in." But such moments were few. He was inspired by the greatness of his task, by his real devotion to India and by the memory of the Queen's last words to him, " Be kind to my poor Indians." There below the line of the hills lay that India where soon he would be diligently from one end to the other, noting, advising, recommending, whether his hosts were district officials or Native Princes.

On these long tours the weather was often trying. At Diu Lady Curzon described how " George was so hot that his collar had gone and he was fanning himself with an immense red satin fan edged with swansdown ", and at

Bombay Lady Curzon almost surrendered, " Oh ! the heat, the heat. . . . Dressing in it is simply awful and with broad swift rivers running down all over you, it is hard to appear dry and smiling at a daily dinner-party." Curzon, however, was, in spite of almost incessant pain, seldom other than urbane and imperturbable. The only thing that roused him to anger was the vandalism that was everywhere doing irreparable damage to the great monuments of ancient India. In Bijapur, for instance, he found that the Public Works Department had saved themselves the trouble of erecting new houses for local officials by converting the old palaces into bungalows, and had torn down many other monuments " to admit air " and the few remaining mosques or tombs were disfigured by " good British whitewash plentifully bespattered about in every direction ". Having dealt suitably with such situations, Curzon could return to Simla as though to an office after a holiday, and shut himself up with the interminable files. Simla society regarded him with awe, not unmixed with a certain malicious amusement at his tremendous pronouncements. One could never be quite certain whether he were in earnest or not ; and Sir Walter Lawrence described how " when he said that no self-respecting woman would allow cold tapioca pudding to be served at luncheon, there was a sensation in Simla ". Many, who felt that the viceregal eye always rested several inches above their heads staring over them at some problem of imperial interests, were inclined to sum him up as a humourless autocrat. But the viceregal eye was more observant than was suspected and the little traits of the officials and their wives amused him. " The red-moustachioed A.", he wrote to Lady Curzon, " wore the same air of blank astonishment at the world in general and read the lessons in church as though they were a Government Resolution ", and his hostess at a tea-party was a " lady with a huge purple feather in her hat, a naughty mouth and a roving eye ".

Though, during his reign, there were many occasions of disagreement between Curzon and the majority of the European community, yet he never faltered in his admiration for " the Englishman in India " and in his speeches he interpreted majestically the ideals and the mission that he attributed to him.

> Oh, that to every Englishman in this country, as he ends his work, might be truthfully applied the phrase, " thou hast loved righteousness and hated iniquity ". No man has, I believe, ever served India faithfully of whom that could not be said. All other triumphs are tinsel and sham. . . . Remember that the Almighty has placed your hand on the greatest of His ploughs, in whose furrow the nations of the future are germinating and taking shape . . . to feel that somewhere among these millions you have left a little justice or happiness or prosperity, a sense of manliness or moral dignity, a spring of patriotism, a dawn of intellectual enlightenment or a stirring of duty where it did not exist before—that is enough, that is the Englishman's justification in India.

* * * * *

Such speeches expressed in magnificent language the conscious maturity of a régime, an almost Antonine sense of permanence. And within a decade had come a series of appropriately post-Antonine developments ; the retreat over the partition of Bengal in face of successful agitation, the capture of the Congress by the extremists, Sir Satyendranath Sinha in the Viceroy's Executive Council, and the experiments of Mr. Gandhi, a Kathiawari barrister who had settled in South Africa, in a new form of resistance to authority which he had evolved from a study of the works of Ruskin and Tolstoi and which he named satyagraha or " truth-force ".

These developments, however, hardly ruffled the even tenor of Anglo-Indian life. There was a good deal of distrust of the new Secretary of State, Morley, which is not surprising in view of his occasional rudeness about Anglo-India. But it was consoling to discover that he no more believed in democracy as a suitable form of Government for India than any Indian army colonel. Discussing the proposed Morley-Minto reforms, he announced, "If it could be said that this chapter of reforms led directly or necessarily up to the establishment of a parliamentary system in India, I, for one, would have nothing at all to do with it." He was happy to discuss the writings of J. S. Mill with brilliant young Indian barristers, but that did not prevent him from becoming the "most autocratic and least constitutional Secretary of State ever seen in Whitehall". He was pleasantly accessible to Indian visitors, however, and Mr. Gandhi on a visit to London (during which he gave a vegetarian banquet to his English admirers and spent £2 on a bottle of hair-restorer) found him affable. But once the visitors had gone the official mask dropped off and Morley could write, "I am an Occidental, not an Oriental. . . . I think I like Indian Mohammedans, but I can not go much further in an easterly direction." Such feelings in a Secretary of State were not, despite the vaunted or dreaded reforms of 1909, likely to lead to much change in the Indian atmosphere and earlier alarm at Morley's Liberal expressions passed away.

What was more worrying than a supposedly Liberal Secretary of State was the increasing nationalist agitation. In the west this was centred in Poona where the Brahman intellectuals looked back to the rule of the Peshwas as to a golden age.

SHOOTING WATERFOWL IN THE JHEELS

CHAPTER IX

POONA had greatly changed since the days when the last Peshwa fled from Parwati Hill or the subsequent era of decay when the old palaces crumbled into dusty ruin and Lady West glanced disgustedly at the ceremonies celebrated with dwindling pomp in the former royal chapel. It was now the headquarters of the Southern Command. Its pleasant climate, the ease with which English flowers could be grown during the rains, the facilities for riding and almost every kind of sport had made it a favourite station with both military and civilian. The Cantonment was well laid out, with wide straight roads (the first car that drove along them was Mr. R. Lamb's 12-h.p. Orleans registered in 1905) lined with shady trees. The river had been dammed by a public-spirited Parsi so that boating could be enjoyed during most of the year. And in the gardens by the dam a band played on warm evenings to the carriages drawn up in rows and the strolling couples by the river bank. A pleasant spot on April or May evenings when the hot wind that elsewhere blew over an ochre landscape was here cooled by the wide expanse of the river.

Rather an eyesore had recently appeared here, a new Parsi house facing the gardens and built in a somewhat flamboyant chateau style ; in the garden a large statue of a lady in European dress with a parasol open over her head, that curious Indian fondness of statuary. It was far worse in Bombay, of course, where in the gardens of many of the biggest houses on Malabar Hill were forests of Venuses and Athenes holding up lamps or pointing to clocks in their stomachs, statues that were a source of pride to their owners who would drape mackintoshes round them during the monsoon.

But it was wonderful how Europeanised many of the Parsis were becoming. They themselves were fond of explaining that this was due to the fact of their not being Indians at all but Persians, and of course during Alexander the Great's conquest of Persia many Greeks married Persians, so you could say that the Parsis were half-Greek really. They were most hospitable people and some of the tea-parties they gave were very pleasant in their way. The paterfamilias with little goatee beard and rimless pince-nez would come hurrying out into the veranda to greet his European guests with a low bow and to lead them into the long drawing-room with its rocking chairs ranged in a straight row, the enormous cut-glass chandelier, the model of the Taj Mahal on a blackwood table, the glass cupboards full of English china, the dark oil-paintings of ancestors, the highly coloured prints of King Edward VII's coronation and of Zoroaster in meditation. On the table a silver teapot even more massive than those commonly seen in European bungalows, and an array of sugared cakes and plates of sandwiches (Uncle Noshirwan had been sent out for the afternoon because he would wander round peering inquisitively into the contents of the sandwiches and then restoring them to their plates with a sniff). And nestling modestly in the shadow of the teapot a plate of Indian potato-cakes. "One of our little native preparations. My wife insisted on making them for you. Oh yes, like sampling foreign dishes." The ungloved hand advanced, selected one of the soft, luke-warm yellowish blobs. A moment of panic; had the cook remembered not to put any chillis in? The Englishwoman's face was inscrutable in the shadow of that huge hat with its pyramid of vertical flowers nodding on green wire stems. A whalebone-stiffened collar enclosing the throat almost concealed the faint swallowing motions. There was an encouraging nod, " Yes, very nice. An unfamiliar taste, of course. And now I will like a cucumber sandwich, please." And after tea the photograph album with the snapshots of their host taken during his visit to England last year ; posed on a promenade in white trousers, blazer and straw hat ; on the racecourse with tilted topper and orchid buttonhole ; in tail-coat with silver-mounted stick tucked under the armpit, drawing on white gloves. And the daughter's collection of pressed wild flowers (" only our common Indian flowers, I'm afraid. Not those glorious blossoms you have at Home "). And the new gramophone with the records recently purchased in Bombay, " When Irish eyes are smiling " and Harry Lauder singing, " I love a lassie, a Bonnie Hielan Lassie "—a catchy tune which set them all swaying a little in their rocking chairs.

It was not till June that it was really fashionable to be in Poona. For then the Bombay Government (having spent the cold weather in Bombay and the hot in Mahabaleshwar) arrived for a four-months' residence. This was the Poona Season. Everyone in Bombay who was anyone came up to Poona for week-ends during the Season, or, in the case of wealthy merchants, rented bungalows for the Season and installed their wives there to avoid the tiresome climate of Bombay during the monsoon. There was then what the Press called a " ceaseless round of entertainment " and the correspondents of Bombay newspapers kept their readers informed about the trend of fashion in the ballroom or on the croquet-lawn. New-comers to the Poona Season were warned not to " do too much ", and above all not to eat too many mangoes, which in the first half of June are most luscious and enticing. Too many mangoes gave one diarrhœa, or as it was carefully called, "Poonaitis". (In Karachi it was called, more allusively but more revealingly, "Karachi Trotters".) And if you were laid low with this unfortunate complaint there was an end for many weeks to the daily visit to Gymkhana where all one's friends gathered. While the ladies drove to the Gymkhana soon after tea, the gentlemen drove there straight from office so as to be able to put in a full hour or two hours at tennis or croquet. Many of the ladies played croquet too, but others preferred to sit on the basket-chairs in the veranda and sew (knitting did not "come in" till the war). They would visit the Club Library, but would be unlikely to find any books there. It boasted of very few books and those were in constant demand. No one under the rank of a Collector's wife had a hope of securing one except by luck. So they would content themselves with gossip about the last ball at Government House, the delinquencies of their servants and the health of their children. And, indeed, what else should they talk about? There were no theatres or cinemas and only an occasional concert. One could exchange news from home, of course, and the ladies who had correspondents in London were able to pass on the information that it had been, or looked like being, a brilliant season; or that it had been a poor summer and really one was lucky to be here, for cold north-east winds in June made England a poor place to be in; or that, as in 1911, it had been a very hot summer, the temperatures in London for weeks on end as high as those in Poona and no Anglo-Indian comforts to mitigate the heat, no fans, no veranda bedrooms, no khus-khus tatties over the doors on which a servant poured water every half-hour so as to keep a cool draught blowing into the bungalow. And the Durbar was a recurrent subject of conversation. All one's friends and relatives in England were anxious for details, and the place swarmed with reporters and Raven Hill had drawn a series of such amusing drawings in *Punch* about India and Indians. There had been produced a moving-picture film of the ceremony, in colours too, which was being shown in London, but it can't have been anything like the Real Thing. One would always remember it ; the King and Queen coming up the steps to the Gateway of India in Bombay, the King in his white Admiral's uniform and the Queen with the ribbon of the Garter and a great hat at a becoming angle, the umbrellas of state, and the rajas in their turbans and sashes and pointed patent leather button boots ; and the King and Queen in their crowns and robes at Delhi, receiving the homage of the Princes and later sitting on the balcony on the palace wall where the old Mogul Emperors sat while the crowds filed past, the royal velvet and ermine and jewellery under the hard white sunlight. It had all been wonderful, they agreed, smiling and nodding on the veranda of the club. Their children rolled and crawled and played on the lawn that was of almost English thickness and was bordered by the banks of many-coloured cannas for which Poona was justly famous and by the blue-grey shrubs of sensitive plant whose leaves withered at the lightest touch (as the children were never tired of demonstrating) and in their delicate decay gave out a faint but unforgettable perfume. By each child squatted a white-cotton-robed ayah and (if the child came from an official household) a red-coated orderly as well. There were a few English and Eurasian nurses and these kept rigidly to themselves, sewing like their mistresses and nodding together over the events at the Sergeants' Dance on Saturday night—those dances in the Canteen at which the etiquette was of terrifying strictness and a girl's reputation was gone if she were not returned to her parents by her partner as soon as each dance was over. And up and down the centre of the lawn, followed by a few of the older children marching in step, paraded the military band. It was generally the band of an English regiment, for of course only English bandsmen could be expected to cope with the really new tunes from England. But for a change the bands of Baluch or Punjabi regiments were often invited. They played bagpipes, really extraordinarily well considering, and to heighten the Scottish effect the men wore bits of tartan, though it was a pity they were so oddly shy about showing their knees and so would not wear kilts. They would play old Scottish airs too with quite a swing; and they sometimes played some of their own border tunes which were surprisingly melodious, unlike these horrid Hindu efforts at music. There was one Pathan marching song which was especially popular. It was called "Zakhmi Dil", which means "Wounded heart", a nice romantic title, and the ladies sometimes showed some curiosity over the words of the pleasant lilting song. But even if the gentlemen knew enough Urdu to interpret them it would have been quite impossible for them to satisfy the ladies' curiosity, for the least obscene lines in the song were those of the first verse which ran, "There is a boy across the river with a —— like a peach. But, alas, I cannot swim."

With the coming of the quick Indian twilight the military band would march off, and inside the club building violins tuned up for a waltz or two-step, for on most evenings (though never on Sundays) there were "flannel dances". They did not last long; since almost everyone had a dinner engagement. As Miss Maud Diver wrote (in a little book, *The Englishwoman in India*, designed to correct stories of Anglo-Indian immorality put about by critics like Kipling)—

> The amount of entertaining accomplished in a year by a Colonel's wife in India would, if set down in full, contrast curiously with the hospitality shown by a woman of the same standing in England . . . India is the land of dinners, as England is the land of five o'clock teas. From the Colonels' and Commissioners' wives, who conscientiously " dine the station " every cold weather, to the wives of subalterns and junior civilians—whose cheery informal little parties of six or eight are by no means to be despised by lovers of good company and simple fare—all Anglo-India is in a chronic state of giving and receiving this—the most delightful or the most excruciating form of hospitality. And who but the hostess is responsible for the destined adjective ? She it is who consigns the nervous *débutante* to the latest joined " thrice-born civilian," who will not stir his little finger to set her at her ease. She it is also who detects the budding love affair and lays her covers accordingly.

Of course the crowd of servants made housekeeping easy, " which enables girls, whose training for marriage has been carried on mainly in ballrooms, and at picnics and tennis parties, to blossom eventually into creditable housekeepers ". The Servant Problem in England (and Mr. Lloyd George's iniquitous new Insurance Scheme) had made Anglo-Indians more tolerant to the failings of their domestic staffs. As Miss Diver remarked, " The worst charges brought against native servants are uncleanliness and a propensity to petty thefts and lies. But, when all is said, are the lower classes of England—despite the advantages of wholesale civilisation —so amazingly clean and honest ? " And unlike the idle hussies in England, Indian servants " never demand an evening out ". Of course, sometimes there were almost too many entertainments.

> It is no rare thing for a girl to go to twelve or fourteen dances in a single season. Save for arranging a wealth of cut flowers,

> laid to her hand by the faithful Mali, an Anglo-Indian girl's domestic duties are practically nil. Intellectual pastimes are not within her reach and religion is left to those who have given up their lives to it. Small wonder that . . . even the more seriously inclined succumb for a while to the irresistible charm, the lightness and brightness of Anglo-Indian social life.

And so at the Poona gymkhana the "flannel dance" was but a prelude to a more elaborate entertainment. The carriages were soon called and drove off down the gravel path of the club. Carriages, and presently a few motors. But these were still unpopular. They frightened the horses and on the whole seemed rather out of place in a country where everyone was supposed to be horse-minded from the subaltern to the Viceroy. Had not His Excellency himself in Simla, abandoning in a moment of commendable enthusiasm all official circumlocutions, minuted on a proposal to maintain the breed of the Burmese pony, "I agree. The Burma pony is a damned good little piece of stuff"? And had not that minute been incorporated in an official communication, "Sir, I am directed to inform you that in the opinion of the Governor-General in Council the Burma pony is a damned good little piece of stuff"? Moreover, the wretched vehicles were always breaking down as soon as they left the smooth roads of Poona and then you would see the undignified spectacle of an official being towed back to his bungalow behind a Maratha peasant's bullock-cart. Indeed some car-owners were so pessimistic as to order relays of bullock-carts to be kept waiting all along the route where they proposed taking an evening drive so that when the inevitable breakdown occurred they would not have to wait long for relief.

European bungalows were still of the traditional kind, steep-roofed with a long low-ceilinged veranda, screened from the road by a huge arbour of trellis work in which pots of ferns and small palms were arranged on green-painted wooden shelves. Many of these bungalows had already been condemned (the judge's bungalow, the building that had once been the British residency in the days of the Peshwa, was condemned as dangerous soon after 1900 and to-day is still occupied by the judge), but they continued to be patched up and renovated ; the modern box-shaped suburban-villa style of official dwelling would have been impossible in days before electricity. Few people bought their own furniture (though many more than in more recent years) for it was easy to hire from the Borah merchants in the bazaar who kept a supply of furniture especially for the bungalows of Europeans. But if in general most bungalows looked rather alike inside they were most completely furnished with sofas and deep arm-chairs and a piano carrying silver-framed photos of a Governor and his lady and of the children at home—perhaps a tinted photo of the girl with her yellow ringlets taken just before the end of last leave, when she had been left with her grandmother or of the boy in his Eton collar and new suit for his preparatory school. In rooms like these guests gathered for dinner night after night, the ladies moving their pink or white ostrich fans and agreeing that it was stuffy this evening or exclaiming at their hostess's dahlias (" You must have a very clever gardener ? "—" Yes, I took him over from Lady Smith. She trained her servants very well, oh a real *sukht burra mem* ") or exchanging hasty tit-bits of *gup* (as gossip was called) while the brass ornament on the mantelpiece and on the numerous gate-legged occasional tables glittered from recent polishing and a faint, faint odour of disinfectant (" those mosquitoes ! ") hung about the corners of the room.

Then the butler, a wrinkled veteran (" been with us for years, knows all my husband's little ways ") wearing a sash and turban-band of regimental, or other service colours, padded in and announced dinner. Forming up by twos in strictest precedence they went slowly, between bead curtains held apart by servants, into the dining-room. The ladies' high-heeled shoes and the patent-leather pumps of the gentlemen made no sound on the thick red carpet (made in the local jail). The senior guests sailed straight to their inevitable places near one or the other end of the table but the more junior hunted about for their name cards that indicated their places (calculated with some care and after frequent consultations of the *Green Book* or Civil List) about the centre of the table. Behind each chair a servant (for the guests would generally bring their butlers with them) helped the diners to be seated and the stiff folds of the heavy white tablecloth rasped faintly as knees jerked forward under the table. If the mosquitoes were very bad, guests might be equipped with mosquito-boots, but ordinarily a light burning beneath the table was sufficient to discourage the brutes. The table-surface was patterned with ropes of flowers which wound between the Indian-silver fretwork-designed dishes of Marzipan, toffee fudge and chocolate creams. In the centre would be a great rose-bowl. Flower-scent hung heavy on the warm evening and blended oddly with the lavender-water of the ladies and the hairwash of the gentlemen. On the walls tigers' heads snarled, the dim figures of a polo team (topi held stiffly against the thigh, a thick unlighted cigarette clipped nonchalantly between the first and second finger) peered out from the heavy blackwood frame. On the mausoleum-like sideboard glimmered silver toast-racks, boiled-egg sets, wedding presents of monumental size, and modest trophies of golf and tennis tournaments. The lamps in their great globes shone on stiff and crackling shirt-fronts with one or two plain gold studs and on white shoulders and lace and velvet dresses. Dresses that the wearers all swore came from England (the senior ladies often felt bound to change, with advancing dignity, to Paris) but were generally made by a bazaar tailor. And nowadays what pains were taken to conceal this ! The tailor had to do his work in the bungalow (for if he was allowed to take away one's material and pattern-book one's friends or their ayahs, in neighbouring bungalows might notice) and in a side-room concealed by a screen in case an unexpected caller chanced upon the plebeian secret.

The long, frayed rope, emerging limply from an iron-rimmed hole far up the wall, now drew taut with a sudden jerk. The punkah moved slowly over the table. In silent procession the servants entered with the soup. These " double khanas ", as dinner-parties were known, taxed the originality of hostesses. There had to be an almost endless array of courses, and it was difficult to think of new dishes. The cook was of little help in this, for he was inevitably a Goanese who had learned his art from a cousin employed in the kitchen of a Bombay hotel, and had few ideas of his own. If you left him to himself you could be certain that the menu would be clear soup, cold pomfret, mutton cutlets with tomato sauce from a bottle, roast chicken, caramel custard and craigie toast. And even if you gave him a menu of your own you had to be very careful that one or other of the cook's own dishes (which gave him so little trouble) did not turn up in place of your suggestion for a course. The cook would generally get the cooks of some of the other guests to help him in his arduous task of preparing a " double khana " and the blame for the regrettable appearance of caramel custard could be laid on one of the other cooks, laid most convincingly with tears and imprecations and references to several Saints who would bear out his tale. The only way to control his flood of falsehood was to threaten to report him to his priest ; for it was assumed that a Roman Catholic priest, and especially a black one, would welcome information about the misdeeds of one of his flock so that he might put a little more pressure on him financially.

So that it was with a sigh of relief that the conscientious hostess noticed that the courses succeeded each other in accordance with her instructions and that the guests seemed to be enjoying the roast duck with the stuffing and apple sauce and roast potato and two kinds of greens.

Conversation was intimate and friendly. They knew everything about each other, their incomes, their hobbies and interests, how much they paid their servants and all the details of the gossip retailed behind the back of every member of that small and closely linked society. Business men up from Bombay for a visit discussed the chances at the Governor's Cup Race-meeting ; or congratulated residents in Poona on their luck in having so pleasant a climate. In Bombay, after a month or two of rain, one was tortured by prickly heat. Did anyone know of a cure for that nuisance ? No, I've tried that. It's as useless as any other nostrum. The thing is incurable. As *Momos* amusingly wrote in the *Times of India* :

In the symptomatic stage, savage warfare did I wage
'Gainst a trifling erubescence on the arm,
For I scratched it night and day, till I heard some idiot say,
That a little iodine would do no harm.
When it spread to hip and shoulder, then I grew a little bolder,
And agreed with all the experts at the club,
That germicidal soap was the only certain hope,
Used gently in the matutinal tub.
But each day I'm getting worse, (which explains this scratchy verse)
So my own advice I'll sell you for a song,
Every nincompoop you meet, has a cure for prickly heat,
And every single one of them is wrong.

So the only thing to do was to come up to the cooler air of Poona for a change ; but one did not look forward to the return to offices in the Fort. Everyone in Poona had some sort of nickname or pet name ; and the idiosyncrasies or mannerisms of other members of the Gymkhana offered a pleasant topic and an opportunity for little stories and jokes. If there were officials among the guests they would talk a certain amount of shop. What on earth did old Tubby get a C.S.I. for in the Birthday Honours ? And when was Jimmy going on leave ? He had hung on to that post far too long and someone else ought to have a shot at it. The ladies were as interested in the shop as the men and they knew all the nicknames of their husbands' colleagues and discussed as eagerly as anyone the chances of an " act " next hot weather when So-and-so went on leave. But though they might know all the men's nicknames the ladies seldom addressed any gentleman except with a formal Mr. even if he were a friend of twenty years' standing ; and the gentlemen were equally formal to their friends' wives. Two ladies who were devoted friends would greet each other with the greatest affection but address each other as Mrs. ——.

They formed a happy united community. The future seemed very sure. Promotion came slowly, but it came regularly. There had been everywhere an increasing prosperity since the turn of the century. The currency troubles and famines of the previous century were almost forgotten. Industry was flourishing and the scale of living in Bombay was steadily rising. The subversive movement seemed to have been brought under control. It was true that there had been that lamentable attack on the Viceroy as he entered Delhi on an elephant but fortunately His Excellency had been spared. He had acted with great courage and consideration. There was even a story (alas, apocryphal) that His Excellency's first words after the shock of the explosion were " Save the elephant ! "

And so in great contentment the diners went slowly through the many courses and sipped their champagne (which was the only appropriate wine for a dinner-party). And after dinner there would be " music " ; a few serious songs by the lady who had brought her music with her and a comic song by the major who had a fine baritone. Or else there would be guessing games and competitions. An hour or so after dinner the butler brought round whisky-and-soda and then it was time to go, though no one could move under any circumstances until the Senior Lady present " made the first move ", as it was called. In the garden, as one drove away, the passion-flowers smelt very sweet. In the distance one could just see the red light burning over Government House, which showed that His Excellency was in residence.

A faint and murky glow came from the direction of the teeming city, the Native Quarter, but that stirred little interest in the departing sleepy guests. Few of them had ever driven through the streets of the city. They were narrow and dusty with probably many disease-germs and there would be an occasional act of disloyalty (though the ladies who returned home excitedly to say they had been " spat at " were usually flattering themselves, having misinterpreted the casual and regular expectorations of the bazaar dwellers). For one's shopping one would sometimes visit East Street or Main Street which ran along one side of the city, straight and dusty roads where Eurasian boys practised bicycling, Parsi shopkeepers gossiped in shirt-sleeves and bored unhappy Tommies trudged up and down in pairs, uncomfortable in their high-buttoned tunics and seldom with enough money for beer. The Tommies would stop for a moment outside a fancy-goods shop (called Cheap Jack's) and, tapping their canes against their legs, stare at the sets of gents' studs, the cheap watches, the children's buckets and spades and the green-lustre vases with pink china rose sprouting from one side and " A Present from Poona " inscribed between two loveknots. Such a vase they would buy one day, they would decide, and send home to Mother or to Mabel (to whom it was so difficult to write in the barracks with the precious stamp one had remembered to buy at the canteen curling up in the heat and other fellows rocking the trestle-table) ; but when payday came the temptation was too great ; and they would stroll without enthusiasm into Mr. Pinto's Billiard Saloon and order a beer, a warm pale tasteless bottled beer, to drink at a froth-bedewed marble-topped table in a corner beside a declining palm, between shelves piled with cheap ping-pong outfits, gym-shoes and bottles of melting acid-drops ; to drink in lonely gloom while Indian purchasers of whangee canes or spotted made-up ties glanced doubtfully at the two representatives of a " brutal and licentious soldiery ". Another beer ; for there was little else to do. Their predecessors in the eighteenth century had found some happiness in irregular unions with native girls. But official morality had changed considerably since then. " Sweat the sex out of you " was the watchword as more and yet more games of football were arranged through the long hot weather ; all parts of the town supposed to harbour " undesirable women " were out of bounds and their approaches patrolled ; the mounting statistics of disease were countered with renewed encouragements to " restraint " and stricter regulations of leave. So that the soldier who had somehow failed to find emotional satisfaction in longer drill and more football, was driven to a whispered bargaining with a tonga-driver for a " four-anna-walla " and an assignment in a ditch.

Beyond East Street and Main Street was the real city, humming with an intense and secret life of its own. Occasionally it overflowed at the great festivals. The Moharrum of the Muhammadans when one's servants begged for leave and then reappeared almost naked, daubed with streaks of black and yellow and sporting a tail of silver paper and one had to simulate a patronising amusement and hand over bakshish—and then on the last evening of the feast the great *tazias* would be dragged through the streets and pushed into the river near the judge's bungalow. The judge would give a tea-party so that his guests could enjoy the quaint sight. The ladies sat about on the lawn looking cool in their flowered muslin and gentlemen gathered near the buffet for a chota peg, while with yells of excitement the flimsy towers, hung with streamers of coloured paper, were toppled over the bridge by bands of black-turbaned devotees ; and they fell with a dull splash and the cardboard crenellations crumpled limply and the swift water bore away the flags and tinselled banners. And then there was Ganesh Chaturthi when Hindus took images of the Elephant-God in procession and ayahs presented the children with little elephant-idols to play with—though this was discouraged in the stricter houses as such heathen customs might disturb the child's Christianity. And Dasara when the servants would paint the tails of one's horses saffron, and one's dogs too, and for this tiresome trick expect more bakshish. And later Diwali when the Native Quarter really looked rather pretty with all the coloured lights.

After the rains it grew hot again in Poona for a few weeks. It would be necessary to run up to Mahableshwar where, in October, the wild flowers were at their loveliest and the

AN INDIAN CADET—MARCHING TO JOIN HIS STATION IN PATRIARCHAL STYLE

air fresh and delightful after the monsoon. But it was in May that Mahableshwar was most crowded; for then Poona was almost unbearably hot and it was difficult to play games or take any exercise in comfort, while in Mahableshwar one could play golf all day. There were other contrasts too, which were neatly expressed by *Momos*:

The Ladies of Mahableshwar
  Have strawberries for tea,
And as for cream and sugar
  They add them lavishly;
But Poona! oh, in Poona,
  Their hearts are like to break
For while the butter's melting
  The flies eat up the cake.

The Ladies of Mahableshwar
  In wraps and furs delight,
And often get pneumonia
  'Neath blankets two at night;
But Poona! oh, in Poona,
  The gauziest wisps appal,
And ladies sleep (they tell me)
  With nothing on at all.

The Ladies of Mahableshwar
  In such sweet charms abound
That doctors say their livers
  Are marvellously sound;
But Poona! oh, in Poona,
  They scold and nag all day,
And contradict their husbands
  Until they fade away.

A sufficiently dramatic contrast. But in days before motors the journey was as tiresome as all Indian journeys. By train as far as Wathar; in the hot weather an exhausting experience. The food in the restaurant-car (if there was one) seldom inspired confidence, so that it was necessary to take all one's food with one, and if a child were travelling too, a goat would be tied in the guard's van and an orderly would hurry off to milk it when the train stopped at some station in the evening. If the train stopped for some time the child would be carried out of the stifling carriage (for the windows had to be shuttered tight against the hot dust-laden wind that blew in sudden gusts), its camp-cot erected on the platform with mosquito net on four bamboo supports, while the Indian passengers gathered round wonderingly, careful not to express any admiration for the child they might feel, for fear of the evil eye. At the foot of the hills there followed a long and slow ascent in carriage, cart or tonga. A steep climb and a steady thrashing of the horses got on the nerves of the more sensitive travellers who would complain to the Government. Government would then issue an order directing that horses should be less cruelly flogged on the ascent. This would lead to a strike of the carriage-owners (mostly Parsis) who refused to run carriages up to Mahableshwar if they were to be hampered and harassed like this, and the order would be allowed to lapse. The road wound round the curve of the ghat until the jagged hills of the Deccan faded into the mist of summer afternoon. As the carriage turned the corner of the ghat towards Panchgani the wind came cool and sweet over the high plateau. The horses were changed here and as the travellers rested under the whispering casuarinas and admired the "neat cottages and villas studded about" which so reminded Colonel Larking of England, hawkers clustered round them trying to sell them young parrots, bunches of wild flowers or home-woven basket-chairs. Presently they set out once more. The road wound slowly over the plateau, the wheels ran muffled through thick red dust, and gradually the trees closed in and the evening was loud with the calls of hill-birds, and they would agree with the enthusiastic panegyrist Mr. K. S. Dastur, who wrote in his *Guide to Mahableshwar*—

> No visitor arriving in this delightful hill-station can fail to be charmed by the foliage and verdure of the trees and the sweet songs of the birds. The trees are of all kinds and there is no space to name them here. Of the notable birds there is the Black Bird, a whistling bird, and the Thrush which has fine tone. Owing, however, to the thick foliage of the above mentioned trees the birds cannot be seen, so it is not necessary to name them.

As they approached Mahableshwar they saw the famous strawberry beds on the left and on the right the lake where the children would be sent with their ayahs to sail their boats and play at fishing.

Most of the servants would have been sent ahead to arrange about the tents and to unpack. For bungalows were scarce and expensive (except for senior officials who could reserve one of the Government bungalows) and hotels were in those days regarded with horror by most Anglo-Indians. And justifiably ; for there were not many European travellers (except the tourists who visited half a dozen northern cities and no one cared how they were housed) who could not stay with friends or at clubs. So that even hotels which were inaugurated with a flourish of advertisement as Up-to-date and Under Entirely European Management, soon declined into seedy disrepair ; the discouraged proprietor shuffled about the dusty sitting-room in shirt-sleeves and bedroom slippers, adjusting here the artificial flowers in a china vase and arranging there a Union Jack-patterned cushion to cover the rusty spring which had worked its way through the faded chintz of the sofa ; and in the bedrooms, where mosquito curtains hung in tatters and a flock-oozing mattress was piled against the wall, unpaid servants squatted over a game of dice.

So if one could not reserve a bungalow the best thing to do was, as in most places in India, to live in tents. In

Poona one would pitch one's tents in a friend's garden; but here one applied to the Superintendent for a plot in the jungle. Snakes and panthers were apt to be a nuisance; but they generally went for the servants or the goats first. With basket-chairs and camp furniture one could make the tents very homely; and to keep away the eyeflies one would burn sticks of insect-incense in vases. It was delicious in the evenings to sit outside the tents. A soft mist crept up from the valley. Thrushes and blackbirds sang. Gentlemen lay back full length in basket-chairs, lit cigars and called for chota pegs. Ladies sipped lemonade and looked forward to a Strawberry Tea at the Club on Friday. In addition to the attractions of the climate and the strawberries there were the wonderful views. Every afternoon the roads, carpeted with red dust and winding between the stunted, enamel-green trees, were filled with carriages taking groups of picnickers to one or other of the "Points" from which one gazed over the jagged hills of the Konkan, half veiled in a steely haze, and caught in the distance the rare flash of the sea. And on the golf-links people discussed the hazard of the Chinamen's Graveyard (a cemetery for Chinese coolies who having been employed in this upland Eden were so eccentric as to sicken rapidly and die) whose notorious difficulty was such that players often wondered with the poet *Senex* whether

> Some subtle spell, exhaling
> Out of their depths, some charm of old Cathay,
> Unstrings the wrist and sets the eyesight failing,
> Just when you think you've got her well away.

And in the red Gothic Club building with its high roof of corrugated iron they would be discussing to-morrow's Badminton Breakfast, a favourite entertainment of pre-war days, at which to refresh the wearied players the servants would hand round barley-water and bacon sandwiches and slices of cut cake. They sat in little groups round the square tables, upon each table was a red and white check tablecloth and, exactly in the centre, a brass bell to summon servants, having on one side an ashtray and on the other a brass match-box holder. Most of the club members had come up from Bombay or Poona, but a few came from farther afield and Colonel Larking, after the shooting expedition in the Nizam's territory which he described in *Bandobast and Khabar*, visited Mahableshwar and was pleased to find that " being the headquarters of the Governor and Commander-in-Chief of Bombay during the hot season, society is a little more sacred, and is, therefore, not such a hotbed of cancans and gossip as the smaller hill stations ". Occasional gossip and scandal there might be, but not on the scale suggested by cynical Mr. Kipling.

> Jack's own Jill goes up the hill,
> To Murree or Chakrata ;
> Jack remains, and dies in the plains,
> And Jill remarries soon after.

And even when there was material for gossip it was important to remember that, as Miss Maud Diver pointed out, " the grass widow in the Hills had pitfalls to contend with ; and perhaps the two most insidious are amateur theatricals and the military man on leave ".

CHAPTER X

THE Great War at first hardly affected the world of Anglo-India, and business as usual remained the prevailing principle throughout its course. For one thing Anglo-Indians had always lived in an atmosphere of greater familiarity with things military than people in England; and to the majority of Anglo-Indians who never went on leave during the war its gravity and the privations of the civilian populations of Europe were hardly imaginable. The papers continued to print optimistic reports of the military operations and sanguine forecasts. So that at first the only sentiments were of pleasurable excitement. The Germans were not unpopular with Anglo-Indians. Indeed, some were never tired of extolling their achievements in their African colonies. But there had been stories of German ambitions in the East and the activities of German agents in the Persian Gulf were not reassuring. Business circles were jealous of German commercial penetration. And the official world had been revolted by the behaviour of the German Heir-Apparent during his regrettable visit to India, during which he was always unpunctual, although punctuality is said to be the politeness of princes. (On the other hand most Indians remained admirers of the Germans throughout the war, Hindus imagining that all Germans were profound Sanskrit scholars like Professor Muller, and Muhammadans remembering with gratitude Germany's help on previous occasions to the Commander of the Faithful and believing in the frequent German expressions of sympathy with the Islamic world.)

It was an exciting moment when the Indian troops sailed for France and dear Sir Pertab Singh (about whose quaint misuse of English so many stories had gone round the clubs) insisted on going with them. The response of Indian Princes was more than gratifying. Almost every day one read of a loyal speech by some ruler, offering his State Army for active service or funds for an aeroplane. From the English Press one learned that the Gurkhas had absolutely terrified the Germans, who were quite unmanned by the way the little Nepalese would crawl over to their trenches at night and attack them with kukris.

Gradually, however, it became apparent that the war would last some little time ; and the unfortunate campaign of General Townshend gave rise for the first time to alarm and despondency. It was no longer an affair of a few battles in Europe. Ladies formed knitting groups and gentlemen enlisted in the Volunteers and spent their Sundays marching about in military formation. The parades of the Volunteers were, it was felt, certain to impress Indians with a revelation of the firm resolution of the European community. Actually they had the contrary effect and Indians felt convinced that the war must now be lost, otherwise why should highly paid merchants and officials voluntarily undergo such discomfort, just as if they were ordinary privates who had no other alternative?

1917 brought the collapse of Russia and new menaces on north and west, the pronouncement of August 20 in the House of Commons, and in November Mr. Montagu's six-months-long perambulation of India.

Leave was now almost impossible to obtain ; and the reports brought by those who returned from leave did not make one repine for a visit to war-time England. The joy of new arrivals from England to find that there were no food-restrictions in Bombay and the eager appetite with which they settled down to " a pre-war breakfast " at the Yacht Club were as pathetic as they were strange. Nor was it only the discomfort of life in England which made leave a doubtful pleasure; the voyage was dangerous. Until the boat reached Port Said passengers from England had to wear life-belts all day and sleep in their clothes at night. Religious services were frequent and well attended. My father relates that a Frenchman, travelling to India on a P. & O., was deeply impressed by the " *sens religieux des Anglais* ". After Port Said, however, life-belts were laid aside and, now that there was no fear of submarines, the services were hardly attended by anyone. On the other hand my father's French acquaintance was more than ever impressed, but this time by the " *sens pratique des Anglais* ".

A faint sense of excitement came to the parties gathered on the Yacht Club lawn each evening, on the terrace overlooking the harbour, to notice that even the P. & O. ships (" such a conservative line, too ") had gone in for this camouflage. But, as the gentlemen remarked, tilting the straw hats over their eyes to protect them from the glare of the setting sun, the camouflage didn't make the ships any harder to see. On the contrary, all those stripes and spots drew one's attention to the ship. Of course, one couldn't tell how it looked through a periscope. But the P. & O. were apt to be very dull and stupid, so perhaps they had used the wrong camouflage. In any case, it brought the reality of danger on the high seas very vividly home to one, and increased a natural disinclination for needless risk.

In consequence, when people wanted a holiday they would go to one or other of the Indian hill-stations or to the increasingly popular Kashmir. Formerly a visit to Kashmir was almost an adventurous undertaking and Lord Baden-Powell relates that he would grant two or three months' leave to young subalterns who wanted to go to Kashmir, and only one month to those who were so unenterprising as to spend their leave in Simla, where they would only waste their time and energy at parties and dances instead of pursuing more healthy activities. Climbing and fishing have continued to be the main resources of Kashmir. On the banks of upland streams pipe-smoking fishermen with slow anticipatory relish select a fly for their next cast. Weather-beaten matrons in green-leather hats and brown-leather jerkins stride briskly down the winding hill-paths. On the door-post of a chaletesque chapel are notices of a Men's Friendly next Sunday afternoon. The chaplain in old school blazer chats genially with a group of Punjabi scouts in khaki shorts and gay turbans, while in the Scouts' camp a young Sikh bugler practises (with a continual menace of quarter-tones) " Come to the cook-house door, boys ". Intellectual majors (fond of referring to " ordinary Army people who aren't interested in Things of the Mind ") lean on alpenstock or rest on shooting-stick and explain " Jove, it's just like Sicily " ; the other majors are reminded of Scotland or Switzerland. And bespectacled missionaries hop off their bicycles and remark with pleasure that in this delightful land even the old Hindu temples have the air of an English parish church of the 'forties ; for so prescient of English taste were those architects of the eighth and ninth centuries that they constructed their shrines with pointed or romanesque arches and trefoil windows and tall sloping roofs, all of the most sedate grey stone, so that coming upon such a shrine in the shadow of pines and fir-trees it is almost shocking to perceive, blatant among so much spinsterish restraint, a marble phallus of Shiva, in the central nave.

But these wilder pleasure-grounds were not the only attractions that a rapidly progressing Kashmir had to offer Anglo-Indians on holiday. An admirable hotel in Srinagar with comfortable bedrooms, and in the lounge probably more paintings of ducks than any other room in the world. House-boats with cushioned chairs, geraniums in pots and chintz curtains which had to remain drawn most of the day to shut out the importunate hawkers who drifted round the canals in their narrow boats offering for sale at each house-boat papier-maché hair-tidies and cigarette cases inlaid with regimental crests. Shops embowered in roses like a painting on a Christmas gift blotter. A jewellery shop whose half-caste owner was a noted palmist and astrologer who held séances in an inner room (it was indeed surprising the number of people who consulted him, their voices drifting through into the outer shop, " You say my Leo influence means too many rich meals, well I've always been fond of good nourishing food . . . but my bad feet you put down to Piscis ? You suggest I should wear more red stones to strengthen my Sagittarius influence, well that does look a very pretty brooch I must say . . ."). An Amateur Dramatic Company whose productions were so good that even temporary visitors were anxious for a part in the next rehearsals (" I've always been fond of acting, though I haven't had much experience except in a performance of ' Aladdin ' we got up in Malta for charity. I was a slave, you know, not a big part, but the make-up was difficult. I had to oil myself all over. Oh, I was much complimented."). Both at Srinagar and Gulmarg admirable golf-courses. And everywhere landscapes of a singular beauty ; the clear blue lakes fed by mountain streams ;

the enormous poplars, the irises in spring and maples in autumn ; sunset on the mountain bastions, the foothills a smoky brown like uncut topaz and the carved white peaks against the paling sky. . . .

CHAPTER XI

IF few Indian cities were profoundly affected by the war, to Karachi it was the beginning of a new era of progress and development. This pŏrt had had little history before the British conquests. Historians dispute whether or not Nearchus, Alexander's admiral, set sail from there on the return to Babylon, but it seems that in early times the chief port for the Indus Delta was Debalbunder, some distance to the east. In the eighteenth century Karachi was the port from which Baluchi and Afghan mercenaries set out in coasting steamers to hire their swords to Hindu princes of Kathiawar. Another profitable export was that of sharkfins and maws for the China market. The principal Hindu banker for the town, Seth Naomal, had been in youth forcibly circumcised by Muslim fanatics and, like many other Hindu malcontents, anxious for British intervention. His services in assisting the invaders were rewarded by the grant of a C.S.I.

Napier, the conqueror, was from the beginning enthusiastic over Karachi's future. "You will be the glory of the East," he exclaimed, "would that I could come again to see you, Kurrachee, in your grandeur!" But for many years it seemed that this prophecy was as unlikely to be fulfilled as so many others uttered by the magniloquent Napier. It was a remote province, administered by a few able but often notably eccentric men. The name of Tyrrhuit (with the inevitable addition of Badshah or king) is still remembered with both awe and amusement in Lower Sind. One hot weather, feeling bored alone in his headquarters at Kotri he sent his acquaintances in Karachi wires announcing his own death. The European community dug out from tinlined boxes black coats and striped trousers and journeyed in great discomfort to Kotri. They were shown the coffin with the corpse in it, and were discussing the virtues of the dead man with the charity usual on such occasions when suddenly the corpse sat up, the door to the dining-room was opened and there was the table laid for lunch surrounded by crates of champagne. On the Upper Sind Frontier the saga of General John Jacob continues to grow, and the extraordinary clock which he made is still the wonder of visitors to Jacobabad. Even in Karachi a certain eccentricity was not uncommon and General Nicholson won bets by crossing Mangho Pir hopping from the back of one crocodile to another till he reached the farther bank. His name, however, is long forgotten, but his wife was to become one of the most popular poets of her time. She wrote under the name of Lawrence Hope ; and tastefully-bound copies of *The Garden of Kama* may be seen in most Indian bookshops or chemists' to-day. She came of a gifted family, for her father was Colonel Cory, the then editor of the *Sind Gazette* and her younger sister was to win fame as Victoria Cross, the novelist. Miss Cross spent her earlier years helping her father who as editor of the only English paper that Karachi boasted had to work hard to supply his small clientèle with news. It can hardly have been from Karachi that the Misses Cory drew information for their romantic writings ; for in their youth it was a dreary place. Steamers from Bombay anchored a mile off-shore and passengers had to climb down into a wide-bottomed sailing boat where they were jostled by negro coolies and dingy Arabs and their luggage was trodden over by the stumbling heavily-veiled

Muslim women and wetted by the green slime of the boards. This boat only took you as far as Manora, and thereafter you had to drive in a horse-carriage to Karachi. The horse went very slowly in the heat, and the springless seats smelt of bugs and human sweat. On the right stretched black mud and seaweed to the distant line of the sea, and on the left a few corrugated-iron sheds broke the monotony of desert. In Karachi the roads were wide and straight and there were a few fine bungalows, but gardens were almost impossible. The soil was sand and if you dug deep a saltish damp oozed up, destroying all plant roots. All you could hope for was a few palms, casuarinas and oleanders. All around was the desert and when the land wind blew the fine white sand banked up against the walls of the bungalows and seemed to fill everything, beds, drinking water, clothes. In the evenings if you went for a stroll you soon came to the end of the town, and there was the sun setting on the grey marshes and the barren outlines of the Baluch hills. There was a church of light yellow stone, and a low-roofed hotel called "Reynold's" with a shelf of bottled beer and a clutter of old newspapers on the ricketty basket-chairs. The Empress Market "a very handsome building . . . in the domestic Gothic style" was opened in 1889. And when the Frere Hall was handed over to the Municipality it was suggested that "the desolate and unsightly appearance of the compound was a reproach to them and so they decided to do something to improve it. To effect this the milk-bush hedge has been uprooted, and stone posts and chains substituted. A new cast-iron Band Stand has also been erected." And there was the Sind Club of which the following description was written in 1890 [1]:

[1] A. F. Baillie's *Kurrachee.*

> The clubhouse is extremely well adapted to its purpose. The verandahs and large entrance hall are cool and comfortable, and the dining-room upstairs is a very handsome apartment. The members are exceedingly hospitable and any traveller properly introduced is at once admitted an honorary member, and permitted to pay a subscription for the period that he remains, which allows him greater freedom than if he was simply a free guest. They " swear " by their whisky, but I might venture to remark . . . that by constantly using the same spirit without any change, the palate loses to a great extent its power of appreciation . . . I have heard that ladies have recently been admitted as members and their more refined taste will have had its effect on the description and quality of the beverages consumed.

The progress of Karachi was inevitable, but for years the progress was slow. There were no roads at all outside the town, and proposals for road-making were turned down by the authorities on the ground that roads discouraged young Englishmen from riding. There was no direct rail connection with Delhi or Calcutta, and the line to Bombay had to run through Jodhpur (with changes at Marwar and Ahmedabad) because the more southerly route proposed would have passed through the territories of the Maharao of Kutch who was a very religious ruler disapproving of railways as much as of Bovril. Up to the war Karachi was considered a pleasant station with an enviable climate, but dull and backward compared to many other places.

The campaign in Iraq brought immense profit to Karachi contractors and with the rise in prices the whole hinterland flourished, remote Baluch notables bought motor-cars and invested money in Karachi banks (one such intending depositor was so enchanted with his first experience of a lift that he spent all day going up and down in it, and returned to his village without remembering to visit the bank). Everyone in Karachi seemed to have money. There was a temporary restraint while the war lasted, and as a measure of economy the Commissioner offered his guests at dinner-parties home-made champagne which his cook had distilled from Quetta grapes. The local Volunteers were well supported and a detachment kept guard at the harbour (members of the detachments would in after-years irritate members of the 1914 Dinner Club who had been exchanging stories of Mons or Ypres, by retailing their own war experiences, the discomforts of a " shake-down " in the Customs Building and the way the harbour searchlights kept waking one up). The war ended, but prosperity continued. New houses and new quarters rose everywhere and the suburbs of Karachi sprawled clumsily over the desert. Champagne, real champagne, reappeared on the tables. There were *dîners dansants* every night at the Carlton Hotel, opposite the station, and on warm evenings the dancers sat in the narrow garden where folding chairs were ranged round bamboo tables. There were picnics every holiday at Manora with hampers from Cumper's Café and in the evenings numbers of new American cars gathered at Clifton (which was already referred to by local patriots as " The Brighton of Karachi ") where a pier had been built, jutting out from the sandhills and, though not reaching as far as the water, affording a view over the sands and the sea, both a little grey with coal-dust from the harbour. There were breakfast and supper parties at the Boat Club, a tall, timbered building rising from the mud flats between Karachi and the port, with a terrace where one breakfasted on excellent cold-storage sausages and watched in an inlet of the sea below the evolutions of the swimming parties and, towards the opposite bank, native herdsmen washing their camels, and there was the Golf Club and the County Club and the Gymkhana and the Karachi Club (but this was mainly for Indians who were

RETURNING HOME FROM A HOG HUNT

not, and I think still are not, admitted to the other clubs) and the Sind Club, all flourishing in the post-war boom. The 1921 slump was a set-back, and several merchants suffered severely, but a sober optimism prevailed and everyone looked forward to the day when Karachi would eclipse Bombay. The authorities were going at last to build the Sukkur Barrage, a far greater undertaking than the Assouan Dam, the barrage that was going to change Sind from a desert into the Garden of India, a great granary, a wealthy province instead of a neglected division of Bombay.

The first aeroplane from England had been announced. There was a whole holiday declared and crowds watched the faint speck over the purple hills of Las Bela grow to the size of a bird, circle in the dry and glittering desert air, and come to rest on the level sweep of sand.

It was the herald of the new town that was to grow up, Drigh Road the air-port, with its neat little bungalows, and mess buildings (R.A.F. Mess and Imperial Airways Mess, too), refreshment room with aircraftsmen, including for a time "Aircraftsman Shaw", regaling his mates, of an evening, with gramophone recitals of Wagner and Beethoven at afternoon tea, factories and workshops, and the great ten-mile road to Karachi with military lorries painted khaki thundering past the huge and cavernous hangar built there in a lonely stretch of sand to house the R101.

Though local patriots were quick to seize on the phrase "Air-Port of India" it was some years before air-travel brought many passengers to Karachi. Even when the regular air-service was started the tired official or business-man who required of his leave, above all things, a preliminary rest and his wife who looked forward to the dancing and deck sports (as I recently heard a lady say " The only way to travel is by British liners, because of the lovely organised games ") and the trip ashore at Port Said for bargains in Chinese shawls and amber necklaces found no attraction in the idea of air-travel. Moreover, after the first rush and confusion of the post-war years the P. & O. began to build some luxurious (and even quick) liners. They were furnished on modern, but not too modern, lines and the décor, quiet (unlike the flashy Italian ships of which a lady said, " nothing but floating night-clubs I call them ") and essentially British, was reassuringly like that of an hotel at a seaside resort which did not encourage trippers ; the dark Tudor lounge with its scalloped Ionic columns and huge arm-chairs, the Renaissance dining-room where one could be sure of bacon and eggs and grilled steak even in the Red Sea, and the Louis Quinze music-room where the ladies played mahjongg and bridge and sipped gimlets or chose a book from the five-shelf library (no nonsense about what ought to be bought, but just the familiar array that one would find at a W. H. Smith & Son's branch, a Naomi Jacob, Beverley Nichols, Donn Byrne and, for the broad-minded, Mary Borden) and where in the evenings they sometimes had concerts, a steward at the little yellow upright piano, another steward with a fiddle and a planter from among the passengers who could play the ukelele. There was also a new rival to air-travel in the overland route by train (or car) through Iraq and Turkey, and this had for its advocate Colonel Cory's successor at the *Gazette*, a brilliant business-man (" the Thruster " he once described himself) who was an ardent apostle of dress-reform among Anglo-Indians and surprised those who had known him formerly as sternly insisting on a stiff collar in the hottest weather by appearing on formal occasions, dressed in white trousers, a patent belt and a middy blouse.

But the institution of the air-mail and the constant passage through India of notable flying figures were an advertisement and encouragement to air-passengers. They gathered in the early hours in the hall of Karachi's new hotel (a fine building, with dome and façade of caryatids and panelled dining-room) and filed into the bus that was to take them to the landing ground and the aeroplane gleaming through the dawn-murk. And then the long, inhospitable shores of Baluchistan ; the Cathedral Rock ; the walled fortress of Sharjah where it was pleasant to find in the waiting-room, guarded by Arab soldiers with chased-silver daggers, copies of the *Sketch*, the *Autocar*, and the *Indian State Railways Magazine* ; the frequent meals, cold-storage sausages after Karachi and afterwards tinned sausages, roast turkey at Bahrein and Basrah ; bridge at the narrow little tables or a book from the library shelf ; the Jordan, Jerusalem (" that's the Mount of Olives " as the informative passenger would know), Alexandria, Athens (" those are the ruins on the hill ") and at Brindisi the pale blue coach, pleasant anticipations of a long night, and reflections on the speed of modern travel that made the terrace of the Karachi gymkhana and the Long Bar of the Trocadero only a few days apart.

CHAPTER XII

ARMISTICE DAY became known in Calcutta as Black Friday. People had on the whole enjoyed the war; the Volunteers' parades, the excitement, and above all, the large fortunes made in jute. These fortunes continued to be made till the early 'twenties but on a decreasing scale. Moreover, the end of the war meant that numbers of young men arrived out as new recruits to the big firms, and their manners and slang and reluctance to wear starched collars in the hot weather deeply disturbed the seniors. "Unstable" was an adjective used several times a day when the elderly gathered together in the clubs for pre-lunch drinks and discussed the juniors in their firms. Just because they had been through the war these young men seemed to consider they had a right to behave differently from their elders and betters and to flout all the traditions of Calcutta society; one always seemed to be having them "on the mat" and telling them that a member of an old-established firm, which prided itself on employing Gentlemen, should learn how to hold his drink (which meant the amiable torpor consequent on a traditionally vast dinner and a succession of dark sherries, madeiras, ports and brandies) and not be heard laughing loudly in the hall of a club or making indecorous remarks in a cinematograph theatre. It was distressing, too, the way the younger men were always in search of novelty and excitement. They did not seem satisfied with the grand old clubs of Calcutta which as everyone knew were the best in India. There was the Saturday Club where one could listen to forty Goanese bandsmen dressed up like Central European ringmasters at work on "Pagliacci" or "In a Monastery Garden", and every Friday night there was a formal ball where you were certain to meet all the other senior people in Calcutta. And on other days of the week there would be dinner-parties at one or other of the great houses. What more could you want?

But in 1918 Firpo's Restaurant was opened and was at once a success. There was a jazz band; the furniture was in the P. & O. Louis Quinze style; and the place was lit in what was considered a very advanced manner. Even some of the seniors succumbed to the lure of this Continental-looking place and entertained their friends to dinner there instead of in their own huge Georgian houses; and this would have seemed, a few years before, a practice subversive of the whole tradition of Anglo-Indian hospitality. There were sporadic attempts to open a cabaret at Firpo's but for ten years the police imposed a ban, to the relief of most of the influential Anglo-Indians who heard with concern of the state of undress permitted to performers in London cabarets and considered that the effect on the Indian public of the spectacle of European girls as professional dancers in a public restaurant would be unfortunate.

There were other changes to perplex the older residents. The old-fashioned houses were becoming too expensive to run. Servants' wages had gone up (for which the military were blamed, especially the "temporary officers who had only come to India for a short visit and weren't accustomed to having servants and so spoilt them and overpaid them"). People were more concerned to have electric fans and running water than a noble façade or a grand situation. Flats became fashionable; and the juniors clattering up and down the long stone staircases to each other's rooms or calling to each other out of the windows seemed generations removed from the traditional Anglo-Indian dwelling in dignified seclusion.

Cars came into fashion slowly. Business-men and brokers went sedately to their offices in the traditional *jaun*, a gloomy box-shaped horse-carriage, till the middle 'twenties.

Towards the end of the 'twenties there was a rage for cocktail parties which the juniors found to be so much more economical than formal dinners, and even if the seniors peered suspiciously into their glasses and talked darkly about American habits and poison and probable effects on the liver, it could not be denied that such entertainments were very fashionable at home, as anyone could see from the photos in the *Bystander* and *Sketch.*

* * * * *

Post-war years were troubled by political disorders. In Calcutta as in Bombay ladies hung about clubs badgering members to contribute to the Dyer Fund, but people in Bombay, who had passed through some very alarming weeks, had perhaps some justification for their subscriptions. This fund has been often and vehemently criticised ; but India is a land of political funds and that was a time when everyone seemed to be raising money for some fund or other. The contemporary Khilafat Fund for which vast sums were collected to restore to his pre-war power a Caliph whose rule was no longer desired even by his own subjects, had an odd and comic history ; and the Caliph must have envied the way General Dyer at least received the money that had been collected for him. In those post-war years most communities in India succumbed to various attacks of hysteria. The boom of the war was followed by a sudden slump. There had been martial law in the Punjab ; a malaria epidemic decimating the rural population over wide areas ;

the recrudescence of the Russian Menace and of the Afghan Question; the launching of the first Civil Disobedience Movement. Stirring times which many English people in India feared were but the prelude to another mutiny. The reforms were held by many to be inappropriate to a period of apparently increasing anarchy. There were some resignations and for a few years it was found difficult to recruit enough Englishmen for the I.C.S. Retired civilians visited the universities to encourage recruiting by painting idyllic pictures of Anglo-Indian Life based on recollections of their own youth in some remote Punjab district in the late 'eighties. One distinguished official, having delivered his recruiting address to an Oxford audience, was asked how a young man with "liberal sympathies" would fare in India. "Well," said the distinguished official with a confiding smile, "I don't mind admitting I was a bit of a liberal myself but once out there you soon forget all about that sort of thing. Too many other interests. Big-game shooting, for instance."

Recruits responded satisfactorily to these siren appeals. Nationalist movements were succeeded by communal riots. And the recommendations of the Lee Commission increased the material comforts of the Indian services. The atmosphere of Anglo-India became much more cheerful.

But it was a strangely changed Anglo-India.

The vast old bungalows were in many districts replaced by neat little villas with electricity, telephones and labour-saving devices. The compound too would be smaller. A garage replaced the row of stables, for people did not ride much nowadays. You could not afford both car and stable, and with tarred roads in the bigger towns riding was much less pleasant than in old days. Besides, one did not remain long in any one district and a car was much less trouble to move than a horse. It was true that some Indians complained that the new motorist-official hardly saw the life of the villages except along the main roads. But that could not be helped ; with so many committee-meetings and increasing work at headquarters it would have been impossible to do without a car. And Indians complained about many things in the new Anglo-India. Some (but these were the elderly) complained that nowadays Englishmen married much too early in India. The old-fashioned administrator with his Indian mistresses had, it has been argued, a knowledge of the people such as his more virtuous successor could hardly hope to gain. . . .

Anglo-Indian life tended now to converge on the larger stations and cantonments, where there was always some company and where the clubs still flourished. Club libraries were far better stocked than before the war. You would find rows of new books ; Priestley, Walpole, and, most popular of all, Beverley Nichols (homesick subalterns found a nostalgic pleasure in those evocations of English country life, the gardens and village characters, and majors' wives thought him charming and unaffected, not like those Sitwells). There might be in the bigger stations like Poona and Lahore French clubs where one might keep up with one's French and not turn into a figure of fun at Marseilles, abusing the porters in Hindustani like the old-fashioned Anglo-Indians one had heard so many jokes about. And there would be other radio fans with whom one could discuss the problems of aerials and the tiresome atmospherics resulting from stormy weather in the Red Sea, which prevented a clear reception of the news, the descriptions of sporting events and the concerts. And there would be people fresh from home leave, for hill-stations were less frequented—you could get home by air in almost the same time as it took to get to Kashmir from most parts of India.

In the smaller stations the Anglo-Indian communities dwindled. The services were increasingly " provincialised ". In the bungalows along the straight and dusty roads of the Civil Lines there would still be cane chairs in the verandas and ferns in hanging pots, but the curtains would be of heavier material, the cushions brighter and in the drawing-room instead of a photo-laden piano there would be the little daughter's German harmonium and on the carved tables a bridal couple photo and ash-trays with college arms. The club would have entered on a period of slow, inevitable decline. Club-addiction is a peculiarly Anglo-Saxon trait ; and the English in India who had usually sent their children home to England to be educated and had in consequence none of the intense devoted family life of Indians, found the same pleasure in gymkhanas as so many Americans in country clubs and in reunions of regular fellows and good mixers. Few Indians drink like Anglo-Saxons ; and even those few have no particular zest for a Bar, for the hours spent perched on a high stool with instep resting on a brass rail. Consequently the drink profits, on which club finances generally depended, declined. One could no longer spend so much on English illustrated papers ; and though the conscientious Brahman official might still dutifully plod through *Sketch* and *Tatler*, digest the Society Jottings, the " Priscilla in Paris ", a time would come when the club would have to be content with only two illustrated papers (perhaps the *Sphere* and the *Sporting and Dramatic*) and one fiction magazine. Subscriptions might be put up and even the price of soda and lemonade raised to compensate for the dearth of orders for whisky and gin, but that gaunt building remained too expensive to maintain ; the diamond-leaded panes of the Tudor windows always seemed to need replacing, the paint was flaking off the two Corinthian pillars of the library and white ants were building in the Gothic fretwork over the pointed archway leading to the ladies' cloakroom.

Sometimes an old Anglo-Indian, who had found his periods of leave and visits to England increasingly unsatisfying (" England seems quite a strange country nowadays. No one seems to have any manners and everyone is in such a hurry ") would have settled down in the station where he had been happy with the golf-course and the friendly gossip in the bar afterwards, and by virtue of his long connection with the club would have been elected secretary year after year without question, and he would now find the changes almost bewildering. Such a one said to me, " Before the old club finally has to put up the shutters I hope I'm dead. I've made it a point in my will that I want to be buried on that little hill overlooking the eighteenth hole, and instead of the burial service I want to have a panatrope play over my grave the Londonderry Air."

* * * * *

The bigger the station the less noticeable the changes. Christmas Week at Lahore was as gay as ever for the soldiers down from the Frontier for a dance and a decent meal at Stiffles' and a cocktail in the mornings (the brisk and misty mornings of Punjab winter) at Lorang's where the band played fairly recent foxtrots and the waiters, wearing sashes and turban-bands of the Belgian colours to emphasise the proprietor's nationality, hurried between the bamboo chairs and the glass-topped tables balancing trays of oysters (brought in cold storage from Karachi) and champagne cocktails and the subalterns fresh from remote outposts remarked on the number of Sikh girls ("surprising percentage of good-lookers") with smart shingled hair and elaborate cigarette-holders who enjoyed their cocktails and beat time to the strains of "Ten cents a dance".

In New Delhi more visitors than ever gathered for Horse-show Week. New and shining cars sped down the long, the bewilderingly long avenues lined by beautiful new bungalows in the Lutyens Colonial style; the avenues whose surface was so wonderfully smooth on account of the ban on all lorry traffic and, in the grander roads where the big officials had their bungalows, even on bullock carts; avenues with well-clipped grass on either side and carefully tended trees; avenues leading nowhere in particular or just out into the rock-strewn wastes around the new city, or to the central avenue from which one gazed admiringly up to the pink cliffs of the new Secretariat and the copper dome of the Viceroy's House and the white circular many-columned Council Chamber, or to the circular road (reminiscent of Bath or Cheltenham) where the shops clustered together, or to the new stadium facing (and concealing) the Old Fort where Their Excellencies would drive in state with lancers and umbrellas to inaugurate the Week, and would mount slowly to the Viceregal Box where in accordance with established ritual the gentlemen of the party would immediately change their white topis for felt hats brought to them on trays by red-robed orderlies. And in the beautiful little houses, furnished in distinctively London style, there would be sherry-parties with well-informed conversation about the ballet, the more modern poetry and painting. These conversations were notable for the absence of Anglo-Indian slang—indeed many boasted of their ignorance of it, like one well-groomed official of many years' service who indicated a veranda and asked,

"Now what's the word they use out here for those little terraces? *Loggie* our Italian friends would call them. . . ."

* * * * *

Post-war changes in Bombay were inevitable and natural. Indians there had always been more Westernised than anywhere in India, and even at the beginning of the nineteenth century Mrs. Graham had noted that relations between English and Indians in Bombay were unusually friendly. Industrialisation had brought together business-men of both communities in alliance against the workers, mostly Marathas from the Deccan plateau who, driven to the cities by poverty, had developed a taste for expensive luxuries like drink and American films and for the incitements of the ubiquitous Bolshevik. The Club-Entry problem had been as long-standing an irritant between the two races as the Temple-Entry problem between the Twice-Born and the Untouchables; but on the initiative of Lord Willingdon a new club was started, open to all communities. Much of the money was put up by Indian princes and there was a lavish expenditure on the golf-course, the tennis-courts and squash-courts. This club naturally attracted those young princelings who generally open their conversation with, "What games do you play, besides golf and tennis I mean?" But the club building was an ignoble structure and the subscription so high that only the rich could hope to be members.

The younger generation of Englishmen brought up on jokes against pukka sahibs developed few racial prejudices. And anyhow it was easy enough to get on with young Indians who were as interested in cars and sport as any English subalterns, who played bridge enthusiastically and read "Sapper" and Edgar Wallace.

Of course there were some intellectuals of both races,

too, and they found many interests in common. They joined the Three Arts Society founded by that cultured Muhammadan lady, Atiya Begum. The reunions would be held at her house on Malabar Hill which had been built to resemble exactly an old Mogul palace. Sometimes a distinguished visitor to Bombay would be present as guest of honour. On one occasion Mr. Bernard Shaw, who had arrived at Bombay on a winter cruise, accepted an invitation and this was justifiably held to be a triumph, though at the meeting a little confusion was caused by the persistence of some of the Indian members in addressing the guest of honour as " Sir Bernard ". There would be on other occasions recitations of poetry, preferably the poetry of Mrs. Sarojini Naidu, The Indian Nightingale.

> O brilliant blossoms that strew my way

(The reciter would make a gesture as of one strewing)

> You are only woodland flowers, *they say*

(But the reciter shook his head. He knew better.)

> I sometimes think that perhaps you are
> Fragments of some new-fallen star !

There would be Indian songs accompanied by Indian musicians and then perhaps a young Parsi would be persuaded to do a tap-dance to the music of a gramophone.

* * * * *

The cordiality between English and Indian in Bombay survived the recurring political tumults when tempers were frayed and old animosities half-revived. The Simon Commission landed to the accompaniment of sharp controversies ; but both English and Indians enjoyed the legend that went round the clubs, that on his return to England after the first six-months' tour the leader of the

Commission had been seen brooding tenderly over a bed of daffodils in Hyde Park and had been heard to murmur with a gentle sigh, " Daffodils. Well, well . . . English daffodils." The returned exile. . . .

Even in the fury of the Civil Disobedience Movement of 1930 Bombay maintained its reputation for friendliness between the two races. While in Calcutta it is said that many of the younger Englishmen joined an association known as the Royalists with gentlemanly-fascist leanings, enterprising Englishmen in Bombay formed a group called the Young Europeans. These were mostly junior members of Bombay firms who prided themselves on a progressive outlook. They gave lunches to prominent Indian leaders and listened with enthusiasm to eloquent speeches by their guests who pointed out that the brotherhood of man was a noble aim and that liberty was preferable to tyranny. They despatched representatives to congratulate Lord Irwin on his policy and were gratified by a viceregal interview. Many, perhaps most of them, were sincere in their desire for a new relationship with political India. Others felt the natural satisfaction of the self-consciously advanced ; the excitement of defying the conservatism of unsympathetic seniors in their own firms and the prejudices of the less sensitive juniors. They had little support among the smarter athletic groups like that exclusive swimming set the Bombay Ducks (with their slogans like " Never let down Ducks " and their annual dinner to the Governor). The more defiant among them flew Congress flags on their cars, which was regarded with wide disapproval. But after the movement was over they could congratulate themselves on their endurance in face of hostile comment (" Yes, we went through a bad time in '30 but we stuck it out.").

* * * * *

British and Indian business-men found a bond of sympathy in approval of "The Cut": the ten per cent. reduction in the pay of all Government servants. Ever since the beginning of the economic crisis there had been rumours of such a measure. Local Service associations were naturally alarmed; for a ten per cent. reduction under to-day's undemocratic Government was a sad precedent to set for to-morrow's democracy. In every up-country club there were anxious discussions as the rumours increased, and the juniors hoped that the "cut" would be carefully graded according to the scale of salaries, while the seniors stressed the importance of the principle of equality of sacrifice. When the final decision was reached to levy an all-round ten per cent. cut there was great disappointment and anxiety among junior officials and soldiers with comparatively small salaries. The reactions of the military included a circular enjoining club members to pay for their own drinks in the club bar and to refrain from "treating". Traditionally each man present in the bar or sitting in one of those wide circles on the club lawn would in turn call for a round of drinks and then sign a chit for that round. According to the new plan each member was only to order drinks for himself and never offer them to his neighbour. This important change, however, was never fully realised; it seemed unnatural never to turn to the others at the bar and ask "What's yours?"; and after a few months the old system had returned despite the frowns of authority. There were other circulars suggesting a parallel cut in servants' wages and committees of military women drew scales of maximum pay; twenty rupees for a subaltern's bearer, thirty for a captain's bearer and so on. But, as the subalterns and captains in line regiments complained, rich cavalry regiments paid little attention to these proposals and so prevented unanimity among employers. The cut was presently " restored " but its memory continued to provoke a certain sense of insecurity.

*   *   *   *   *

An Anglo-Indian of the 'seventies or 'eighties of the last century who returned to Bombay to-day would miss, at least in the " Fort " area, the traditionally vast dark drawing-rooms, the verandas wide as a liner's deck, the great gardens. The spaciousness of Anglo-Indian life had always been a much-vaunted compensation for the discomforts of the climate ; and though our visitor from the 'seventies might be impressed by the amenities of frigidaires, English baths, built-in radios and electric cooking ranges, he might wonder whether Anglo-Indian life had not lost much of its distinctive character, and whether these bright little flats with tiled floors and imitation-Heal furniture were not more appropriate to New York or Berlin than to Bombay.

He would probably, however, find even more to cavil at in the style of Bombay's post-war architecture. The Georgian palaces of the eighteenth century were as appropriate to the age of the Nabobs as the red Gothic of the nineteenth century to the age of the evangelical administrators. But to what kind of age, our visitor would wonder, could these new buildings be said to be appropriate? Styled by local admirers " modernistic ", these blocks of flats are shaped like biscuit-tins, their walls adorned with a few insignificant geometric designs which begin to change colour after the second monsoon ; there are bits of arty trellis-work and balcony railings designed with the purposeful rusticity of garden-seats ; flat roofs with an imitation pergola and a coloured plaster gnome or two ; doors in unexpected places with quaint door-handles and knockers ;

entrance-halls like grottoes in Selfridge's annual display of Santa Claus Land. Even the sedate hotels which in their gloomy solidity had seemed pleasantly typical of nineteenth-century Bombay had, our visitor would find, yielded to these new architectural fashions ; had opened cocktail bars in " Riviera Style " and many a little alcove or " Kozy Neuk " leading from the main hall whose pointed arches offered a remarkable contrast to the new eruptions of chromium and moulded glass. And our visitor would hardly enjoy his luncheon (no longer tiffin) or dinner in the sea-green glitter of the dining-room, silver stars and a laughing moon on one enamel-green wall, green glass pillars all round, no fans or punkahs (no longer necessary with the air-conditioning apparatus) and on the dais a deafening noise from a jazz band. For luncheon they would play old favourites, perhaps Gilbert and Sullivan or selections from the works of Mr. Hermann Finck, but for dinner jazz would be inevitable. Many of our visitor's fellow-diners would dance as soon as, or even before, they had finished dinner. Others would be off to the cinema. Bombay now boasted seven or eight cinemas devoted exclusively to American and English films. Most of them, it is true, were converted theatres, with the annoying result for those who had paid the top prices for the best view, that they also got the most uncomfortable seats, but films were often shown at the same time as the London première, or even earlier, so that one had the comforting feeling that one was not an exile.

For an exile in post-war Bombay one was, more than before, likely to feel. Too many things seemed to be inferior, yet nostalgia-inducing, imitations of London . . . The negro band that played in " The Taj " in the cold weather and made a speciality of " swing " music, to which luckily it was, however, quite easy to dance the same old fox-trot one always had danced; the football matches on the Cooperage ground—though England could boast nothing so picturesque as the forest of fezzes and turbans that rose skywards whenever Muhammadan Sporting scored a goal; the Bombay Symphony Orchestra's concerts, with the Police Band in charge of the "brass" and Parsi ladies fiddling away for dear life; the B.B.C.I. (Bombay, Baroda and Central India) electric railway; the new double-decker, red-painted buses; all tended to have the same effect, an effect reinforced by the weekly arrivals and departures of the P. & O. mail-boats.

Leave was a staple topic of conversation at all gatherings and particularly—for many ladies went home every year—at those "bridge and gimlet" parties at which the married women whiled away the later hours of the morning. Another favourite subject now was patent medicines, a topic not confined to the women. Gone were the vast meals to which our nineteenth-century visitor had been accustomed and on which he had thrived. Even the more frugal, cold-storage fare now provided proved too much, in Bombay's climate, for twentieth-century digestions. Our visitor would be startled by such outlandish words as "Bemax", "Energen", "Vitalin", repeatedly recurring in the conversation, alarmed at "Are you still on strychnine? I've gone on to arsenic", disgusted by the food served to him at a meal where all his fellow-guests were taking a course of Dr. Hay's famous slimming diet.

As of old the Anglo-Indian Press chronicled the various festivities in which the city indulged. Bombay's "gay social whirl" (as one girl described it to me) reached its apex for many at Christmas and the New Year. The welcome accorded to 1937 was thus described by *The*

Evening News of India in its society gossip column called "The Bombay Man's Diary":

> The host of New Year's Eve revellers last night must have totalled thousands and the voice of jubilation swept through all the city and its suburbs. It roared its loudest and merriest at the Taj where there must have been not much short of two thousand souls bent on making the welkin ring with echoes of a very good time. An elaborate programme had been arranged by that enterprising duo Faletti and Framrose, who devised between them a host of ingenious ideas to keep everyone interested and entertained . . . a choice menu of mirth, beautiful decorations, quantities of gewgaws, baubles and noisy instruments, first-rate cabaret music and what not. The result was a proper Bacchanalian rout in which the most sedate and sober pranced and capered with the zest of two-year-olds at a birthday party.

Yet was this Bacchanal essentially more vulgar than the routs and orgies in eighteenth-century Calcutta so much more literately described by Mr. Hickey?

One more difference perhaps our visitor might mark, and it would comfort him—the contrast between life in the "Fort" area and life on Malabar or Cumbala Hill. On the two latter lived the Civil Service and the Judiciary, the world of officialdom, the "Number Ones" of business firms and the rich Anglicé Parsis. Here were still spacious bungalows, many of them with views over the lovely Bombay coast-line. In them formality and precedence still to some extent held sway, their inhabitants seldom figured in "The Bombay Man's Diary". "The sun"—to vary Mr. Noel Coward's lyric—"had *not* set on Government House."

The advent to power of Congress brought to this world new social as well as political problems. Should one attempt to "mix", risking the snub of refusal which Congress Headquarters wished the Provincial ministers to administer? Should the Sheriff of Bombay go to the station to meet the new Premier on his arrival from Poona? Should the European members of the Bombay bar attend a dinner in that Holy of Holies, the Byculla Club, to the new minister for law and order, risking the possibility that a hot-tempered Irishman might strike the cigarette from the mouth of a congressman who was smoking during a loyal toast? And there was the alarming scare that the seat of government was going to be moved altogether to Poona. It was all rather difficult, but meanwhile life for the majority went on much as before. Probably a social *modus vivendi* could be achieved; after all congressmen were human beings, and it was satisfactory that the ministers had not, after all, insisted on the police wearing Gandhi caps and *dhotis*. Anyway, one must wait and see. . . .

And in that position we must leave the British in India. Times have changed rapidly for them since 1918—even their designation of "Anglo-Indian" has been taken from them and by Act of Parliament bestowed upon those who had previously been called Eurasians. Indianisation proceeds apace and Indian independence has become a practical possibility rather than the extremists' dream. The spacious days when the Englishman, be he Governor-General or District Officer, was supreme in his own sphere have vanished. To-day may be looked on as a transitional stage. One may hazard that in the future the British in India may be less noticeable for their eccentricities, their conscious superiority, but that it is extremely unlikely that anyone will ever mistake them for citizens of any nation but their own.

THE END

INDEX

INDEX

INDEX